MURRAY WALKER
INCREDIBLE!

www.penguin.co.uk

Also by Maurice Hamilton

Niki Lauda The Biography
Formula 1 The Official History
Formula One The Champions
Formula 1 The Pursuit of Speed
Grand Prix Circuits

MURRAY WALKER

INCREDIBLE!

A Tribute to a Formula 1 Legend

MAURICE HAMILTON

BANTAM PRESS

TRANSWORLD PUBLISHERS
Penguin Random House, One Embassy Gardens,
8 Viaduct Gardens, London SW11 7BW
www.penguin.co.uk

Transworld is part of the Penguin Random House group of companies
whose addresses can be found at global.penguinrandomhouse.com

Penguin
Random House
UK

First published in Great Britain in 2021 by Bantam Press
an imprint of Transworld Publishers

A CIP catalogue record for this book
is available from the British Library.

ISBNs 9781787635593 (cased)
9781787635692 (tpb)

Typeset in 11.25/16.5pt Bembo by Jouve (UK), Milton Keynes.
Printed and bound in Great Britain by Clays Ltd, Elcograf S.p.A.

The authorized representative in the EEA is Penguin Random House Ireland,
Morrison Chambers, 32 Nassau Street, Dublin D02 YH68.

Penguin Random House is committed to a sustainable
future for our business, our readers and our planet. This book
is made from Forest Stewardship Council® certified paper.

CONTENTS

FOREWORD BY MARTIN BRUNDLE

I t was a wonderful privilege to have known and worked with Murray, and indeed to have driven in races on which he commentated. He remains undoubtedly one of the best sports commentators of all time, a man who transcended Formula 1 to become a passionate soundtrack and national treasure to fans all around the world.

A natural communicator, ably confirmed by his very successful tangential career as an advertising executive, he was also a man whose glass was permanently half full. He had a kind and supportive word for everyone in the business and his warm, open and enthusiastic personality made him welcome throughout the paddock.

He was so respected that, remarkably, he was even more loved for making errors during his coverage of our relentlessly data-driven sport which continuously strives for perfection. His 'Murrayisms' are comedy gold and he was smart enough to play along and make a virtue of what he claimed were 'not mistakes but prophecies which immediately turned out to be wrong'.

In 1997 I became his apprentice in the commentary box, and to learn a little about broadcasting from the maestro himself was like having Pelé teach you how to kick a ball. Before the first season got under way we had dinner together and I asked him for advice on this business of F1 broadcasting. His humility made him reluctant to suggest he knew all the answers, and after some cajoling he said: 'What I can tell you is to remember that we are only there to inform and entertain, nothing else.' Simple, clear advice I repeat to myself a quarter of a century later.

One of the smartest decisions I've ever made was to stand up alongside Murray for the entire race, which he liked to do so that he could bounce around, animatedly point at the screen, and keep his diaphragm and lungs opened up. We worked well together, although it was sometimes difficult to get his attention such was his engagement in the race. The arrangement was that I would put my left hand on his right shoulder when I wanted to say something, but in reality he only noticed if I dug a fingernail under his tendons! I became convinced that if I crept out of the commentary box he wouldn't notice until after the race, such was his focus.

His pre-race preparation was legendary with copious notes and diligent homework both at the track and back in his hotel room, and he remained pin sharp, knowledgeable and enthusiastic about F1 to the very end of his life.

A life well lived and well loved, and a career which will be celebrated and remembered for a very long time – unless I'm very much mistaken.

COLOSSALLY, THAT'S MURRAY

'*ROSBERG OUT! Keke Rosberg! Out of the Australian Grand Prix! If this isn't a sensation, I'd like to know what is.*'

Just ninety-three seconds later, Murray Walker received a spectacular answer to his query. In one of the most dramatic incidents, arguably, in the history of Formula 1, a rear tyre exploded on Nigel Mansell's Williams-Honda as he reached 180mph on the main straight.

'*AND LOOK AT THAT!*' bellowed Walker, stabbing a finger at the monitor in the BBC booth. '*Colossally, that's Mansell! That is Nigel Mansell. The car absolutely shattered. He's fighting for control. You can see what's happened. Now – this could change, and will change, the World Championship.*'

Indeed it could. Indeed it did. Mansell's failure to win the 1986 world title at the eleventh hour on the streets of Adelaide would enter the annals of motor sport spectacle just as surely as the excited declarations of the man commentating on it.

'Colossally, that's Mansell!' Who else but Murray Walker could have said such a thing?

When it came to motor sport, everything was a derivative of colossal in Walker's book. Rosberg easing to the side of the track and coming to a gentle halt compared to Mansell's hair-raising departure at a hundred times the speed may have been similar to contrasting a chilly draught with a raging typhoon. But, as far as Murray Walker was concerned, the fact that Rosberg had lost a commanding lead in what would be his final Grand Prix was a 'sensation'. It was a thought he wanted – desperately needed – to share with viewers in the UK and in several countries around the world taking the BBC broadcast.

The fact that retirement for Rosberg had become a familiar sight in half of the preceding fifteen races was an irrelevance as far as this commentator was concerned. Rosberg was leading a race for only the fourth time in 1986 and there was a certain poignancy attached to this one; a pathos that Walker would have not merely noted but unashamedly embraced.

Rosberg's spectacular style in the cockpit appealed to Murray just as much as the Finn's insouciance when out of the car. Keke had been a popular world champion in 1982. The fact that Rosberg had won just a single Grand Prix that year added to his aura of cheerful indifference.

This race in Australia would be Rosberg's 114th and final appearance. It may have been a comparatively brief Formula 1 career (Lewis Hamilton reached twice that number of races in 2018) but it did not detract from the F1 community's wish – articulated so passionately by Walker – to see Rosberg end it with a win.

Apart from losing a comfortable lead, there was nothing particularly sensational in the strictest visual sense about the McLaren coming slowly to a halt. But whether he recognized it or not, Walker's emotional connection with this driver on this particular circuit had been cemented twelve months before when Rosberg was the colourful victor of the inaugural Australian Grand Prix.

An Australasian element to the international F1 calendar had been a long time coming. It was to be one of the most popular additions for many years after that first race weekend in early November 1985. But Walker loved it for reasons that went beyond the surprisingly good quality of the temporary race track and its facilities.

Adelaide, keen to lay down a sporting benchmark in the face of established competition from Sydney and Melbourne, made a bid to hold the Grand Prix. A track was mapped out through the suburban streets, beginning and ending in the Victoria Park race course. Instead of dividing the community in a physical and philosophical sense, the locals were united by the prospect of such a vibrant and internationally acclaimed sporting series coming to the so-called 'City of Churches'.

If Adelaide could pull this off, it would be one in the eye for the states of Victoria and New South Wales – a thought that was quickly grasped by John Bannon, Premier of South Australia, of which Adelaide was the state capital. Dispensing with formalities, Bannon flew to London, where he laid out his plans before Bernie Ecclestone, the de facto head of Formula 1. Ecclestone liked what he saw. Bannon then flew straight to Japan to secure backing from Mitsubishi. The race was on.

F1 personnel arriving at Adelaide in 1985 quickly realized two things: the small airport had only been handling regular international travel for three years, and the fans waiting by the fence were not just there to welcome star drivers as they walked across the tarmac. There was a sizeable 'Murray Walker Fan Club' presence – an indication of the following for both the sport and one of its lead commentators despite live transmissions from Europe having regularly been beamed into Australia at 2 a.m. on a Monday morning.

Murray had become part of F1 folklore. He had been commentating on Grand Prix racing for BBC Television since 1969, the unique and unmistakable timbre of his delivery making Walker the 'Voice of Motor Sport' in the same way that the gentle tones of John Arlott represented cricket, or Bill McLaren's Celtic burr and phraseology immediately brought rugby union to mind. Murray's identification with his subject would become so harmonious that he would be the only key member of the BBC team to make the switch when ITV took control of F1 broadcasting in 1997. And all of this despite a propensity for making errors in excitable moments – of which there were many – during commentaries on motor sports as diverse as rallycross and touring car racing. Walker was soon to discover that the Australians had in fact embraced his gaffes as part of the broadcaster's British charm.

'I was at the course during our first visit [in 1985] when a fellow came up to me,' recalled Murray. 'He was holding a T-shirt. "Me and my mates have done a few of these," he said. "We're going to wear 'em on Sunday. I thought I ought to show you, to make sure you're not offended." I looked at the T-shirt. On the front was my face and under it, the lettering MURRAY WALKER FAN CLUB. On the back, it said: "Unless I'm very much mistaken . . . Yes, I am very much mistaken". I said I didn't see how I could take offence at that. "It's very flattering," I said. "Thanks very much."

'We were in fact working with Channel 9, the host broadcaster. When David Hill, our Australian producer, saw the T-shirt, he said: "That's going in the programme, mate!" Which he did – but not quite in the way I had expected.

'David went and found a girl with an enormous bosom and got her to wear the T-shirt. Her role after each commercial break was to shimmy up to the camera, with the image of my cheeks looking rather more chubby than usual, then turn around and display the message on the back. That was my cue to bring in the viewers. I couldn't think of a nicer way to do it.'

Walker and his co-presenter, the 1976 world champion James Hunt, commentated on a lively race in 1985. This was the year that marked the arrival of Ayrton Senna as a man to watch. In his first season with a leading team (Lotus), the hugely talented Brazilian had led at least six races but claimed victory in just two of them. He won pole position in Adelaide for the seventh time that year but the almost desperate desire to finish the campaign on a high saw Senna leave the road more than once and then collide with the eventual winner, Rosberg, before retiring. The efficient running of the Grand Prix capped a hugely successful weekend, summed up by the headline in Adelaide's *Advertiser* the following morning: KEKE IS KING, BUT ADELAIDE YOU ARE THE NUMBER ONE.

As the newspaper's motoring editor, Bob Jennings had been deeply involved in the Grand Prix and Murray Walker's role within it. 'It's fair to say that Australia was probably more prepared for Murray Walker than he was for Australia,' recalled Jennings. 'Australian F1 fans were well accustomed to the F1 commentaries of the diverse duo of Murray and James Hunt following the upsurge of interest in the sport – and its TV coverage – brought about by [Australian] Alan Jones's World Championship victory in 1980.

'On his arrival in Adelaide, Murray was soon aware of the fan club T-shirts. He was delighted with his celebrity status and amused by the T-shirt although I'm sure it must have been a two-edged sword as he would rather be recognized for his commentarial abilities than his famous gaffes. Initially, just a few of the shirts were made by local photographer and motor sport enthusiast John Lemm, for some of his mates.'

'People kept on asking for them at the merchandise stands and of course they didn't have them,' said Lemm. 'So they started asking the blokes wearing them where they came from. My brother Phil [a race mechanic] and I used to race home at the end of each day and print up a whole lot more in our shed, then sell them the next day from the back of one of the race trailers in the support paddock. We gave one to Murray and he loved it, but Channel 9 borrowed it from him and put it on a fairly shapely girl and used shots of her whenever they went to an ad break. Murray never did get the shirt back but years later we found a few in the shed and I was able to give one to him.'

'Murray was enlisted by then motoring writer and cartoonist John "Stonie" Stoneham to write F1 reviews for the now-defunct *Adelaide*

News daily newspaper,' continued Jennings. 'The two became firm friends, Stoneham [infamous for an earlier Niki Lauda cartoon] having been an F1 enthusiast for many years.

'Both Murray and Stonie were inveterate collectors and during one of their chats Murray lamented that his collection of *Autocourse* annuals was missing the rare 1978 edition. On his first trip to Australia, on the way to Adelaide, Murray had called into the renowned Motoring Bookshop in Sydney. Thinking he wouldn't be recognized and taken as an innocent punter looking for this book, he asked the grey-haired bloke behind the counter: "Er, I don't suppose you have a 1978 copy of *Autocourse*?" "Of course not, Murray – nice try!" replied Fred Vogel, the shop's celebrated owner. Even then, anybody involved in racing in Australia knew the sight and sound of Walker!

'The story has a happy ending. Stonie later discovered a copy in a Melbourne motoring bookshop and bought it, along with several other editions. Stonie and Murray had dinner subsequently in Adelaide and Stonie produced the '78. Murray was thrilled. "How much?" he asked. "It cost me a hundred," said Stonie. Murray quickly peeled off a hundred. But it was pounds sterling, not Australian dollars, which were worth far less. "Wrong denomination," said Stonie. "You've overpaid me." "Don't worry about it," said Murray. "It's worth it."'

There was no doubt that the *Advertiser* felt coverage of their first Grand Prix had been worth the effort. An eight-page wrap-around supplement of the broadsheet newspaper carried reports on the race from every angle. The only sour note concerned a review of the television coverage. 'Despite the barrage of TV technology and the unrelenting hype, the furious attempts to turn the Grand Prix into a television spectacular ultimately failed,' wrote Jason Daniel. But he did concede that 'The only compensation was Murray Walker's masterful commentary. He was gushy and sentimental but always tried to rip up some enthusiasm for the proceedings.' It was perhaps no surprise that

Daniel had written this curmudgeonly piece from his armchair in Sydney.

There could be no question that Melbourne and Sydney were hurting. The *Advertiser*'s Des Colquhoun summed it up in a column under the heading WINNING WAYS OF A DEAR CITY. 'Rightly or wrongly,' wrote Colquhoun, 'it has reflected on Mr Bannon. If he doesn't announce the election date during this morning's euphoria, he must be politically bonkers.'

Walker, in fact, had come close to meeting the South Australia Premier in a move not without an element of Murray faux pas. 'It was arranged on race day that I should do my in-vision introduction from a balcony in the VIP area,' Murray recalled. 'This was in an elevated part of the pits. Despite all my cards and credentials, I had a great deal of difficulty getting in there but at last I did, and we filmed the intro.

'I was making for the exit when I came across a very fierce-looking Australian security man who was standing ramrod-like to attention. I went over to him and jokingly said: "Keep on your toes, old chap, because there are going to be all sorts of people trying to get in this place who have absolutely no right to be here." Through the corner of his mouth he hissed: "Would you move aside, sir, and let the Premier through." I swung round and there was John Bannon, waiting behind me. G'day!'

2

LOOK AT THAT!

Any concerns Bannon and the Adelaide Grand Prix team may
have had about improving the show twelve months later were
helped enormously by the way the 1986 World Championship
was working out. Whereas in 1985 the title had been settled in favour
of Alain Prost several weeks before, this time it was going to the wire
in Australia. Not only that, but three drivers – Prost, Nigel Mansell
and Nelson Piquet – were in with a shout. In 1985, the author had
been the only British national newspaper representative to make the
trip. Twelve months on, the Grand Prix media office was inundated
with applications, seemingly from anyone with a portable typewriter.
Adelaide had become the hottest ticket in international motor sport.

It was a natural fit for the *Observer* to commission Clive James –
one of the best-known Australians at the time – to write a piece for
the Sunday newspaper. James's typically astute and dry observations
included a mention of Walker. It was difficult not to, given the broadcaster's popularity and increasing notoriety for what had become
known as 'Murrayisms'.

'Adelaide is a very pretty city,' wrote James. 'Laid out spaciously on
flat land with the hills in the background strictly a backdrop, it is mostly
one storey high. Two storeys rate as imposing and any public building
with a clock tower counts as a landmark. Flowers cascade over wrought-
iron balconies. Outside of Grand Prix time, not a lot happens except
the Adelaide Festival, which has won international fame in the literary

world but understandably doesn't generate the same fizz among the local girls as handsome young men dicing with death, etc. No doubt Julian Barnes, guesting at the festival next year, will set hearts beating, but he would be the first to admit that when reading aloud from one of his books he doesn't crank out as much aura as Nelson Piquet doing 200mph, or even two miles per hour. Piquet just has to stand there and the young ladies bite the back of their hands.

'They are also very fond of Gerhard Berger, Alessandro Nannini and almost anyone else with his face in the official programme, including Murray Walker, the BBC race commentator who knows everything but gets it mixed up in moments of excitement. The Grand Prix circus, knowing that Murray loves the sport, is collectively very fond of him, but from Murray's angle what makes Australia so remarkable is that the fans are fond of him too. Murray Walker is a big star in Australia. When the sunlight bounces off his bald head, he gets mobbed.'

Channel 9 did not hesitate to make the most of Walker's presence, Murray regularly donning the TV channel's trademark pale blue polo shirt and appearing on camera when not required for commentary duty. He was invited into the trackside studio at lunchtime on Saturday and asked to preview both qualifying and the race, and say who he thought would become world champion.

In 1986, qualifying was split in two: a one-hour session on Friday, followed by another on Saturday afternoon. Mansell had provisional pole with a time half a second faster than anyone else. This seemed logical since the Williams driver was leading the championship and a clear favourite to win it. All the Englishman needed to do was come home third or higher and the title would be his, no matter where Piquet or Prost finished.

Walker knew all of this when he arrived in the studio. He was also aware that Prost, second fastest in the first qualifying session, had been quickest in the free practice session that had just finished. Clasping his hands around his middle, Murray sat back and gave his prediction. 'I've been sticking my neck out and saying Prost for the World Championship. And I've been saying it in a situation that's been very contentious because Nigel Mansell is the favourite. But I think it's very significant that Prost has got his McLaren going well enough to set the fastest time this morning. He's more than four seconds faster than Rosberg's lap record from last year; faster than Mansell's [provisional] pole position yesterday; he will be faster this afternoon and I'm still sticking to my last [prediction].'

Walker's confidence in a driver widely considered to be the outsider was seen to be even more well-meaning but naive when the Williams-Hondas went on to dominate final qualifying, Mansell ahead of Piquet. Prost was fourth, more than a second behind Mansell and slower than the Lotus-Renault of Senna, who could be guaranteed to make life doubly difficult for Prost as he tried to go after the Williams duo.

Murray, meanwhile, stuck to his guns. He would have the last laugh – but not in the manner either he, Prost or anyone else could have truly predicted. Not that the finishing positions would matter greatly to John Bannon as he was joined in his suite by the Australian Prime Minister, Bob Hawke, to watch the race and add the final touch of credibility.

As the cars formed on the grid, Walker was following his usual dramatic routine by standing in the commentary box, as eager to get going as the twenty-six drivers ranged beneath him.

'*And it's GO! And a superb start from Nigel Mansell. Senna goes through into second place ahead of Piquet. The two McLarens* [Rosberg and Prost] *slot in behind them. Into the chicane – is anybody going to go off this year? It looks to me as if they're bunching up well. No problems at the chicane – and Senna is challenging for the start* [meaning "lead"] *and he goes through and he takes the lead. Senna takes the lead on the right-hander at Wakefield Turn.*

'*Now up to East Terrace Bend, the left-hander. It's Senna, Mansell,*

Piquet ... and ... the McLaren going through ahead of the Williams. It is Ayrton Senna in the lead. It is PIQUET second, it is Rosberg in third position, Mansell is down to fourth position – well there's a turn-up for the book, because Nigel Mansell has lost his lead.'

Mansell, in fact, had only held the lead briefly, Walker missing the glimpse on screen as the Williams, struggling momentarily for grip, dropped back on the approach to East Terrace. Meanwhile, positions had changed yet again at the front.

'... and Piquet going through and trying to take Senna! One Brazilian passes another. We've got a third leader before even one lap has been completed! And it is Piquet, Rosberg, Senna, Mansell, Prost.'

Lap 2

'Piquet leading for Williams-Honda. Then Senna – there he is. Rosberg is going through [into second place]. *Keke Rosberg. He means to win this one.'*

Lap 3

'And there is Mansell ahead of Senna. So it's Mansell third, Senna fourth, Prost fifth. We've still got a long way to go. Watch the action.'

There was plenty to see. Rosberg took the lead from Piquet, with Prost gradually moving into third.

Lap 22

'AND OFF SPINS PIQUET! WHAO-EE! Now ... Piquet goes off, Prost goes through. Now ... we have the two McLarens first and second. Rosberg leads. And – Prost – is – second! This could change the race.'

Although Rosberg was very keen to bow out with a win, the Finn had made it clear he would do what he could to assist Prost in his title bid in the face of such strong competition.

The story of the race then began to turn in a less predictable direction. Light contact when lapping the Benetton of Gerhard Berger resulted in a punctured front tyre on Prost's McLaren. The deflating Goodyear lowered the front of the car and made it difficult for a McLaren mechanic to slide the jack beneath the nose.

Lap 32

'Alain Prost on lap 33 [32] *is into the pits for his expected tyre change at about the right time. And this is a bad change by modern standards, over seventeen seconds. And that is not good. That could be critical.'*

It would indeed be critical, but not for the expected reason. With tyre life in this eighty-two-lap race being an unknown, the Goodyear technicians grabbed the opportunity to assess wear on Prost's discarded tyres. From what they could see, wear was not a problem. Word was passed on that drivers could run non-stop.

As the race settled down again, Walker was able to choose his words rather more carefully than usual, particularly when it came to predicting a successful outcome for Rosberg in the leading McLaren.

During the weekend, Rosberg had asked to have a word with Walker. Since they were not exactly buddies, Murray did not know whether this was good or bad. Had he said something in a previous commentary to upset the phlegmatic Finn? Rosberg, in fact, was concerned about what he *might* say on Sunday afternoon. Having confirmed that Murray was aware this would be the Finn's last race, Rosberg stated the obvious by saying he wished to end on a high note. Again, this was no surprise to Walker. 'But Murray,' continued Rosberg, 'if I *am* doing well, for Christ's sake don't say anything about it!' Given Rosberg's dry sense of humour, it was said tongue in cheek, but with an undertone prompted by Walker's known habit of frequently putting a jinx on a driver by speaking highly of his progress.

On this occasion, it was difficult not to pass comment on the manner in which Rosberg had been commanding this race for fifty-five laps. If nothing else, there seemed no reason for it to be ended by tyre trouble, given Goodyear's earlier assurance about the integrity of their tyres.

That promise began to unravel when Rosberg came to that 'sensational' stop described so excitedly by Walker. It was some time later that a replay would show a shard of flailing rubber at the rear of

Rosberg's car. Had that happened thirty years later, sensors and on-board cameras would have picked up the failure immediately, word would have gone out and the outcome of the championship might have been very different.

On 26 October 1986, Williams were none the wiser and both their drivers pressed on. Until lap 64. Then, 'colossally', it was Mansell.

Piquet was now leading both the race and the championship. Having seen Mansell's dramatic tyre failure, however, Williams reluctantly took the precautionary step of bringing in Piquet for fresh tyres – allowing Prost to take the lead.

Lap 82

'And Alain Prost is virtually within sight of his twenty-fifth Grand Prix win, his second World Championship. An absolutely superb achievement. You have seen the crowd rising to this popular little Frenchman, demonstrating yet again that he is the driver of the day, and he takes the chequered flag. He wins the Australian Grand Prix. He wins the World Championship of 1986. Absolute euphoria in the McLaren pits. Look at him. He can hardly believe it himself.'

That last statement was even more apposite than Walker could have imagined as he watched Prost come to an immediate halt, climb from the cockpit and leap in the air. This was an era when performance was heavily restricted by the amount of fuel each car was permitted to carry. For the final five laps, Prost's dashboard read-out indicated he had no fuel left. The memory of spluttering to a premature halt at Hockenheim three months earlier loomed large. He had no alternative but to press on and hope. The McLaren ran out as Prost crossed the line.

Walker's pre-race prediction had been 100 per cent correct even though he had been as fortunate as the winner at the end of a hugely dramatic race. Meanwhile, Mansell was understandably crestfallen when interviewed by Murray in the paddock.

A few days later, Nigel and his Williams were in Japan for a scheduled goodwill appearance and some demonstration runs at the Honda
factory. Murray and a BBC cameraman accompanied Nigel. John
Cadd, one of Mansell's mechanics, overheard a conversation, instigated
by a typically breezy Walker.

'Do you realize, Nigel, if you'd had the shunt earlier and hit the
wall and stayed in the middle of the circuit, the race would have been
stopped and you'd have been world champion [based on the running
order at that time]?'

'Christ,' responded an understandably unamused Mansell, 'I don't
want to hear that, Murray.'

'Oh ...'

3

HEROES

n the wake of their failure to win a Formula 1 championship that ought to have been the first for Honda, Nigel Mansell and Williams were understandably reluctant to make that pre-arranged trip to Japan. Murray Walker couldn't wait to get there.

A bubbling enthusiasm for anything related to motor sport notwithstanding, when Murray referred to Honda as 'an absolutely fantastic company', he meant every word. He was thinking specifically of Honda's domination of motorcycle racing, a branch of motor sport that consumed his boyhood ambitions and dreams long before the Japanese company had planned their clinical onslaught in the 1960s.

Murray's passion was inevitable, given the exploits of his father, a man he adored. Graham Walker made his living through racing motorcycles – an existence as rare as bikes themselves in the opening decades of the twentieth century. Wounded when operating as a dispatch rider in the First World War, Walker Senior put aside the difficulties of braking with a permanently injured left foot to become a works rider for Norton, the fabled British firm. Such was his success, Graham was appointed competitions manager for Sunbeam (a company that described itself as 'the Rolls-Royce of motorcycles') before moving on to Rudge-Whitworth.

'That's when my father became really good,' recalled Murray. 'Rudge, Norton and the rest of Britain's motorcycle manufacturers who dominated the world were in a head-to-head battle for sales. The promotional benefits, both at home and overseas, that came from sporting supremacy were immense, so racing success was vital. At Rudge-Whitworth, my father was sales and competitions director – and he really got down to it with a will.'

The Isle of Man TT (Tourist Trophy) was as significant as it was difficult. There was no equal to the 37.73-mile Mountain Course, a demanding mix of tight turns through towns that linked fast sweeps across open countryside and lofty moorland. In the 1928 Senior TT, Walker's leading Rudge was forced to retire with 14 of the 268 miles to go. What had been a titanic battle with the Sunbeam of Charlie Dodson was resumed a few months later at the Ulster Grand Prix. After two and a half hours of wheel-to-wheel racing on the 20.5-mile Clady circuit, Walker stayed in front for the final time on the notorious 7-mile undulating straight to win by eleven seconds. Such an impressive result strengthened the *Boy's Own* image of Murray's dad.

'My father happened to be what you might describe as a peculiar mixture,' recalled Murray. 'He was 100 per cent a motorcycle man and in addition to racing, he tuned engines for people who wanted to compete against him. It's hard to believe that sort of thing happening today when you think about how suspicious and single-minded competitors are when, in their view – and quite rightly – winning is everything. With regard to my father, the thing is that all of this was on top of his commercial role in sales and distribution for Rudge and the other great names he worked for. In fact, when Enzo Ferrari set up his own motorcycle racing team in 1932, he chose Rudge-Whitworth bikes. And it was my father who sold them to him – something Mr Ferrari would remind me of when I got to meet him in later years.'

Upon retirement from racing, Walker Senior added another string to his substantial bow by becoming editor of *Motor Cycling*. The fact that he had no journalistic training did not seem to be a hindrance as the trade's leading publication went from strength to strength, along with Walker's reputation as a fair but forthright expert in all things motorcycling.

Keeping a close watch on racing at home and abroad, Graham would have become aware of Tazio Nuvolari, a wiry little Italian whose early progress had been punctuated with success and broken bones in equal measure. Unlike Walker, Nuvolari also had a desire to race cars. A trial for Alfa Romeo at Monza in 1925 had ended in disaster when the gearbox on the P2 seized, spinning the hapless Nuvolari into the trees. Doctors declared his injuries to be severe enough to preclude riding at Monza in the Nations Grand Prix in six days' time. Nuvolari would have none of it and persuaded the doctors to bandage him in such a way that he could adopt a riding posture. Such ambition seemed even more absurd when Nuvolari shuffled towards his machine and had to be lifted on board. When he won the race, there was no further discussion. It was a chilling demonstration of a determination to compete and succeed, whatever the cost. There was to be a similar episode when Nuvolari came to race in Britain in 1938. A wide-eyed fifteen-year-old Murray Walker would be there to see the moment – and remember it for the rest of his days.

Grand Prix racing, in some disarray, had been ripe for picking in the early 1930s when the Nazis came to power in Germany. Seeing motor sport as a powerful propaganda weapon, Adolf Hitler put up a grant large enough to tempt Mercedes-Benz and Auto Union to go head-to-head and produce some of the most spectacular and powerful racing cars ever seen.

All the more reason, then, for Nuvolari to take great pleasure in using his consummate skill in a less powerful Alfa Romeo to humble the might of Germany in their home Grand Prix on the twisting 14-mile Nürburgring Nordschleife in 1935. Three years later, following the loss of their star driver, Bernd Rosemeyer, Auto Union managed to persuade

Nuvolari to join them. This was a tasty prospect for British motor sport fans, starved of decent international racing for far too long and having enjoyed a taster on their doorstep in 1937.

Graham Walker would have been familiar with a circuit that had been laid out for motorcycle racing on gravel paths and farm roads within the Donington Park estate in the Midlands. The plan for a more substantial track led to the introduction of car racing in 1933. Enthusiastic work by the owner of the land, guided by the Derby and District Motor Club, brought sufficient improvements to warrant major events and, eventually, the Donington Grand Prix. Full credibility was guaranteed when Mercedes and Auto Union accepted an invitation to take part in the inaugural event in 1937. Graham and Murray Walker needed no prompting to see these 600bhp silver monsters tackle the undulating challenge of the 3.1-mile track.

In an interview with the writer Christopher Hilton, Murray recalled his first sight of a Grand Prix car. 'I remember walking about the track and being absolutely flabbergasted at Melbourne Hairpin when the German cars shot over the hill and braked for the hairpin and then shot up the hill again.

'I walked about the paddock. I don't know if it was difficult for everybody to do that then or whether I had some sort of special privilege. We had a great family friend who'd been in the army of occupation in Germany after the First World War. He'd married a German girl and stayed on. Whenever Mercedes and Auto Union went racing in English-speaking countries, he went with them to act as interpreter. Naturally, he was at Donington and I got drawn into the environment as an interested, enthusiastic schoolboy. I remember being in the paddock and being close to the drivers. I don't remember having any difficulty getting autographs.'

Walker returned in 1938, intent on adding Nuvolari's signature to his collection and keen to see the Italian in action for the first time. 'I remember being impressed by the publicity material being handed out by the Germans,' Murray recalled. 'They were gigantically switched on and they handed you all sorts of photographs. They were giving away things. You know people do brass rubbings in churches? Well, they gave you papier-mâché that you could put a piece of paper over and rub with a pencil and you got these beautiful pictures of the drivers and the cars. They had badges and brochures – things which did not exist in our world. Nuvolari had a tortoise as his emblem and Auto Union produced a limited run of those. I was given one – and wish I'd still got it. But I do remember being struck by how tiny Nuvolari was. He didn't seem capable of handling this enormous car with its long tail and engine in the rear. He looked such a diminutive little figure behind that big steering wheel.'

Any doubts over Nuvolari's capability were quelled when he qualified second fastest and put the Auto Union D-Type among a trio of Mercedes W154s on the four-car front row. It had been an eventful few days for Nuvolari, not least on the previous Monday when, during a test session, he had hit a stag that had wandered out of the woods. Nuvolari was found stroking the poor animal but there was nothing that could be done. He asked to have its head stuffed and mounted, and placed alongside other mementoes and trophies in his study at home in Mantova – all of which added to the mystique surrounding the little man.

Nuvolari's reputation as a racer would be magnified spectacularly during the race. After holding the lead for twenty laps, a pit stop for a change of plugs dropped him to fourth. When a British entrant's car blew its engine and deposited oil on the approach to a bend, several drivers spun into the undergrowth, one demolishing a fence. Since the British driver had cruised to a halt beyond the corner and marshals had been oblivious to the imminent danger, there had been no warning. Nuvolari, who had been first on the scene, had somehow sensed danger, backed off and allowed the Auto Union to run its course across the grass before continuing unscathed.

After fifty laps, Nuvolari was third, fifty-eight seconds behind the leading Mercedes. For the remaining thirty laps, he mesmerized the crowd, sliding the silver car at will and slashing the lap record time and again as he took second place and reduced the leader's advantage. Going faster still, Nuvolari closed in remorselessly. 'I don't remember what lap it was,' recalled Walker, 'but I do remember the reaction from the crowd when he took the lead. The place went absolutely mad. I'd never seen anything like it. Incredible!'

Nuvolari appeared overwhelmed by the reception from the crowd. He spoke neither English nor German but the look of delight on his face said all that was necessary as he was carried shoulder high.

'What we didn't know,' said Murray, 'was that Nuvolari was in pain. I was not alone in discovering quite some time afterwards that he had actually broken a rib during that incident with the stag. He didn't like hospitals or medical people apparently and he hadn't said anything to his team. He had bandaged himself up very tightly but I'm sure Don-ington's bumps – of which there were many – must have taken their toll. And I should also point out that the race lasted for more than three hours. It was a fantastic performance. Absolutely incredible.'

In years to come, when asked to name his favourite driver, Murray would always nominate Nuvolari. 'He is the best who ever lived,' Walker told Frank Keating in an interview for the *Guardian* in 1986. 'I remember like yesterday him winning at Donington in 1938. A dare-devil? Crikey, yes! He was a right scruffy 'erbert; an engaging, archetypal, arm-waving, laughing, hysterical Latin. In the car, he was all arms and elbows and thrills, four-wheel drifts round corners and smiles as he realized he'd arrived 50 miles an hour quicker than he should have, all opposite lock and brakes and dust. Nuvolari was the guy we queued up all night for, unquestionably the greatest of them all.'

Murray's clear preference may also have been a handy way, in future years, of side-stepping the ticklish problem of offending the current top drivers he knew and respected. But there can be no doubt that the race he witnessed on 22 October 1938 made a deep impression.

When the German national anthem rang out over Donington that afternoon, the crowd stood respectfully to attention. There was enthusiastic talk of another Grand Prix at Donington the following October. By then, however, 'Deutschland Über Alles' had taken on a more sinister meaning.

4

WAR ZONE

The International Six Days Trial (ISDT) was considered to be a supreme test of motorcycle riders and their machines. Covering more than 1,250 miles of public roads, competitors from many nations had to obey strict rules while running more or less non-stop, adhering to crippling time allowances and carrying out their own repairs on modified road bikes. Graham Walker had captained the British team to success in 1926 and finished runner-up on three other occasions. Having reduced his involvement as a competitor, Walker was a natural choice for the British War Office when looking for a manager of the Army entry in 1939. With Britain having hosted the ISDT for the previous two years, Austria was earmarked for the date in late August. Politically, it would turn out to be an unfortunate choice.

'I accompanied my parents on this wonderful trip,' recalled Murray. 'The event was based amid the absolutely glorious scenery you would expect in and around Salzburg. The only problem was, following its annexation by Germany [in the spring of 1938], Austria was totally under the control of the Nazis. Tension was rising but we had reassurances that everything would be OK. It was while we were in our hotel that news came through that Germany had invaded Poland. You can imagine how we felt after hearing that.

'My father immediately went off to find Korpsführer [Adolf] Hühnlein, who was the boss of German motor sport and who I had last seen turned out in tweeds in the paddock at Donington. He was looking rather different now in his breeches, brown boots, military jacket and pill box hat! Hühnlein told my father that, even if things did turn nasty, he personally would guarantee the team safe passage out of the country. My father then asked him: "Can you tell me where you are in the government hierarchy?" When Hühnlein replied that he was number ten, my father asked: "What happens if numbers one to nine say we've got to stay?" That's when we upped sticks, and the team didn't actually finish the trial. There was the question of whether to go to Switzerland – which you could reach quicker, but faced possible internment – or take a chance and dash to France. And that's what we did. It was an eventful journey, to say the least. We walked into our home in Enfield [in north London], turned on the radio and heard [Prime Minister] Neville Chamberlain giving his declaration of war.'

About to turn sixteen the following month, Murray was dispatched to Devon, chosen by Highgate, his north London public school, as a suitable evacuation point for its pupils. Describing himself as 'average', as a student Walker applied the same diligence later seen in his role as commentator. He came away with the equivalent of today's A levels and the ability to play the bugle while rising to Company Sergeant Major of the School Corps, with the added distinction of having been made a prefect.

His education complete, Murray was keen to play his part in the war effort. 'I volunteered for the Army,' he explained in an interview with the British Automobile Racing Club's *Startline* magazine in 2008. 'If you volunteered, you were accepted to what you had volunteered for. If you waited for your conscription number to come up, you went where they sent you, and I didn't want to end up in the infantry or lighting smoke generators in Wolverhampton! I volunteered for tanks, and I was accepted. Then I found I had a year to spare before actually joining the Army simply because at that time during the war they literally hadn't got enough equipment to train people on. All the equipment was going directly to the fighting troops and I had to hang around for just under a year. So I got a business scholarship with Dunlop, which put me through all the various branches of what a big organization does.'

Typically, Walker downplays the fact that he had been granted one of only a few annual scholarships handed out by this major global force in the rubber business. He would look back on this period as an invaluable grounding that would serve him in two ways in his future career: first as an executive in advertising, and second as a motor sport commentator reporting on tyres being taken to the extremes of endurance.

Before then, however, he received the keenly anticipated call in the form of a telegram instructing him to report to the 30th Primary Training Wing (PTW) at Bovington on 1 October 1942. The camp in Dorset would mark the bottom of a massive curve as Murray learned as much about himself as he did about driving a tank. Eighteen character-building months later, Second Lieutenant Graeme Murray Walker, Royal Armoured Corps, passed out at Sandhurst, taking the salute from General Dwight D. Eisenhower, Commander in Chief of the Combined Allied Forces being made ready for a landing on the northern coast of Europe.

'I was very lucky to join the Royal Scots Greys,' recalled Murray. 'This regiment had a proud history, having fought in Palestine and in General Montgomery's Eighth Army. It had fought its way through France, into and out of Belgium, and was at Nederweert in Holland, where I joined it as a young, totally inexperienced new boy.'

Walker had the rough edges knocked off the pip on the shoulders of his uniform as his unit moved to the so-called Second Front.

Murray later recounted his initial experience when talking to Kirsty Young on the BBC's *Desert Island Discs*. 'When I joined the regiment, my Squadron Leader greeted me,' recalled Walker. 'He said: "Nice to have you with us, George." And I said, a bit haltingly: "The G stands for Graeme actually, sir. But my friends call me Murray." He said: "I thought it was Murray-hyphen-Walker." And you felt that he was quite disappointed that it wasn't Murray-hyphen-Walker. He said: "You will be responsible to Sergeant McTavish." I was fresh out of Sandhurst. I've got this single pip on my shoulder and I thought, What's he think this is? Confetti? And he said: "I know what you're thinking: you're God's gift to the British Army because you're fresh out of Sandhurst. You know nothing. McTavish has been with us since Palestine, as he was right through North Africa. I've benefited from that man's experience. And it's probably because of that I'm alive and talking to you now." And, of course, he was absolutely right.'

The learning process continued its rapid and uncompromising climb as the Allied forces advanced towards the banks of the Rhine and the German border. While coping with this fraught existence, Walker was to receive the surprise of his life.

'The going was very tough indeed with the Germans resisting every inch of the way with anti-tank guns, rivers, ditches, snipers, blown bridges and Panzerfausts [hand-held anti-tank weapons],' said Walker on *Desert Island Discs*. 'Then I had this quite incredible experience. We were having a pretty bloody time clearing the approaches. And every so often we used to have to come back to replenish fuel and ammunition. As we drove along towards the replacement depot, I saw four people standing there and I idly thought to myself, Gosh, that bloke looks just like my father. And as we got closer, I saw this man in military uniform – my father was not in the Army – was actually my father. I stopped and jumped out. I can't remember what I said; it was probably something like:"What the hell are you doing here?" Because we were half an hour away from extreme shot and shell.

'Cut a long story short: as a magazine editor [of *Motor Cycling*], as he was then, he had used his contacts. First of all to get accredited as a special correspondent, and secondly – and I don't know to this day how he found out where my regiment was – he'd got up there. I was pretty worried because the last thing I wanted to see was my father where he was. We took on what we wanted in the way of fuel and ammunition, and I trundled off again.'

'Do you know why he did it?' asked Kirsty Young.

'Because he wanted to see his little boy, I expect,' Murray replied quietly. 'I was very fond of him. And he was very fond of me. And hopefully he wanted to see me again.'

During the following weeks there were moments when Murray wondered whether he would see his parents again, particularly when faced with conditions which he described as 'Dante's Inferno' as the Germans stoutly resisted this attempted breach of their border. The feeling of euphoria when he eventually saw a crude piece of sign-writing declaring YOU ARE NOW ENTERING GERMANY would soon be subjugated by what lay ahead.

Murray's unit was part of an Allied advance ordered to beat the Russians (advancing from the east) to the Baltic coast, but progress was slow and painful. On 2 May 1945, the Royal Scots Greys eventually reached their goal at Wismar. The war came to an end not long after.

Assuming a peacetime rank within the armed forces proved difficult as politics came into play. Murray had to fight hard for his overdue promotion to the role of Captain with the recently formed British Army of the Rhine. He was stationed at the Royal Armoured Corps Training Centre at Belsen. By the time he reached this infamous place in October 1946, all traces of the former Nazi death camp had been expunged. 'It became,' said Walker, 'a good place to finish one's Army career and a dramatic contrast to the utterly unspeakable place it had formerly been.'

Six months later he was on board a ship, bound for Hull and a return to civilian life. It was the end of a period which Murray would only speak about if asked during his future years in broadcasting.

'He tended not to talk about the war years,' said Tony Jardine, who worked with Walker as a pit lane reporter. 'But we would obviously have dinner together when covering a Grand Prix and that's when you could tease out the stories. One I remember very well concerned the advance across the German border and on towards the Baltic. He was in the lead tank of this convoy. So, he was in charge, and you can imagine him saying: "This way, boys. C'mon, follow me!"

'According to Murray, the roads got narrower and narrower, to the point where he could go no further. So there he was, stuck, with forty-odd vehicles jammed behind him. He had his little map or chart or whatever it was, and he'd gone the wrong way. He had to get the whole lot to reverse something like three or four kilometres. Think about doing that in a tank! As he said, it wasn't hard to imagine the comments from the other lads: "Who's bloody leading this thing? What sort of idiot has done this?" Apparently, his superiors tore a strip off him for that.

'It obviously wasn't funny at the time, but he was laughing about it over dinner. Of course, that led to jokes from the rest of us on the ITV team. We'd say Murray should never do the voice on a satnav because he'd be shouting: "Look at that! It's a junction. Incredible! Turn right or turn left. It's one way or the other. Unless I'm very much mistaken, turn right. No! What am I saying? It's left! Left!" He loved that. Absolutely classic Murray.

'He was a wonderful raconteur. Apart from entertaining us so brilliantly, you could see, from the way he talked, how he'd been so good in business before he became a full-time commentator. He knew all about how to sell himself and get the point across. It was no surprise he'd been so good in advertising. It was easy to forget he'd made – as Murray might say – "an absolutely gigantic" success of that as well as everything else he'd ever done.'

5

THE HARD SELL

M urray Walker could have written a manual based entirely on his life in the advertising world. He could also have produced a travelogue covering a sales trip to India and Ceylon (as Sri Lanka was known at the time) that would make your eyes water as readily as the curries Murray grew to love. The thrust of the narrative would have embraced experiences ranging from the extravagant and patronizing gin-and-tonic style of life post-British Raj in Bombay, to shared toilets in ramshackle lodgings off the beaten track – all in aid of selling Aspro pain relief tablets to a teeming and vibrant population.

Capping this bizarre eighteen-week journey would be the failure of his company to act on a single recommendation outlined in Walker's lengthy and carefully crafted report. Apart from enriching Murray's understanding of the wider world, the trip had been a complete waste of time. It was an unsatisfactory conclusion to his second foray into advertising. The first had come almost as soon as he arrived back in England after the Second World War and returned to civilian life, as he recalled during an interview in 2008.

'At the end of 1947, I joined – as opposed to rejoining – Dunlop because I was not a student as I had been before, but a full-time employee,' said Murray. 'I worked in the advertising department of the tyre division. I got promoted and moved from Fort Dunlop in Birmingham to their headquarters in St James's Square in London, where

I found myself in the Public Relations Department. I switched back to advertising and became the manager for Dunlopillo latex film cushioning and general rubber components such as conveyor belts, rubber buckets and all sorts of industrial things. After I had been with Dunlop for eight years, I belatedly realized that it was a "Live, horse, and you'll get grass" sort of company where, if you hang around for a long time, you'll receive a reward that doesn't amount to much.

'I was clearly never going to get very far, so I left and joined Aspro and, almost immediately, I was sent off to India and Ceylon to take a look at the market out there. One of the many things I learned on that trip was that a lot of the folk in India believed Aspro increased sexual power. I'd never been told that was the case although maybe if you believed it enough, it actually would. I have to say I never tried . . .'

Walker's disappointment at the lack of interest in his findings from the Far East venture was soothed somewhat by a pay rise and promotion to advertising manager for Aspro Home Products Division. This covered, in Murray's words, 'a rag bag' of items ranging from Lifeguard Disinfectant, starch and air fresheners to pet products. Lifeguard ran a promotion offering the top prize of a house worth £30,000 – a substantial reward (worth £850,000 today). Having suffered the privations of war a decade before, Walker was startled by the response of the winner, a housewife from Croydon.

'I went to see her with a giant dummy cheque and a photographer to record her surprise and delight when she opened the front door and got the good news,' recalled Murray. 'I may as well have told her she'd won a bar of chocolate for all the emotion she showed.

'"Will you tell me who you bought your winning bottle of Lifeguard Disinfectant from?" I asked.

'"Why?"

'"Because – great news! – whoever sold it to you has won a superb Ford Popular car."

"'Well, it was the chap down the road, and if I'd known I was going to win, I wouldn't have bought it there because I don't like him.'"

If he was honest, Walker didn't much care for the company he worked for. He was happy to double his annual salary to £2,000 and accept an offer from the advertising agency McCann Erickson to promote motor products – on paper and given his interests, a more suitable arrangement. Once again, however, Murray had steered into a career cul-de-sac. Two years later, he found reverse, changed direction and accelerated towards a job that would last for twenty-three years.

Walker had come into contact with Masius & Ferguson when the aspiring agency had dealings with some minor products manufactured by the Aspro group. A growing familiarity between Murray and the agency over the years made a chat about job prospects in 1959 almost a formality.

Walker's first client would be the Mars confectionery and pet-foods company, named after its owner, Forrest Mars. In 1932, the American had set up his chocolate business in Slough, with the pet-foods division established in Melton Mowbray. Murray was impressed by the tough but efficient business ethic employed throughout the company and knew he would have his work cut out to meet Mr Mars' demands when it came to advertising and sales.

'Forrest Mars didn't think or act like other people,' said Murray. 'His company was the first in the UK to work to the USP [unique selling point] philosophy, involving intensive research to find out what potential buyers wanted from the product and, from that, the creation of a USP. Hence, among the brands I worked on, we had "PAL – Prolongs Active Life" [dog food], "Opal Fruits – Made to make your mouth water" and "Liver-rich Lassie gives head-to-tail health". I would constantly be described in later interviews as also being the originator of one of the greatest USPs of all time – "A Mars a day helps you work, rest and play" – but I wasn't responsible for that one. Unfortunately!'

Walker was, however, the inspiration behind two of the cleverest catchphrases in the pet food industry. When considering what would appear to be the bland and limited scope of bird seed, Murray came up with 'Trill makes budgies bounce with health'. In fact, he had made a rod for his own back. Trill was so successful it dominated sales, leaving the agency to ponder how the market could possibly be expanded.

In 1964 his firm became Masius Wynne-Williams. John Ayling joined as a graduate in the media department not long after. 'Murray was one of my first board account directors; an enthusiastic, witty, albeit humble leader,' wrote Ayling on the 'More About Advertising' website in 2021. 'On a Friday in 1966, Murray called a meeting with one of the account group teams to spend the weekend considering a major issue on one of our brand leader products. I was a bit out of my depth in this early discussion in my career, but excited to be part of the team. The product was Trill, a massively profitable brand at a time when virtually every home had a budgerigar, and Trill dominated the market. The client had asked us to review improving profitability on such an outstanding successful product. Television was crucial to its success. Meeting again on Monday, with the creative guys pretty subdued, Murray, as always, bounced into the room. "I think I've cracked it," he said, smiling at the highly paid creatives: "An only budgie is a lonely budgie." Genius! Lateral, strategic thinking at its best. Many homes in the UK purchased a second pet for their birdcage and even my mum in deepest East Grinstead supported her impoverished son's agency. It was an example of Murray's team ethic.'

Staying loyal to the firm and showing belief in clients' products at one stage produced a strange and potentially difficult test: Walker and his colleagues would regularly eat dog food in public. Murray explained the oddity to Kirsty Young on *Desert Island Discs*.

'It was my job – our job – to convert the British housewife from feeding the dog household scraps on which the dog was seemingly perfectly happy and fit. We had to persuade her to go to a shop, buy a can, carry it home, open it up, give it to the dog, not knowing what was in it. And we had to get the trade to stock the stuff and sell it. They suspected that the can was full of factory floor sweepings, when it wasn't. It was actually very high-quality stuff. In order to convince the trade how good it was, in extremis, we would open a can and eat some in front of them.'

'And how was it?' asked Young.

'Nothing wrong with me – ruff, ruff!'

Supermarket shelves stacked high with tinned dog food of every flavour subsequently justified the assault on Walker's taste buds in the interests of canine cuisine. Such dedication would bring increasing rewards as Masius Wynne-Williams expanded rapidly to become the largest agency in Britain, opening branches around the world. Jack Wynne-Williams, formerly a partner but now in full command, was keen to encourage young blood within his burgeoning company.

'I had joined as the lowest form of animal life – an account director in the advertising business,' recalled Murray in 2013. 'When I joined in 1959, we had a billing of £6 million a year, which was a lot of money. There was a London and a Hamburg office to service. Twenty years later, we had offices in twenty-four countries and a billing of £1.5 billion a year.

'Jack had what he called his "Young Turks". There were four of us and he called us in one by one. He said to me: "You talk a lot. D'you want to put your money where your mouth is? I'm going to sell you a bit of the business." He said it would cost £30,000, which was – and still is – a lot of money. I didn't have thirty thousand washers. He told me that Warburg, the agency's bankers, would be happy to assist by offering a loan at 10 per cent interest. At that time, 10 per cent was actually very reasonable as these things go. But we were talking about £500,000 by today's values. He said: "You know what this business is like; we're doing all right now but we could lose business at the drop of a hat." Being a pretty cautious sort of chap, I gave this a lot of thought and reasoned that the agency was going, and would continue to go, from strength to strength. So I accepted. The agency did indeed continue to prosper. I'm happy to say it was by far and away the best financial decision I ever made!'

Walker rode the wave of success, dealing with a broad portfolio of clients. His enthusiasm and clever thinking were applied to Baby-cham, Imperial Tobacco, Nescafé ('Coffee with life in it!'), Woolworths, Wilkinson Sword razor blades, Weetabix, the Beecham brand Phyllosan ('Fortifies the over-forties!') and road safety campaigns for the Government's Central Office of Information ('Don't ask a man to drink and drive' and 'Clunk, click – every trip').

Many of the foregoing, however, had to be delegated when Murray was put in charge of the newly acquired Vauxhall Motors account. Being keen on motoring, Walker knew the depth of this particular challenge since the Vauxhall models were more notorious for chrome and rust than elegance and performance. He would later describe the top-of-the-range Viscount as 'the ultimate in a soft-suspension, personality-free Squidgemobile. It oozed along with effortless smoothness – but absolutely zilch in the way of automotive charisma.'

Walker may have laboured hard on presenting a fresh image, but his well-worked words would be undercut by painful reality when it came to promoting Vauxhall sales abroad. Apart from being firmly established Opel territory (part of the same General Motors group as Vauxhall), the various European countries had their own problems. In a twelve-month period, a grand total of forty-seven Vauxhall cars had been sold in France – and all of them at heavily discounted prices to GM employees. When Murray got to Stockholm, the despairing

Swedish boss gave a vivid demonstration of his difficulties with the British company. There, in the service department, was a Vauxhall Victor, delivered from the factory in Luton with drum brakes on one side and disc brakes on the other. No amount of advertising blurb could cover such a lamentable failure to produce a reliable motor car. Walker, for once, was lost for words.

Things became politically fraught when Vauxhall's American owners began to play a more influential part in European sales, Masius Wynne-Williams eventually being shovelled to one side. But if Murray found that difficult, he was to be tested even more by the acquisition of the Co-op account. This brought him into contact with a company he described as 'a massive sprawl, loosely integrated by common ideology that was like a handful of sand – very difficult to get hold of. And it interfered with the machinery. The advent and growth of supermarkets was making the Co-op, with its self-governing individual societies, banks, farms, milk business, funeral services and tea business, look ponderous, old-fashioned and irrelevant.'

All of this was adding to a sense of increasing frustration. By the end of 1979, Walker was fifty-six and had been with the company for twenty years. As the eighties dawned and keen young executives made their presence felt, Murray found he had less to do and, as a result, no longer felt the same sense of achievement. He sold his shares, took a full pension and in 1982 said a cheerful, if reluctant, goodbye.

Rather than retire quietly, Murray Walker's life was about to engage an extra gear and take off in a completely different direction. The only similarity was that the ability to talk would continue to be his greatest asset – even if, in this new role, he didn't always say the right thing. Murray's final audition for this new job had actually taken place thirty-three years earlier in the middle of a windswept field in the Midlands.

6

A WORD IN YOUR EAR

'*That very healthy note you heard just then was Frank Gerard. He's driving, as usual, his inimitable race.*'

The voice was that of Murray Walker. The sound, like the urgent tearing of calico, was an ERA. The elderly British racing car was, in fact, driven by Bob (not 'Frank') Gerard. No matter. Walker pressed on with his BBC Radio commentary covering the final laps of the 1949 British Grand Prix.

'*He* [Gerard] *was second . . . he won, I'm sorry . . . in Jersey only last week, as you know. This is the same car that he used then. And this ERA is well over eleven years old. In fact, I believe I'm right in saying it's twelve years old. Which is a pretty astounding record. It's up against the cream of modern European racing cars today and the very greatest credit is due to Gerard.*'

The green ERA (English Racing Automobiles) was an indication of the parlous state of international motor racing just four years after the end of the Second World War. Neither Formula 1 nor the F1 World Championship, as we would come to know them, had been invented. This Grand Prix, the second at Silverstone, would be for a hotch-potch of machinery, much of it dusted down following the end of hostilities. Gerard's venerable ERA, lovingly prepared, was a case in point.

The Maserati of Baron Emmanuel de Graffenried was leading Gerard by more than a minute after almost four hours of racing. Walker had been positioned throughout at Stowe corner, on the opposite side of Silverstone from the pits (then located between Abbey Curve and Woodcote); the main commentary point was manned by Max Robertson, a professional sports presenter.

'*Now, Max,*' continued Walker, '*I think de Graffenried has either just gone past you or will be very shortly with you. Can you see him?*' (Walker, in fact, had mistaken the similar Maserati of British driver Fred Ashmore for the leader, who had already passed Robertson's commentary point. Ashmore was three laps behind, in sixth place.)

'*De Graffenried is on his last lap now,*' responded Robertson. '*He should be very nearly up to you. In fact, Bob Gerard will also be passing us very shortly also on his last lap ... and here comes Bob Gerard! He's driven extremely well, only coming into the pits once for refuelling. He's driven exactly as he has done every race; a purposeful, steady race from the start, lapping at about two* [minutes] *twenty* [seconds] *to two twenty-two, whereas de Graffenried has been able to lap at about two eighteen. De Graffenried I think is just passing you now; I see a red streak going down there – so over to you for the final description.*'

'*Yes, Max, I'm sorry,*' said Murray, '*it was Ashmore; it's liable to be a bit confusing. De Graffenried is now taking Stowe corner for the last time this afternoon. He bounces a bit as it goes round with his yellow wheels spinning. And he's motoring ... as he goes down to the chicane* [introduced before Club Corner, never to be used again] *he looks back to see if there's any opposition. And de Graffenried is one of the few people that doesn't change down for the first corner on this chicane. He's entering it now and I'll follow him through.*

'*He's going up to the hairpin bend, taking no chances this time. He crosses his right hand right over his left in the peculiar way that they do. Round the 180-degree bend and into the 90-degree one – and is now heading up the straight to the Abbey Curve ... and I think in about three seconds, Max, he'll be into your sight to take over the finishing line.*'

'*Can't see him,*' said Robertson. '*Is he going to come? Yes, he's here!*

Flashing into sight. Is this the last lap? Yes, it is ... Up goes the chequered flag ... and he's the winner!'

Robertson stopped talking and allowed his microphone to pick up the plummy voice of the track commentator, speaking to no fewer than 120,000 spectators who had been desperate to watch an international motor race with cars driven by competitors with foreign-sounding names. Max Robertson had not been so keen to make the journey to Silverstone.

'I was about as expert on cars as Murray was about fly fishing,' recalled Robertson. 'Silverstone was not my spiritual home. The chap in charge of outside broadcasts thought, because I could do tennis, which was fast sport, I could do that. He was totally wrong! I hated the noise. I hated the smell. I think my undoing eventually was when I said something like "There goes Ferrari in a Farina ..." People often ask me what a radio commentator − or a commentator of any sort − needs for a sport. The answer is, you've got to know the sport, you've got to be keen on it, have real enthusiasm and be able to communicate. Murray had all those in super-abundance.'

Walker's zeal had received one stern test that afternoon during his Silverstone mini-marathon at the microphone. 'There was an unpleasant incident with a chap called [John] Bolster,' he recalled in 1996 during an interview with the journalist Robert Philip. 'Bolster was a very flamboyant bloke, wore a deerstalker hat, had a walrus moustache and spoke in a very distinctive, plummy voice. He was a prominent motoring journalist and he was racing an ERA on that day. I was commentating for the first time at Stowe − don't forget, there was only a rope and maybe a few straw bales between the cars and spectators back then − when he came barrelling down Hangar Straight towards me. He loses control, goes end over end, and is flung out of the car, landing more or less at my feet outside the commentary box with what looked like blood pouring out of him. I thought, Cripes, they never told me what to say about this sort of thing. Accurately, but understatedly, I said: "Bolster's gone off!" I thought he was dead. In fact he recovered and went on to become a pit lane reporter for the BBC. As far as I was concerned, I had stumbled through my first commentary as a professional – if that's the right word.'

Murray's first experience with a microphone had occurred a few weeks earlier and could be attributed to his father. Having stopped competing in 1935, Graham Walker's voice and experience as a rider blended perfectly when he was asked by BBC Radio to commentate on the Isle of Man TT and the Ulster Grand Prix motorcycle races. From time to time, BBC Radio also covered minor events such as a hill climb for cars and motorbikes at Shelsley Walsh, a classic event in Worcestershire that had been running since 1905. When Walker had to drop out at the last minute, the BBC asked the circuit commentator to take his place. Since the resulting void in the event's information service for spectators was more or less Walker's fault, the organizers asked Graham what he intended to do about it.

'Why not try the boy?' he asked, pointing his ever-present pipe towards twenty-five-year-old Murray. 'I think he'll be all right. Even if he isn't, it won't be a disaster because he'll only be talking to the spectators and they'll be able to see what's going on anyway.' This was true enough. With cars tackling the short climb at one-minute intervals, there would not be the continuous wheel-to-wheel action associated with a race track.

Once Murray had been accepted to make his speaking debut with such a relatively straightforward job, he had his eye on a much bigger prize. Walker's target audience would be the BBC producer, Jim Pestridge, not the spectators lining the 1,000-yard course. If anything, the paying public would feel they were getting more than their money's worth as Murray babbled incessantly, giving every conceivable detail about competitors and their machines while, at times, describing

blindingly obvious on-track sequences as if the spectators were somewhere else. Moreover, according to this voice booming from the
loudspeakers, many of these happenings seemed to be blessed with
more excitement than they truly deserved.

Proof that Walker had hit his mark came with an audition to join
the BBC team commentating on a motor race at the Goodwood circuit in West Sussex. He proved acceptable and spoke well enough to
be invited to try the more demanding and high-profile support role
to Max Robertson at the British Grand Prix. The prospect of following in his father's footsteps brought one mild dilemma: Murray would
have to give up riding in motorcycle trials.

'There was a lot to be said for that form of motor sport,' recalled
Walker. 'It was tough and demanding; a real challenge for man and
machine on cross-country terrain that, in places, you wouldn't want to
walk over, never mind attempt to ride a motorbike. I loved it. Apart
from getting you out of the house and into stunning countryside,
there was a tremendous camaraderie – probably because we all thought
we were slightly mad to be doing this, often in the middle of winter.

'I did it for about two years – lots of trials and six-day enduros. I
won a gold medal in the International Six Days Trial in 1949, rode in
the Southern Experts Trial and won a First Class Award in the Scottish
Trial. I was good, but I wasn't brilliant. If I'm really honest with myself,
it didn't matter enough, or I wouldn't have given up, particularly
when I was trying to carve out a career for myself in advertising and,
at the same time, the work with television increased.'

Walker and Robertson had been assisted at Silverstone by F. J.
Findon, the editor of *Light Car* magazine and a commentator on vari-
ous motoring events in the Midlands. The *Radio Times* listing on
Saturday 14 May showed, under the heading Light Programme (later
to become Radio 2), 'Sports Parade' beginning at 1 p.m. with cricket
(Glamorgan v. Worcestershire and Leicestershire v. New Zealanders),

interrupted by thirty minutes with the Richard Crean Orchestra and a twenty-five-minute sector on 'New Books and Old Books'. 'International Motor Racing' was scheduled for 2.25 p.m., the fifteen-minute slot followed by a further sixty-five minutes of cricket. Then came forty-five minutes of 'Band Call' with the BBC Variety Orchestra, which led to a fifteen-minute update from Silverstone at 4.30 p.m. The finish of the race was covered during a thirty-minute session at the end of the afternoon.

Clearly satisfied with Walker's performance at Silverstone, the *Radio Times* ('Journal of the BBC – Price Twopence') on 26 May listed 'The British Empire Trophy with commentary by Raymond Glendenning and Alan Clarke, assisted by Murray Walker and Leslie Adams from the Grandstand and Cronk ny Mona, Isle of Man'. Murray would return to the island not long after to take up commentary duties alongside his father at the TT motorcycle races.

Murray was at home in every sense. An annual visit to the Isle of Man had been part of the Walker family's routine, Murray having been taken there as a babe in arms while his father raced. Now they were working together, Graham located in the start/finish commentary box while Murray took his microphone, earphones, wires and the inevitable clipboard to various points on the 37.7-mile circuit. In 1949 he stood in a slip road at Ballacraine, 7 miles from the start. Walker nearly came to grief when Les Graham, a leading rider, overshot the corner and the clutch lever of his AJS threatened to disembowel the commentator, who somehow remained standing – and speaking.

Graham and Murray moulded into an outstanding team. 'Even though we couldn't physically see each other, we quickly reached the point where one knew precisely when the other was ready to come in with something to say,' recalled Murray. 'But whatever was being said, I completely and happily bowed to my father's knowledge and experience. At the TT, he knew every lump and bump in the road; he knew every turn that was critical, and he could explain why that turn was critical in terms that were easy to understand. I know I'm obviously biased, but he had an electrifying voice and a delivery that generated excitement. We – I should say "he" – pulled in huge audiences and the BBC, of course, loved it. And what helped – and helped me enormously – was that my father knew absolutely everybody that was worth knowing in the world of motorcycle racing.'

Murray would not be slow in building up his own contacts book thanks to an outgoing, friendly demeanour and the fact that the Isle of Man TT was the ultimate race for bike riders. He was on the best of terms with Geoff Duke, Phil Read, Giacomo Agostini, John Surtees and, his favourite of them all, Mike Hailwood. 'I make no bones about the fact that, in my opinion, Mike Hailwood was the greatest of all time,' said Murray. 'Apart from being an extremely modest and likeable chap, he was a natural-born genius in the saddle – and an engaging hell-raiser out of it! I watched his rise to the very top and commentated on every one of his twelve TT victories. He was a very dear friend, great fun to be with, and, rather like me, he would never have made it had it not been for the support of his father.'

Murray was devastated in 1962 when his father died after a short illness at the age of sixty-six. 'My mother and I were plunged into grief,' he said. 'I can tell you, I adored my father. He was a wonderful man; kind, generous. People would look at me and say, "That's Graham Walker's little boy." I do actually remember thinking I would love the time to come when someone looked at my father and said: "That's Murray Walker's dad." It's not the sort of thing I would ever have said to my father – that I'd love to be bigger than him one day. I don't think he'd have been hurt. I think he would have understood. But he would probably have thought I was being big-headed. My father – in terms of fame, achievement and any other measure – was a much, much bigger person than I am.'

Nonetheless, Murray quickly established a reputation that, whether he recognized it or not, was based on his father's ethic of hard work and enthusiasm for his subject. Murray's experience astride a competition bike in the late 1940s meant he was ideally qualified to commentate when the Independent Television network (ITV) decided to cover trails riding. Murray had got married in 1957 and his wife Elizabeth was to play a significant supportive role as he integrated a full-on commentating schedule with his Monday-to-Friday commitments to the advertising agency.

'I look back in amazement at what I did,' said Walker in 2013. 'I don't know how I did it, but the answer is, if in life you want to do something badly enough, you find a way, don't you? This was when ITV were doing what is now called motocross but what was then known as scrambling. Every Friday, I'd leave the office in St James's Square at 5 p.m. and get on the Tube to Cockfosters, at the northern extremity of the London Underground system. Elizabeth would be waiting in the car, loaded up with the dog and provisions, and we would then drive to Yorkshire – and this was before the motorways and the M1 – to somewhere like Wakefield, Ripon or Leeds, work all day Saturday for the national network, and then on Sunday, with the same riders on the same bikes at the same circuit, do the whole thing again for the northern TV network, ABC. When it got dark at 4 p.m., I would drive back in our Triumph Herald estate with the boxer dog in the back.

'It makes my blood run cold to think about this, because we had one of those gas stoves which Elizabeth had in the footwell. She would heat up some stew, which I would eat on the move. On Monday morning, I was back in the office. One year, we did this for thirty-two weekends in succession. And I loved it! Adrenalin conquers all.'

Come 1969, that insatiable sense of excitement was about to find a completely new outlet. The harbourside at Monte Carlo, shimmering in the sunshine, could not be further removed from the mud and murk of a Yorkshire hillside in winter. Or, indeed, a pokey commentary box on the flat expanses of Silverstone. The captivating effect of Walker's adrenalin surge, however, would remain exactly as before.

7

LIFT-OFF

On 18 May 1969, at the Kennedy Space Center in Florida, final preparations were being made for a Saturn V rocket to lift off and begin the Apollo 10 mission to the moon. Views from a previous space flight were shown on BBC Television's *Sunday Grandstand*. A besuited and serious-looking Cliff Michelmore leaned towards the camera. Speaking with quietly dramatic effect, the seasoned presenter summed up: '*A view from space. Some find it frightening; others, thrilling. Some find it fruitful; others, wasteful. But the Apollo programme goes on. We've now, today, reached Apollo 10. There is, at this moment, less than an hour to go until lift-off.*'

The eight-day mission would be a success. While astronaut John Young remained in the Command Module, Thomas Stafford and Eugene Cernan would fly the Apollo Lunar Module to a descent orbit within 8.4 nautical miles of the moon's surface. It would be the final dress rehearsal for the first lunar landing two months later.

Michelmore's solemn description of the Apollo 10 countdown preparations had been inserted into the afternoon's programming that included, as its sporting highlight, three visits to the Monaco Grand Prix. This, in its own very small way, was a venture into the relative unknown for Murray Walker. He would be broadcasting live from the Monaco trackside for the first time.

The BBC had felt that such a glamorous occasion would be worthy of a taster before the start of the *Grandstand* programme. With the sound of racing engines echoing around the harbour, the camera had panned across the yachts and surrounding white architecture to come to rest on Murray, arms folded and wearing a light-coloured jacket over a polo shirt buttoned to the top. '*This,*' he began, with heavy emphasis on the opening word,'*is the fabulous location for what is going to be the third Formula 1 World Championship event of 1969. The Monaco Grand Prix, held here at Monte Carlo, this fantastic 1.9-mile circuit which plunges and rises, twists and turns round the harbour in Monte Carlo and where, in spite of that, the lap record, held by Richard Attwood, is nearly 80 miles per hour. And here this afternoon, the world's leading drivers are going to race on this course which has seen men like Nuvolari win here. And you will be joining us at about ten to three to see the 1969 Monaco Grand Prix.*' Then a fixed smile while the picture held for what must have seemed four very long seconds before returning to the studio in London.

Walker would then have made his way along the harbour, bustling as normal, many years before the quayside became the F1 paddock. In 1969, the eleven F1 teams were based in garages dotted in and around the Principality.

The main talking point that year had been whether there would be a race at all. The teams had arrived fresh from the previous race in Barcelona where a pair of Lotus cars (driven by Graham Hill and Jochen Rindt) had crashed heavily following rear wing failures. This had prompted much discussion about rear aerofoils which had grown to such a ridiculous degree they were mounted on stalks.

The Automobile Club de Monaco, as organizers of the race, had canvassed the teams about removing the rear aerofoils. Everyone had agreed, with the exception of Ken Tyrrell, who felt he would have too much to lose because his Matra-Ford MS80 had been designed spe-cifically with the wings in mind. The cars had therefore run as normal during practice late on Thursday afternoon. In the meantime, enough members of the sport's governing body – the Commission Sportive

Internationale (CSI) — had been mustered. They agreed the wings should be banned with immediate effect on the grounds of safety. The lap times set on Thursday were declared null and void.

The teams had not taken the decision well. At one point on Friday morning, Monaco had been quiet as arguments raged when there should have been official practice. Murray Walker was not alone in being relieved when an agreement was reached: the cars would henceforth run without rear wings.

Having done his homework in the usual thorough manner, come Sunday morning Walker would have been more concerned about his place of work for the afternoon. Calling it a 'commentary position' would be like describing a basement flat without windows as a panoramic penthouse.

Broadcasters were plonked on the pavement lining the main straight and across the road from the pits. They would sit on folding chairs behind a bench. A flimsy cloth canopy overhead would supposedly provide shelter if it rained but would offer no deterrent when it came to preventing glare on the 12-inch monitor and its images — which were in black and white. Two layers of low-mounted crash barrier in front of a roll of split-hazel fencing (draped in advertising banners) separated the commentators from the track and racing cars under full acceleration. The noise was unspeakable. A lip microphone was barely adequate. In between shouting his commentary, Walker would be hard-pressed to hear cues from London in his earphones. With the race yet to start, however, Murray was able to listen while Michelmore linked the end of a profile on Graham Hill (the reigning world champion) with the start of the race.

'*That film profile of Graham Hill,*' said Michelmore, '*was made to celebrate his second winning of the World Championship last year in Mexico. He is also the man who, at the moment, lies fourth in the present World Championship league table after two of the races have taken place. Today, for the glamorous and gruelling Monaco Grand Prix, he's also fourth on the grid. To see how he's doing on the grid today, to see how others in front of him at the moment in the World Championship, people like Jackie Stewart, Bruce McLaren and Denny Hulme, are going to do in the next 156 miles and two hours – the race is due to begin in a few minutes – let us go now to Monaco and join* [slight pause] *Murray Walker.'*

The TV image showed Prince Rainier III and Princess Grace of Monaco stepping as regally as they could from a Lamborghini Espada after arriving on the start/finish straight. Princess Grace was wearing a headscarf in recognition of conditions that were as grey as the TV picture flickering on Walker's monitor.

'*Welcome to Monaco,*' said Murray. '*Where, if the conditions are slightly overcast, they are nevertheless just about ideal for racing as His Serene Highness Prince Rainier of Monaco and Princess Grace, who have just completed a tour of inspection of the superb 1.9-mile circuit, retire to the Royal Box to watch the eighty laps of the Monaco Grand Prix, which is to come and which starts in just about ten minutes' time.'*

As the mobile camera switched to the pole position Tyrrell Matra-Ford and its driver, Walker kept pace.

'*There is the man that many people expect to win today. Young Jackie Stewart in his MS80 Matra, who has put up an electrifying lap in practice, one minute 24.6 seconds, which is no less than 3.5 seconds faster than the official lap record put up last year by Richard Attwood in the BRM, who this year is driving a new V8 Lotus.*

'*And there is Graham Hill's car, and tremendous drama today when this car was brought out of the transporter because Graham Hill has got on the back of the car a special spoiler; Graham Hill, incidentally, is in fourth position . . . in practice.'*

Murray hesitated slightly when he sensed something was amiss as a pair of what he thought were Lotus mechanics leant into the cockpit and blocked the view of the driver as they helped secure his seat harness.

Fortunately, Murray realized his error seconds before the mechanics straightened up to reveal Chris Amon in the cockpit of a Ferrari.

'*In second position is Chris Amon – and it's Amon's car that we're looking at now, the V12 Ferrari which, like Hill's car, has got that special spoiler on the back.*' (These spoilers were makeshift crude aerodynamic devices incorporated overnight to compensate in some small way for the rear wings that had been banned.)

'*And there,*' Murray continued as the camera panned down the remainder of the grid, '*are the rest of the fourt—fifteen competitors in this event because as usual sixteen competitors in this Monaco Grand Prix. Car number eight there is Jean-Pierre Beltoise in his V8 Cosworth-Ford-powered French Matra and Beltoise is third fastest in practice – but, sitting alongside me now is a man who knows as much as anybody about this superb circuit because he has driven on it so many times himself: Innes Ireland. And, so, as the competitors get ready now to start their 80-mile* [lap] *stint, let's hear some-thing about the circuit from Innes himself.*'

Walker's comparatively slow and deliberate diction was replaced by the languid tone of the Scottish former Grand Prix driver. Ireland's best result at Monaco had been ninth in 1960, his worst experience undoubtedly a year later when he selected second gear instead of fourth in the tunnel, locked the transmission of his Lotus and emerged into the daylight by flying through the air without his car, which was destroying itself against the tunnel wall.

Ireland went into detail about the furore over the removal of the rear wings that made the cars handle, according to him, '*comp-lete-lay different-lay, and so they had to start beck at squarr one*'. Having gone on to explain why the narrow grid at Monaco required cars to line up in a two-by-two formation (as opposed to three-two-three), Ireland then proved he was no more immune than Walker to slips of the tongue by saying '*I'll naow hand beck to Rodney Walkerley*' (a British journalist of Ireland's acquaintance).

Murray picked up without hesitation, pointing out that a helicopter would provide *'fantastic shots'* from overhead. Then he began to run through the grid order. As he did so, the cars were called forward from the so-called dummy grid on to the starting grid proper (there was no warm-up lap), Walker's increase in pace matched by a rise in volume, both from himself and the cars rolling past a few metres in front of the commentary position.

The blazered starter stood in the middle of the road and signalled his assistant to raise the 'thirty-second' board – which the man immediately fumbled, dropping the board, its numbers spilling on to the track. While urging his assistant to sort himself out, the starter began moving towards the side, clearly poised to wave the national flag.

At which point the screen went blank. Murray immediately went into cover-up mode. *'And there's tremendous excitement now,'* he enthused. *'The crowd is on its toes . . .'* Then a flicker – and the picture was back, just as the starter dropped his flag.

'There we go! And . . . the Monaco Grand Prix is on. Into the lead straight away goes Jackie Stewart – up to Ste Devote, the fast climb up to Casino Corner.'

The shot switches to a camera looking down towards Ste Devote in the distance as one grey car after another comes out of the corner and accelerates up the hill before flashing past the static camera – an impossible kaleidoscope without the colour. But Walker is on the case.

'It's Jackie Stewart in the Matra, straight away into the lead, followed by Chris Amon. The battle is on. The two fastest men in practice . . . not unnaturally leading and . . .'

Walker's voice tails away as a car pulls to one side in the distance.

'And somebody in trouble. I can't identify him until we get closer.'

Murray quickly and correctly calls the driver as Jackie Oliver in the BRM, and as he does so, the director switches to the helicopter camera. The moment Murray begins talking about the view of cars streaming out of Casino Square, the picture returns to Oliver – except the view from the pavement-mounted camera is now obscured by photographers and assorted hangers-on running towards the stricken BRM. It is a commentator's worst nightmare. There's a race going on and the picture is of trousered legs running down a hill. Walker deftly goes with the flow.

'*And Oliver in real trouble at Ste Devote on the first out of eighty laps. It looks like his suspension has collapsed because the nose is right on the ground . . .*'

The producer has caught up with the action as the field streams towards Portier and on to the waterfront. Walker follows suit – and then gets his 'Jackies' confused.

'*And meantime, as they go down towards the Station Hairpin on the first lap and to rejoin the course at Portier, it's Jackie Oliver in the lead. There's Bruce McLaren* [Beltoise, in fact] *in third position, Amon is in second position and Graham Hill is in fourth place. Streaming into the tunnel now, into the 130-yard – flat out in fourth gear, as far as Jackie Stewart is concerned – tunnel and now very shortly down to the chicane. There they are, and out of it.*

'*And Jackie Stewart, the man who put up the fastest lap in practice, is leading on lap one, and he's leading from Chris Amon, who is in second position. As they go down towards the Gasometer Hairpin* [the present loop around the swimming pool and Rascasse was not introduced until 1973], *the slowest corner on the course, to complete the first lap out of eighty in what, as usual, is going to be a tremendously gruelling event . . .*'

Murray continues for another six laps then hands back to the studio in London, Michelmore reminding the audience that there will be a progress report before returning once more for the final laps.

Walker's ten-minute catch-up includes news of the perpetually unlucky Amon's race lasting no more than sixteen laps before the Ferrari's differential failed, followed, seven laps later, by Stewart's retirement with broken transmission, leaving Hill in the lead. A return to the studio brings further discussion on the lunar mission and pictures of the Earth taken from Apollo 8, the first crewed spacecraft to have left the Earth's orbit the previous December. The sequence ends with Michelmore's brief homily on Apollo's colossal contribution to human endeavour. Then he seamlessly shifts to the next item.

'*All goes well with the countdown for Apollo 10 for its blast-off. But how well do things go in Monaco? Right at the beginning of this programme, we called this an exacting race, and it's certainly proved to be that. Sixteen started. At the time when they did begin, Stewart was leading the sixteen. Halfway through Graham Hill was leading and there were only eight left. Murray Walker, at that time, asked could Graham Hill, already a four-time winner at Monaco, hold on and make it five? Now, during the closing stages, let's go and find out in the final minutes that really matter how well things go now, direct from Monte Carlo and Murray Walker.*'

The picture switches to Piers Courage, entering Tabac in the Frank Williams Brabham–Ford. In the background, the distinctive echo of racing engines bouncing off the walls and buildings, and then a voice that, over the next two decades, would become just as familiar and warming to motor racing fans. Walker begins with a typical double affirmative of a single thought.

'*Well, the incredible Graham Hill not only can hold on, but is holding on. Forty-year-old Graham, the oldest man in the race, is still leading and now has only four laps to go. He is about to complete – in fact, has completed now – his seventy-sixth lap and we are looking down on him in his Lotus 49B and, here he is, going past the Hotel Metropole, braking hard, round the right-hander at the Hotel Mirabeau, braking even harder for the sweeping left-hander hairpin at the station, now into the right-hander, approaching Portier, under the railway bridge, on his seventy-seventh lap in the eighty-lap race. And he is about twenty-two seconds ahead of Piers Courage in the Brabham, who at one time was closing on Graham Hill. But Graham, crafty, wily, experienced tactician that he is, immediately speeded up a little and has now pulled away a little and as I talk to you with Graham Hill almost at the end of his seventy-seventh lap, as he approaches the Gasometer Hairpin in fourth, third, second – now down to first gear, goes right the way round the right-hander, straightens up, accelerates away to complete lap seventy-seven and start his seventy-eighth lap.'*

Walker goes on to reiterate that Hill leads Courage by twenty-two seconds, the Brabham holding a similar gap over Jo Siffert in Rob Walker's privately entered Lotus, followed by the works Lotus of Attwood, these being the only four on the same lap. With just seven cars remaining, all of them widely spaced, there would appear to be little to talk about. Murray has other ideas.

'And here is the leader, on lap 78. And the drama can really start to build up now because it is the closing stages of the race that are the most worrying for a driver . . . Graham Hill plunges down past the Metropole Hotel on his seventy-ninth and penultimate lap. And now Graham will be really worrying because if anything is at all weak on the Lotus and it breaks, it would be heartbreaking.

'Graham has already won more Monaco Grands Prix than anyone in the history of this event which began in 1929. This man has won four Monaco Grands Prix. And Graham Hill is now through and on his last lap. He has considerably less than two – only a mile to go now. Past the Metropole Hotel for the eightieth and last time. Down to the Station Hairpin for the eightieth and last time. And Graham, who is an imperturbable, phlegmatic man with a wonderful sense of humour, must have his heart in his mouth now. He's down to the lowest part of the course – no more climbing to do . . .

'And here's Graham Hill, through the Tabac for the last time. Paul Frère is getting the chequered flag ready. And Graham Hill [Murray, a tremor in his voice, has gone up a couple of octaves] *comes down to the Gasometer Hairpin for the last time. It's going to be five victories at Monaco for this incredible forty-year-old Londoner. He accelerates away. And* [shouting now] *he's coming up to the finishing straight! And the 1969 Monaco Grand Prix*

HAS BEEN WON for the fifth time by Graham Hill! The Lotus mechanics justifiably LEAP into the air with delight.'

Walker's commentary decelerates in company with the winning Lotus as Hill removes his crash helmet and waves to the crowd. Murray runs through the finishing order, gives an update on the championship and hands over to Innes Ireland for his impression of the race. By the time the former Grand Prix driver has paid warm tribute to Hill's canny and measured performance, the British national anthem can be heard in the background and Walker, speaking at a more reverential pace than before, remarks on what a wonderful occasion it has been while clearly hoping there will be pictures to match the background music.

The director, meanwhile, has not been able to show any shots of Hill climbing from his car and stepping up to the Royal Box to receive one of the most sought-after trophies in motor sport. Having apparently lost interest, the director flicks from one trackside camera to another, showing a hotch-potch of spectators walking on a track that has already been reclaimed as a public thoroughfare.

Walker must keep talking. He covers the state of the World Championship, restates the result, going slowly through each finisher in great detail. Rarely has a driver finishing last, three laps behind, received so many words as Walker covers Vic Elford's career as a rally driver and sports car exponent, and now a Formula 1 driver of some repute in Murray's eyes.

'*Monaco has come, and it has gone,*' he continues, almost in desperation. '*The crowd* [i.e. all he can see on his screen] *poured into the circuit this morning and it will now be hours . . . and hours . . . before they are clear of it. The roads of the Principality will be clogged for a long, long time. They've seen two more cars finish the race this year than finished last year. Because, out of the traditional sixteen that always start the Monaco Grand Prix, only five cars started last year.*'

His error can be excused because the producer has finally found something other than a view of people aimlessly milling around. Walker's voice rises and accelerates once more. *'And here, being pushed in, a dismal sight, particularly for Jackie Stewart, the car that was leading for twenty-three laps . . .'* And so begins a description of the Matra MS80, its engine, Stewart's progress in the race and why his car had to be abandoned and is being pushed to the pits by the Tyrrell mechanics, Stewart's lap record (down to the last tenth of a second), the significance of how many gear changes he made per lap, and how Monaco *'is probably, if not definitely'* the most demanding circuit on transmissions out of all the circuits that are used for World Championship events. Which allows a neat segue into listing the remaining eight races on the calendar.

There is no respite for Walker as the screen once again shows the aforementioned crowd continuing to clog the streets and no hint of a return to the studio in London. Murray picks up the theme of how much Hill enjoys champagne and the chances of a *'typical Graham Hill champagne party'* before describing how Hill will soon be off to America for the Indianapolis 500 and how the life of a racing driver today is a very, very busy one.

Finally, a call to wrap up after filling with unflappable aplomb for seven minutes that must have been made to feel interminable thanks to the haphazard work by the local television production company. Walker repeats the result and concludes his first Grand Prix commentary: *'So, the end of a brilliant 1969 Monaco Grand Prix. And we say, from Monte Carlo, goodbye to you.'*

8

WHAT *AM* I SAYING!

Murray Walker had been fortunate on two counts. His role behind the microphone at Monaco had come about thanks to the regular motor sport commentator, Raymond Baxter, being busy elsewhere, largely because the BBC's decision to cover Monaco had been last-minute. Baxter, mentioned in dispatches as a Spitfire pilot during the Second World War, was booked to commentate on the Biggin Hill International Air Fair, one of the largest civilian air shows in the world at that time. BBC *Grandstand* was scheduled to take a fifty-minute broadcast from the Kent aerodrome in between Monaco and discussion about the Apollo space programme.

The inclusion of the Grand Prix on the BBC schedule was a surprise to many, not least *Autosport*: the weekly magazine's preview of Monaco listed transmissions on London Weekend Television (a surprise in itself) but made no mention of the BBC. Rather than an oversight by *Autosport*'s punctilious reporter Simon Taylor, this was an indication of the Corporation's continuing state of flux over advertising on F1 cars. While Walker grabbed this chance to show his worth, the irony was that Graham Hill's winning Lotus had indirectly led to this scheduling confusion in the first place.

Prior to the end of 1967, advertising on racing cars had been restricted to trade sponsors. While support from Shell, BP, Dunlop and the like was welcome, it was no longer considered sufficient as F1 teams became more adventurous and committed. When the CSI waived the rule for 1968, the governing body was not only potentially expanding race teams' bank accounts but also opening a can of worms.

Colin Chapman immediately proved he could think outside the box commercially as well as technically when he unveiled his Lotus cars with the red, white and gold branding of John Player (a division of Imperial Tobacco that owned the Gold Leaf brand). Traditionalists were horrified. The television companies, mindful of negative connotations associated with tobacco advertising, vowed not to show Grands Prix. But, in the same way that financial imperatives underscored thinking within F1, so it was in broadcasting when the commercially driven independent television networks began to screen the occasional F1 race.

The BBC, meanwhile, was receiving substantial stick from its licence payers for not showing the British Grand Prix at Brands Hatch in July 1968. A knee-jerk reaction one month later led to the BBC trucks rolling into Oulton Park in Cheshire to televise the Gold Cup. The non-championship F1 race was won by Jackie Stewart's Matra (with, as it happened, no tobacco branding), followed by Chris Amon's Ferrari (ditto). But the cameras could not avoid giving exposure to Hill's Gold Leaf Lotus, starting from pole position but lasting no more than seven laps before the mobile cigarette packet was stubbed out with transmission failure.

F1 was racing into the future with cars advertising anything from tobacco to toiletries. The BBC was stumbling in its wake, spurred on by rivals televising an increasing slice of the action and stepping on 'Auntie's' toes in May 1969 by daring to show the Monaco Grand Prix, previously the BBC's highlight in a desperately thin annual roster of F1.

Tradition continued to play its part in the BBC's planning post Monaco 1969. Motor sport had been included in their Easter Monday programming since the late 1950s with coverage of a popular meeting at Goodwood. When the Sussex circuit ceased racing in 1966,

Thruxton in Hampshire assumed the holiday date by hosting a round of the European Formula 2 Championship. Not only did Murray find himself there in March 1970, he also had the winner of the 1969 Monaco Grand Prix as his co-commentator. It turned out to be an object lesson for Graham Hill.

'It [commentating] is really difficult,' Hill told journalist Eoin Young. 'I must say, I admire a chap like Murray Walker. You wouldn't believe how hard it is to identify cars on the little monitor screen we had in front of us. You've got to do your homework very well in practice or you can't tell which car is which, never mind rattle on about them. We were cramped shoulder to shoulder in this little box trying to watch what was happening on the track in front of us, what was happening on the monitor, and all the time listening to the chap directing the cameras who was rabbiting away doing a little commentary of his own. This was coming through our headphones the whole time, so we really had to be on the ball.'

It is not recorded whether Murray took the opportunity to explain how the commentary box at Thruxton, for all its limitations, was luxury compared to the al fresco kerbside table and chair he had had to work with while Graham was otherwise engaged at Monaco.

Walker, as we have seen, had been delighted to accept the call to the French Riviera. He was also the subject of televisual change that was turning out to be just as agreeable.

Having decided that motocross (or 'scrambling' as it was more commonly known) had run its course, the BBC had been making a gradual transition to rallycross, which very broadly speaking was muddy racing for cars. This idea had actually been born through necessity rather than through a television executive's foresight.

For many years, the RAC Rally had been recognized as one of the toughest events on the international rally calendar. The event in November 1967 had been no exception, attracting 150 entries, including a works Ford Lotus Cortina for Graham Hill as, not for the first time, the F1 driver switched disciplines. Competitors from Lancia, Porsche, BMC (British Motor Corporation), Ford and the rest had assembled at a London Heathrow hotel before setting off on the four-day event, the competitive element consisting of 400 miles spread across sixty-nine special stages. On the night before the start, however, a man from the Ministry of Agriculture arrived with some bad news: the event would have to be cancelled because an outbreak of foot-and-mouth disease was affecting many of the areas through which the rally was due to pass in England, Wales and Scotland.

This was a dilemma for Associated Television (ATV). In a brave venture, ATV had committed eight outside broadcast units to the event, the plan being to have Dickie Davies present the programme from Rally Headquarters. The sports department had even persuaded the powers-that-be to allow the programme to go out on a Sunday evening at a time when there was usually a religious break.

In the light of the cancellation and in an attempt to give ATV some return for their trouble, it was hastily arranged to have the top competitors gather at what would have been the first special stage on Ministry of Defence land (away from rural areas and unaffected by foot-and-mouth) near Camberley in Surrey. There, in front of TV cameras, competitors raced against the clock on a collection of mixed surfaces. The first Rallysprint, later to evolve into racing known as rallycross, had been run through happenstance.

The international rally teams thought no more about it as they moved on to focus on the Monte Carlo, the East African Safari and other iconic rallies far removed from an artificial event for television. But the attraction of rallycross, particularly in the winter months when circuit racing had finished for the season, appealed to a few small but energetic car clubs, none more so than the Thames Estuary Automobile Club (TEAC).

There had been a few one-off events elsewhere, but the enterprising TEAC officials set up a rallycross championship. It would be run through the winter at Lydden Hill, a small but tricky little race track in a valley just off the A20 near Dover. The TEAC then stole a major march on rival clubs by arranging sponsorship from Embassy cigarettes (owned by Imperial Tobacco) and tempting the BBC to televise it.

This was good news for Murray Walker on two counts: the advertising company he worked for happened to handle the Imperial Tobacco account; and the BBC realized rallycross and Walker's crash-bang-wallop style of commentary were made for each other.

The *Radio Times* listing for *Grandstand* on Saturday 5 October 1968 showed rallycross opening the afternoon's entertainment, returning to Lydden Hill twice in between swimming, golf and the classic Cesarewitch Handicap horse race at Newmarket.

There was no shortage of action for Walker during three transmissions lasting between fifteen and twenty minutes. The varied entry, populated mainly by Ford Escorts, Lotus Cortinas and the ubiquitous Mini Cooper S, would provide sideways entertainment from start to finish on a one-mile circuit made of tarmac, grass and chalk surfaces. As rallycross quickly evolved over the winter, so did entrants' ingenuity when looking for ways to make their cars go faster.

'In motor sport terms, rallycross was a relatively cheap way of going racing,' said Walker, when reflecting in 2013. 'By that I mean you could take a road car – a well-used road car – and modify it. These chaps, many of whom were in the motor trade, were adept at doing this sort of thing. As a result, you would arrive in the paddock at Lydden and be amazed at some of the things they got up to – and were allowed to get up to thanks to the generous and rather loose regulations.

'The Mini was an extremely popular choice because they were widely available, there were plenty of spare parts, they were easy to work on and it didn't cost a lot of money. On top of that, the Mini possessed superlative handling. But that is not to say the Mini dominated. Over time, it seemed these chaps would have a go at anything. And when I say anything, I mean anything. We had front-wheel drive, rear-wheel drive, four-wheel drive, front engine, rear engine, turbo-charged, supercharged, normally aspirated. I always liked to get to race meetings early to do my homework. With rallycross, you *had* to get there early to find out what was going on, not just under the bonnet but throughout the motor car. It may have said "Ford Escort" on the entry list but, very often, that's where the similarity ended with the Escort on your local Ford dealer's forecourt.

'The other absolutely fascinating thing about rallycross was that the drivers were often as individual as their cars. The grid at Lydden was about as far removed as you could get from a grid full of F1 cars and superstar drivers – but every bit as enjoyable in a very different way.

'And you could by no means compare the facilities at a Grand Prix – even the worst facilities, and I have to say there were some fairly average ones in those days – with what you had to deal with at Lydden. Ramshackle is a fair description. And that's being kind. There was a canvas screen separating the men's and the ladies' and I remember someone had put up a handwritten note saying:"Gentlemen, keep your voices down – the ladies can hear every word you say!"'

Murray had plenty to say on the day he was given a ride as a passenger in a Ford Escort driven by John Taylor, the ex-National Hunt jockey who had turned his hand to horsepower of a different kind and would become European rallycross champion in 1973. The Englishman's Escort may have had a full-race Ford Cosworth BDA engine under the bonnet, but it had no seat alongside the driver. Walker, very excited about commentating at speed, found he had to hold on to the roll cage and whatever else he could find while making the best of a makeshift perch where the passenger seat should have been.

Taylor did not hold back, power-sliding at will and bouncing and bucking across the bumps and uneven surfaces as the Escort crossed from tarmac to the grass/chalk infield and back again before climbing Hairy Hill. Then the flat-out rush downhill and sideways through Paddock Bend at the bottom, skimming a stout earth mound (known as Mabbs Bank) as he did so.

Murray continued to babble animatedly, even when he felt an agonizing pain in his side as they started the fourth lap of this high-speed slalom. A visit to the circuit doctor would reveal a broken rib. Viewers later in the day would not have an inkling about the commentator's continuing discomfort.

Walker was at least grateful that the car had remained in one piece. Spectacular incidents were not only part of the sport but also fertile ground for a growing collection of oft-quoted 'Murrayisms' as Walker tried, in a hurry, to describe what he was seeing.

Keith Ripp, a multiple rallycross champion, provided an example when he was comfortably leading a race in his Mini. A dull, wet afternoon was about to become even more miserable for the British driver. Murray described what happened next: *'The Mini of Keith Ripp accelerates away, over 100 miles an hour; flings it sideways, on to the chalk, keeps it there, avoiding Mabbs Bank . . . which HE DOES NOT DO!'*

As Walker uttered those words, the yellow car, having struggled for grip on the mud, was hitting the bank at high speed before being launched into the air. Walker's summary of the fast-moving drama was a masterpiece of understatement. *'Keith Ripp in REAL trouble,'* he shouted as the Mini cavorted in a terrifying series of rolls before eventually landing in a very sorry state on what was left of its wheels. *'The car flies apart. Off comes the fibreglass roof AND the doors. And Keith Ripp, strapped in the car, looks to be perfectly all right. And THAT is a demonstration of how the wrong line at that corner can cause real trouble. Thankfully, and mercifully, Keith Ripp is all right.'*

Walker's genuine concern for a driver's well-being was also called into play during the final of the 1980 British Rallycross Championship as John Welch and Tony Drummond fought tooth and nail for the title.

'And it's Tony Drummond leading John Welch . . . two sinister black Ford Escorts . . . they are pulling away . . . and Welch is now on Drummond's boot lid – great stuff. These two cars are very, very evenly matched . . . Oh, John Welch is – now he's getting aboard! [The two cars touch.] *That's it! That's it! Bang! Bang! And off! Off! That's it!* [The Escort thumps the grass bank and bounces in the air.] *John Welch's race is over. I'm afraid that looks a nasty one. And they are stopping the race. Oh dear – to put it very mildly indeed.'*

When Welch failed to emerge from the car, Walker knew no more about the driver's condition than his viewers. Modulating his tone considerably, Murray reminded the audience that the cars had to be built to the highest safety standards. He also commented on the fast response of the safety team and their specialized skills, his quiet authority providing reassurance. By the standard of previous rallycross wrecks, Welch's car was reasonably intact. But the fact that the driver remained within it caused enough concern for Walker to hope that he had just been winded by the violent impact with the bank. That appeared to be the case when Welch was eventually helped from the car.

'Well, there's a very, very, very deep sigh of relief from me because, as you can see, John Welch is very conscious; he's obviously very dazed, poor chap. That's the doctor in the yellow cap; as usual the right people are in the right place at the right time. [The doctor stands back and signals to race control.] *And thumbs up! John Welch is OK. Thank heavens for that.'*

On another occasion, the race appeared to be without incident and Walker had managed to avoid any verbal trip wires as the chequered flag appeared. Murray was winding down as the Dutchman

Piet Dam began to cruise back to the paddock. '*Piet Dam wins, looks through a completely clear windscreen – that's the big advantage, of course, of being in front.*' No sooner had Murray said those words than the BMW failed to negotiate the next corner, went straight on and rammed the bank directly beneath the television camera.

Watching cars attack the Kentish scenery had become a familiar scenario, as Murray related during an interview with Robert Philip in 1996.

'In one particular meeting there were probably a hundred people taking part, of whom I knew twenty,' he said. 'As I had to be able to talk knowledgeably, entertainingly and authoritatively about them all, I got to the track as early as possible and talked to as many people as possible.

'I was chatting to this chap whose name was Richard Hastieloe. How old are you? Thirty-two. Where do you come from? Wigan. What do you do for a living? Computer programmer. Have you had any success? No, I do it for fun. Is there anything I ought to know about the car? Yes, I'm glad you asked. My Mini has a Perspex windscreen into which, using my skill and experience as a computer programmer, I have caused a large number of holes of different diameters to be drilled to a random pattern. As a result of which, whenever mud lands on my windscreen, there is always a hole I can see through. I said: "Thank you, Richard – we'll let you know." I thought nothing more about it.

'To my great surprise, however, this chap was actually in the lead during a pretty dull afternoon's rallycross. So I say: "Here's something interesting. Richard Hastieloe, number 27, who by the way is a thirty-two-year-old computer programmer from Wigan, has used his skill and experience as a computer programmer" – at this point the camera zeroed in on the Perspex windscreen – "to cause a large number of holes of different diameters to be drilled to a random pattern, as a result of which there is always a hole he can see through."

'As I said this, he plunged off the circuit, sailed over a bank and disappeared through a plywood hoarding, leaving a nice, neat hole in the perfect outline of a Mini. Which is why the commentary actually ends with me screaming "... always a hole he can see through ... WHAT *AM* I SAYING!"'

9

HERE COMES HUNT

M urray was scheduled to commentate on the opening round of the 1970 British rallycross season on 17 October. A fortnight before that, he had covered a different form of motor racing at a race track far removed from the chalky expanses of Lydden Hill.

Passengers emerging from the railway station at Crystal Palace on 3 October would have been puzzled by what appeared to be the sound of loud and angry bees attacking Anerley Hill and the surrounding south London suburb. Race fans, however, would have been in no doubt that they had arrived at one of the most picturesque, if unlikely, motor racing venues on the British calendar.

The Crystal Palace track worked its way through a public park, the roads being too narrow for F1 and barely acceptable for the 100mph average set during a round of the European F2 Championship in May 1970. The 1.39 miles were considered perfect, however, for smaller, more agile Formula 3 cars, the sense of drama being heightened by their high-revving engines.

F3 was a significant stepping stone for young drivers, important enough for Lotus to run a works team of two cars (duly decked out in Gold Leaf colours, in a perfect mimic of their larger F1 brothers). The twenty-eight-car entry for the Daily Express Trophy (a round of a major British F3 championship) included nine drivers who would eventually make it to F1. Some made fleeting appearances; others had season-long contracts; two, Alan Jones and James Hunt, would become world champions. In October 1970, however, neither of them seemed destined for greatness – particularly Hunt.

In common with many of his rivals, Hunt had run out of funds during the summer. By living in a tent as the F3 circus criss-crossed Europe, the lanky Englishman, often going without a square meal, managed to survive on the small sums paid by organizers for starting their races, boosted occasionally by more substantial prize money. James had earned a sporadic share of the latter thanks to a couple of wins (occasionally in Formula Libre races elsewhere) and podium finishes. It was touch and go whether he could reach the season's end. The opportunity to race at Crystal Palace, a short journey from Hunt's family home, became essential when the BBC decided to include the race on their Saturday *Grandstand* schedule.

By finishing second in his heat, Hunt ensured a place in the final. Apart from the works Lotus of Dave Walker being the favourite, it was anyone's guess who would join the Australian on the podium. Principal contenders were Hunt (Lotus), Dave Morgan (March), Mike Beuttler (Brabham) and Tony Trimmer (Brabham). With each lap taking less than a minute, there was a lot of talking in store for Murray Walker.

Lap 1

'*And this is the end of lap one, with nineteen to go; it's Walker, Beuttler, Trimmer, Morgan and then James Hunt. And Walker is really piling on the pressure now, pulling out a bit of a lead. He's got two-fifths of a second lead; that may sound ridiculously small but even a fifth of a second in Formula 3 is really something. Look at that battle for second place between Beuttler, Trimmer and James Hunt!*'

Lap 3

'*And look at Trimmer! Trimmer is going to go through and take Beuttler for second position. Tony Trimmer has done it! Now, can Tony Trimmer, who is in the lead of the Shell Motorsport Formula 3 Championship, catch Dave Walker, who is in second place in the Shell Motorsport Formula 3*

Championship? And can Mike Beuttler in the yellow Brabham and James Hunt in the red Lotus ... and Beuttler is going to take Trimmer — he won't [do it] *there — and Hunt is going to go through and pass Beuttler!'*

Lap 9

'Hunt, trying to take [Trimmer on] *the inside at Ramp Bend, and failing.'*

Lap 10

'And the lead now is one and two-fifth seconds for Walker — and James Hunt is through! Hunt is up to second place now. James Hunt, from Sutton [in Surrey], *twenty-three years old, been driving for three years. And here he is, in the red Lotus. Behind him, Tony Trimmer — and Dave Morgan is up to fourth place. And Beuttler is right back to sixth position!'*

Lap 11

'The leader is now two seconds ahead. The fourth to seventh place cars are virtually together. And Trimmer is back ahead of James Hunt. What a fantastic scrap for second place! And Hunt is back in front again! 91.99 miles an hour is the fastest lap we've had so far today.'

Lap 14

'Here is the leader, Dave Walker. Now, James Hunt, second. And up into third place has come Dave Morgan in the March.'

Lap 15

'Morgan going through to take second place from Hunt ... And Hunt is going to go through and take — Hunt puts both his wheels on the grass! And gets through. But not for very long because Dave Morgan immediately retakes second place and waves a laconic hand over the windscreen at Hunt as he does so, as much to say, "Don't do that again, my friend!" But James Hunt will try again.'

Lap 17

'James Hunt going through, to try and take — and he's going to do it! He takes second place from Dave Morgan by nipping through on the inside at Ramp Bend!'

Lap 18

'*James Hunt in second place. Up into third place has gone Beuttler, down to fourth place has gone Morgan.*'

Lap 20

'*Dave Walker, from Australia, is on his last lap. There he goes . . . And it's Beuttler up into second place! Beuttler has taken Hunt! Morgan is fourth. Here's the leader, almost home, up to the last corner. And there's Morgan, going to go through on the outside* [of Hunt, going into the final corner].'

The producer cuts from this battle to show Walker taking the flag.

'*Walker wins . . . AND A TERRIFIC SHUNT ALL THE WAY DOWN THE FINISHING STRAIGHT! And Beuttler has finished second and there are bits of Formula 3 motor car all over the track! Let's see and identify who they are. I can tell you for sure that Tony Trimmer is in third place . . .*'

The camera, meanwhile, has swung to the right and, in the distance, Hunt can be seen energetically evacuating the cockpit of a car beached in the middle of the straight with both right-hand wheels missing. He breaks into a brisk trot, heading for Morgan's damaged March, which has come to rest against the wall on his right. Morgan climbs out and begins to walk away, unaware of his advancing rival. Caught by surprise and a swift right hook, Morgan is felled with a single blow before Hunt strides off.

While all of this is going on, Murray, seemingly oblivious to the unscheduled pugilism, is looking at his lap chart and informing viewers that Hunt and Morgan are not finishers. By the time he looks back on track and verifies his logic by identifying the abandoned cars, Hunt has disappeared and Morgan is back on his feet. It has been a colourful introduction to a driver who would come to play a major role in Walker's working life.

James Hunt would eventually join forces with Lord Alexander Hesketh's team, the flamboyant ensemble making its F1 debut at Monaco in 1973. This race was covered, as usual, by the BBC through a series of brief transmissions with Raymond Baxter as commentator. In addition to Monaco in 1969, Murray had been called upon to stand in for Baxter at the 1969 and 1974 German Grands Prix at the legendary Nürburgring Nordschleife.

In 1976, Walker would be asked to join the BBC Radio team covering the British Grand Prix at Brands Hatch. It seems surprising now, but the BBC had no plans to televise the race, having got their politically correct knickers into another twist.

The tricky question of tobacco advertising may have been quietly forgotten but the British broadcaster had been thrown into more moral panic early in 1976 when the Surtees team turned up with F1 cars boldly carrying Durex logos. A stand-off at a non-championship race (coincidentally at Brands Hatch) in March had ended when the BBC team (with Murray scheduled to be commentator) packed up and went home when John Surtees refused to threaten the – dare it be said – protection of his small team by removing vital sponsorship. There would be no change in attitude on either side as the 1976 Grand Prix season continued. Which was unfortunate for BBC Television because public interest in F1 had exploded exponentially with the exploits of James Hunt.

10

THE CLASS OF '76

Sometimes, things are meant to be.

With Hesketh having been forced to withdraw from racing for financial reasons at the end of 1975, it seemed James Hunt's F1 career had also been washed up. It was his good fortune that Emerson Fittipaldi had chosen that moment to leave McLaren in the lurch at the eleventh hour as the Brazilian went off to join his brother and run their own F1 team. Hunt had done enough with Hesketh to prove to McLaren and their sponsor, Marlboro, that he was worth a punt. In truth, McLaren had very few options, and James had none at all.

Hunt had gone on to justify his choice for the 1976 season by challenging the reigning world champions, Niki Lauda and Ferrari: after the first eight races, he had notched up four pole positions and two wins, at Jarama in Spain and at the Circuit Paul Ricard near Marseilles. Hunt and Lauda may have been reasonably close when struggling through F3, but that friendship was being tested as Lauda led the championship when they reached Brands Hatch in the middle of a searingly hot summer.

The rivalry was manna from heaven for the British sports media as they extolled the virtues of the cavalier young Brit with the flowing blond locks, ranged against the aloof and serious Austrian; one driving for a young team of 'good blokes' based on a trading estate directly beneath the Heathrow flight path, the other being seen to represent a motor sport icon that had forever been a thorn in the side of British teams. The animosity, real or media-engendered, would reach a new level of loathing based on extraordinary events within minutes of the British Grand Prix getting under way.

Before the start, Hunt's problems had been twofold. Lauda not only claimed pole position but was also allowed to choose from which side of the front row he would start. Apart from being an unusual concession, this was critical at Brands Hatch, where the start line featured a downward-sloping camber with the right side being particularly steep at the point where, logically, pole should have been located (the first corner being a right-hander). Lauda had no hesitation in choosing the left-hand side as his starting point. Not only did he make the best getaway, but Hunt's problems were multiplied when Lauda's team-mate, Clay Regazzoni, came charging through from the second row. Which is when the trouble began.

Carrying too much speed and enthusiasm into the first corner, Regazzoni locked his brakes and struck a rear wheel on Lauda's car. Regazzoni's Ferrari went sideways, and in the ensuing mayhem Hunt's McLaren became airborne and, for a scary moment, looked like overturning.

Hunt managed to continue but quickly discovered he was in trouble thanks to the McLaren's steering being awry. Thinking his race was over and his championship seriously compromised, Hunt was relieved to see flag signals indicating that the race had been stopped because of the chaos caused by other cars becoming involved at the first corner. Hunt managed to nurse the McLaren through a rear entrance to the pits.

Now the race entered a grey area of the rule book. Would there be enough time for McLaren to fix the broken steering? If repairs could not be carried out, would Hunt be permitted to take the restart in the spare car? And, if so, could he assume his original grid position? Had he broken the rules by, unlike the remaining runners, failing to complete the first lap thanks to taking the shortcut? Questions, questions.

The pit lane was a hive of mildly chaotic activity. In its midst, Murray Walker was festooned with headset, microphone and the accoutrements necessary to stay in communication with the BBC Radio commentary box as well as the outside world. Walker had no more idea than anyone else about what was going on. But that did not stop the producer from tasking Murray with getting reaction. But from whom? The race organizers were in the control tower, urgently thumbing through the regulations. Judging by the frantic activity at McLaren, there was no hope of expecting any team member to have either the time or the inclination – assuming they knew the answer in the first place. Ferrari would, as a matter of course, rule out any positive outcome for McLaren while extolling their innocence in all things.

Then Murray spotted a possible saviour. Running down the pit lane, pursued by a posse of journalists and cameramen, James Hunt had abandoned his car and was heading for the McLaren garage. Murray takes up the story.

'I wasn't a regular commentator in 1976 – few of the races were televised – but I was acting as a pit lane reporter, something I was happy to do. I was going to be at Brands Hatch – wild horses wouldn't have stopped me – so it was good to not only have something to do but also maintain my contact with the BBC.

'It had been a fabulous season and the drama was being ramped up spectacularly by the first-lap incident. I had absolutely no clue about what would happen next. The rules in 1976 were not, and had never been, as clearly defined as they are now [2013]. It was getting pretty tense in that pit lane.

'So, I see James coming towards me and tell the producer to come to me as quickly as possible. I'd spoken to James before, obviously, but this was not the time for pleasantries and a cheery hello. I had to get straight to the point. I stuck the microphone in front of him and asked: "Can you tell us what's going on?" And James replies: "There's a race going on, dear boy." And he keeps walking. That was it.'

It may have been the end of that particular interview, but the story was far from over. Teddy Mayer, the McLaren team principal and also a lawyer, bought time by arguing with officials for long enough to have Hunt's car repaired. James took the restart and won the race. Two months later, Ferrari successfully protested and Hunt's victory was wiped out.

In the meantime, Lauda had not only survived a fiery accident at the Nürburgring that came close to killing him but, having missed two races, he had also made a truly remarkable comeback at Monza six weeks later. Hunt then pulled off two very impressive wins in Canada and the United States to ensure the championship would run to the wire at Fuji in Japan. The BBC's attitude to Durex sponsorship may have continued to prevail but, in truth, few could have foreseen the Japanese race in late October as being essential live broadcasting. Yet this was being billed as the championship shoot-out of all time.

The BBC sent a radio team (Simon Taylor, assisted in commentary with the sometimes colourful observations of motorcycle world champion Barry Sheene) to the Fuji International Speedway, 60 miles southwest of Tokyo. Murray, stationed at BBC Television Centre in London's Wood Lane, watched the feed supplied by the Tokyo Broad-casting System and prepared to dub selected clips for twenty minutes of highlights, due to be shown at 4 p.m. on the Sunday afternoon, several hours after the race had actually finished. Walker's words would be interspersed with clips of recorded live commentary by freelance journalist and broadcaster Barrie Gill.

Any questions viewers might have had about how this was being done were answered when Murray's voice came over loud and clear while Gill sounded, as you would, 6,000 miles away at the other end of a scratchy telephone line. There was no signature tune for the high-lights package ('The Chain' had yet to come), just a fast but nondescript orchestral piece as the camera showed grey and gloomy images of the pit lane.

'*It couldn't be worse at the Fuji circuit,*' began Walker's almost exaggerated staccato delivery, as if reading from notes. '*Pouring rain, thick mist – and it's a delayed start. So, is the Japanese Grand Prix on or off? James Hunt, there getting undressed – and that's an omen. Niki Lauda, the Ferrari ace, looking totally relaxed, and looking as though HE doesn't expect the race to start either. And just look at that rain pouring down.*'

Five seconds later: '*But the race IS on . . .*'

Pictures of cars leaving the pits allow Murray to set the scene before what had been Gill's live commentary is slotted in as the field begins a warm-up lap to explore conditions that would never be tolerated today. As the cars return to the grid, Walker steps in.

'*This, then, is the clincher. The World Championship decider. Three points separate the leader, Niki Lauda in the Ferrari, and Britain's James Hunt in the McLaren. It's gonna be a FANTASTIC race.*'

Back to Gill, who had clearly drawn the short straw as the race started and he tried manfully to determine who was following Hunt through the spray and mist swirling behind the leading McLaren. Gill managed to successfully get through the first two laps, his voice then rising several octaves as he announced Lauda's sudden arrival in the pits. At which point Walker's dubbed commentary takes over.

'*Yes, this amazing 1976 World Championship series is maintaining its drama because Niki Lauda, leading the World Championship, is OUT OF THE RACE!*'

Any lingering doubts about whether Murray is 'live' in Fuji are immediately dispelled when he knows everything there is to know about Lauda's Ferrari.

'*But,*' he continues, '*amazingly enough, there is nothing wrong with his car! Niki Lauda talks to Daniele Audetto, the Ferrari team manager, and says the conditions out there are too bad – I've had enough. And who can blame him after his dreadful accident in Germany? So, now, James Hunt, number 11, only has to keep going to win this year's World Championship. But, behind him, there's a terrific scrap going on for second place between number 5, Mario Andretti in the John Player Special, and number 9 – there – Vittorio Brambilla, the Italian, in the March.'*

Walker continues for another two minutes before an editorial cut jumps to lap 21 and rejoins Gill's commentary.

A minute later, Murray returns to describe a lurid moment that almost costs Hunt the championship. Brambilla, having dealt with Andretti, tries to overtake Hunt, spins and narrowly misses the McLaren. It is manna from heaven for Walker.

'What a fan-tastic miss for James Hunt! Let's see it again and hear James say whether they touched.'

Then follows Hunt's languid, dismissive tone, recorded after the race – and, it's a fair bet, far removed from what he might have said at the moment the gyrating orange March came within inches of taking him out of the race. Walker's commentary continues as the Grand Prix passes half distance, Gill coming in again at lap 61 as Hunt continues to lead until the six-wheel Tyrrell of Patrick Depailler moves to the front. Walker takes over.

'So! Depailler leads and Hunt is second, but how much longer is he going to be second because Andretti is right behind him ... and Andretti has taken second place from Hunt!'

On lap 65, Gill describes Andretti's move on Depailler to take the lead, and the Tyrrell's subsequent pit stop with a punctured tyre. With the rain having stopped, the drying racing line is causing havoc with the worn wet-weather tyres. Knowing that Hunt is about to have trouble at a crucial moment, Walker's commentary takes precedence with five laps to go.

'*And Hunt! Hunt is in the pits in second place! And if he drops below fourth, his World Championship is going to be in danger. What an incredible change of fortune. And just look at the way the McLaren mechanics are changing those wheels* [said in admiration when, in fact, because of a deflating front-left tyre, the mechanic responsible for that corner could not get his mini-jack in place; by the time the other mechanics had rallied round and lifted the car, the stop had taken twenty-seven seconds]. *Andretti, into lap 70, the leader. Hunt is still in the pits. And two wheels are changed. James Hunt gets away. Now he is in fifth position and out of contention.*'

It is at this point that Walker would have been grateful for the power of hindsight. Lap charts at the time were in some disarray, as was the official illuminated scoreboard. Had Murray been commentating live, he would have been unsure of Hunt's position – a vital requirement given that James needed to be fourth or higher to claim the title.

'*And Hunt is passing* [Alan] *Jones* [in a Surtees]; *Hunt is fourth! And Hunt moves up to third position. And James Hunt IS going to win the World Championship if he just keeps going in the place he's in now . . .*

'*And James Hunt is on his way to third place and World Championship victory, there he goes. James Hunt. Holding the flag up for Britain, driving a superb race in far-off Japan. And Mario Andretti coming up to take the chequered flag and win the 1976 Japanese Grand Prix – AND HE DOES IT!*'

Then a switch to Gill's commentary as he describes Hunt's McLaren coming to a halt in a sea of mechanics and well-wishers. The transmission ends with a recording of James reflecting on his championship.

Retirement seemed a long way off for twenty-nine-year-old Hunt with the world at his feet. With a growing sense of disapproval, Walker would read stories of Hunt's bad behaviour as he turned up late (sometimes not at all) for functions, usually in unsuitable attire and not acting in a manner a former tank commander would expect of a fellow in a position of influence and responsibility. In common with many members of the British media, Murray was not sorry to see Hunt suddenly quit racing part way through the 1979 season.

Thinking he had seen the back of the renegade racer, Walker would be startled and dismayed to discover twelve months later that they would have to work together. Despite Murray's initial misgivings, this would be the beginning of what would be a frequently tempestuous but widely celebrated commentary partnership. First, though, BBC Television had to step up its Grand Prix game considerably.

11

THE CHAIN GANG

The impact of the Hunt v. Lauda story in 1976 had not been lost on Jonathan Martin. As editor of BBC's *Sportsnight*, Martin had noted growing interest as the duel gathered pace through the hot summer and had the nation on tenterhooks as the finale was played out thousands of miles away on a chilly Sunday morning in October. F1's impetus was maintained in 1977 by Lauda continuing his extraordinary comeback and winning the championship, and Hunt scoring a hugely popular win in the British Grand Prix at Silverstone. Hunt's subsequent news value – both good and controversial – raised Formula 1 even higher on the sports agenda. It would be the catalyst for the BBC's *Grand Prix* highlights programme and, by association, the beginning of Murray Walker's rise to commentary legend.

'It was a time when television coverage was developing,' recalled Martin. 'In the early seventies, it was pretty haphazard and broadcasters had limited facilities – compared with what goes on now, it's just unbelievable. The coverage of sport in general was pretty prehistoric by today's standards. For the BBC, it started to evolve around two sports: downhill skiing and Grand Prix motor racing. They allowed exciting coverage and, at the same time, personalities emerged; in skiing it was Franz Klammer, and in F1 it was James Hunt and Niki Lauda. They gave us the impetus. BBC2 was developing as a channel and looking for content. That allowed me to push the door open and get *Ski Sunday* and *Grand Prix* on the air. In both cases, we had to take what we were offered by Eurovision, which we would record. *Grand Prix* would be a half-hour highlights programme later that night.

'There was never any question about who the motor sport commentator would be. I thought Murray had a voice that transcended his sport; his voice *was* motor racing. It growled like an engine; it was brilliant.

'Murray would go off on a Wednesday or Thursday to the venue and spend from then until Saturday at the track and then fly back that evening. We would edit the race coverage on Sunday to a half hour, which made a nice, compact show. We weren't quite confident enough to give it an hour and a half, or two hours, because the coverage was . . . a bit dodgy.

'My assistant producer, Bob Abrahams, found that fabulous piece of music – from "The Chain" by Fleetwood Mac – to start *Grand Prix*. It had the throbbing start, which was the cars on the grid; then, suddenly, it exploded into action. It was perfect.

'Murray would have come back from wherever the race was, armed with notes and facts and figures. *Grand Prix* was very clipped; we used to cut it quite quickly. Editing was slower in those days and we'd have a shot list. And then we went on air for the thirty minutes or so.

'Sometimes Murray didn't dub it; we might have had a time problem, in which case he would do it live as it went out. He'd have had a chance to view the programme beforehand, so he'd know what was coming. I'd tell him to pause, because I'd be ahead of him, warning him. But sometimes he would get himself into a groove and wouldn't be quite ready to pause for the next segment. I'd have to shout: "Murray! Pause! Pause! We need a voice edit here – we're jumping from lap 15 to lap 40."'

Martin chose to have Monaco as the first race covered by *Grand Prix* – a logical decision, not only because this race had all the obvious attractions as a popular classic, but also thanks to being the first European race on the 1978 F1 calendar.

Accompanying the gentle introductory bars of 'The Chain', the opening shot for the debut of *Grand Prix* brought a moody low-level clip looking up at James Hunt pulling on his balaclava, then quick glimpses from a similar angle of Mario Andretti (pole position and winner for Lotus-Ford in Argentina) and Niki Lauda (pole position for Brabham-Alfa Romeo in South Africa), followed by pit lane scenes of cars being started and cockpit shots of Jody Scheckter in his Wolf-Ford, Ronnie Peterson (pole for Lotus in Brazil, and winner in South Africa), Andretti and Lauda. Then came a melange of action sequences and glimpses of Colin Chapman, Ken Tyrrell and Bernie Ecclestone. By the time 'The Chain' was up to speed, the title 'Grand Prix' (in yellow italic capitals with contemporary go-faster streaks in front of the 'G' and 'P') flashed on and off a couple of times before the caption 'from MONACO with Murray Walker' brought a voice that would be forever associated with F1 long after the short-lived graphics had been superseded.

'*Welcome to Monte Carlo and the famous Monaco Grand Prix,*' says Murray. '*One of THE classic events in the Grand Prix calendar. This year back in its traditional place as the first European Grand Prix of the season. A season which stretches ahead of us now, through to Monza in Italy in September. And here, on BBC2, throughout the summer in this special* Grand Prix *series on Sunday nights, we'll be bringing you highlights of the races that, once a fortnight, count towards the Drivers' World Championship.*'

Murray goes on to update viewers on the championship positions with Andretti and Ferrari's Carlos Reutemann joint leaders.

'*And there is the grid,*' he says, stepping up a gear in the dubbed commentary. '*In pole position, Reutemann. Then* [John] *Watson* [Brabham], *Lauda, Andretti,* [Patrick] *Depailler* [Tyrrell-Ford], *Hunt* [McLaren-Ford], *Peterson and* [Gilles] *Villeneuve in another Ferra—the red lights go on. When the green flashes, the Monaco Grand Prix – will – be – on.*'

Three seconds later: '*Go! And a great start. It's Depailler coming up, but it's John Watson leading into Ste Devote – and JAMES HUNT RAMS THE BARRIER! As they go up the hill towards the Hotel de Paris, it is John Watson leading Patrick Depailler . . . Niki Lauda . . . Reutemann . . . Andretti . . . Scheckter, and then the rest.*'

The first two laps are covered, allowing time to include Hunt limping into the pits with a punctured front tyre.

Lap 12

'*John Watson – and you can see that he's building a bit more of a lead over number 4, Patrick Depailler. Number 1, Niki Lauda; two Alfa Romeo-powered cars – and look at the battle for fourth! Andretti, Scheckter,* [Alan] *Jones* [Williams-Ford], *Peterson, Villeneuve. As Mario Andretti goes through the tunnel . . . and the noise in there is INDESCRIBABLE, with some five 500-horsepower engines BELLOWING their way through at 120 miles an hour.*'

The commentary continues to allow Walker to cover the demise of Jones's smoking Williams before cutting.

Lap 36

'*And John Watson in the lead is closing up on Emerson Fittipaldi, who is nearly a lap behind him. Watch for the yellow Copersucar of the double ex-world champion. Emerson Fittipaldi – and the leaders are much closer to each other. There is Reutemann* [ahead of Fittipaldi and also about to be lapped]*, there is Fittipaldi . . . and there are the leaders. And it's Watson, Depailler, Lauda, virtually together as they come down to La Rascasse* [actually Loews Hairpin] *and this is where the race could change because the three cars ahead of them could baulk them.*'

Murray covers the leaders dealing with the backmarkers.

Lap 38

Watson has a sideways moment exiting Casino Square. As Lauda looks to challenge Depailler on the downhill run to Mirabeau, the Tyrrell driver ducks out of the leader's slipstream.

'And Depailler trying to pass Watson! What a race! The Monaco Grand Prix. It's living up to its fantastic reputation. Lauda challenges Depailler. Gets the nose of the Brabham right under the rear wing of the Tyrrell, then has to drop back a bit. And into the tunnel again . . .'

At which point Walker, as if to accentuate the drama, manages to cast what could be interpreted as a commentator's curse, even though he knows not only what's about to happen next, but the reason behind it.

'And John Watson is still holding that first place in this GREAT Grand Prix he is driving – AND WATSON OFF! Watson off at the chicane. Watson's brakes are failing and he's gone off at the chicane. Patrick Depailler is into the lead.'

Following a re-run of Watson's demise (seen in the distance), the report jumps to lap 43, Walker noting that Reutemann is holding up the leaders as they attempt to lap the Ferrari.

Lap 45

'There is Depailler, and . . . and . . . Lauda is dropping back . . . As the leader, Patrick Depailler, flicks it through the chicane, you can see now that the gap is spreading out. He's got the whole of the swimming pool complex and the straight behind him clear . . . Lauda is obviously in trouble . . . And Depailler, absolutely on his own; the race is in his pocket if he can keep going – and Lauda goes into the pits. In trouble. Off-side rear tyre going flat and he's got to go in and change it.'

Leapfrogging through various stages in the next twenty-one laps, Murray notes that Watson has moved up to second place and trouble for Andretti means that third is being disputed by Scheckter and Peterson until his Lotus retires. The story shifts to Scheckter closing on Watson, who eventually falls to fourth with continuing brake trouble.

Lap 70

'If Depailler wins this race – he's had a second place and two thirds already this season; beaten on only the very last lap in South Africa when he ran out of petrol. And if he wins this race, he can go up – he WILL go up – to lead

the World Championship. A wonderful reward, not only for himself but for Ken Tyrrell, his team leader, and for Maurice Philippe, who designed this brand-new car to replace the six-wheeler.'

Lap 74

'*And there is Jody Scheckter in second place ... Well, the race seems to have adopted a pattern – AND DOES IT? LOOK AT LAUDA! Niki Lauda is closing RIGHT UP. Niki Lauda, this tremendously gutsy, determined Austrian; he has now really got the bit between his teeth. He sees a chance for the second second place in two years come to him: he was second last year. And look at the way Scheckter is trying! But it seems to me that Scheckter must be in some sort of trouble to allow Lauda to close up in the way that he has.* [Scheckter can be heard struggling to find a gear as the pair accelerate on to the pit straight.] *LAUDA'S THROUGH! Lap 74, Lauda is going to go through – AND HE DOES! Takes second position – and a new lap record.'*

Lap 76

'*And Patrick Depailler only has to do this lap to win an incredible race. And if he does, the whole of France will go raving, justifiably mad. An ENORMOUS amount of French money has gone into this car. Much of the car is French, although, of course, it is a British-built car and a British-built Cosworth V8 Ford engine.*

'*Depailler, then, almost home. The chicane ... accelerate away ... down to third gear for the Tabac, 100 miles an hour. Up to the swimming pool, 85 miles an hour, second gear. Up into third, 100 miles an hour. Back into second, 85 miles an hour. Up to La Rascasse, the slowest first gear corner, 60 miles an hour. Foot hard down, the finishing line is almost in sight, the crowd waves him on.*

'*And Patrick Depailler can almos—AND KEN TYRRELL, OUT INTO THE ROAD! The team goes mad – and well they might. And Patrick Depailler takes the chequered flag to win the 1978 Monaco Grand Prix in absolutely brilliant style.'*

Walker talks Lauda and Scheckter home in second and third places and then runs down the rest of the finishing order. Scenes of a jubilant Depailler on his slowing-down lap, accepting the plaudits and flag-waving from the orange-suited track marshals. Murray uses a re-run of the start to show how the Tyrrell driver did much for this win by jumping from the third row of the grid and neatly slotting into second place at the first corner.

This is followed by a crowded scene in front of the Royal Box as Depailler is interviewed by Jackie Stewart, not only a former Tyrrell driver but also a previous winner of this race. Stewart's understanding of the significance of Depailler's first F1 win – particularly at this track – is clear. The soft-spoken Frenchman, for his part, looks charmingly modest and slightly overcome.

As Depailler receives his trophy from Prince Rainier and Princess Grace, a graphic shows him leading the championship, and Murray wraps up the programme.

'*After Monaco, in two weeks' time, the Belgian Grand Prix at Zolder, and we will be back for that. But today, at Monaco, it was, at last, Patrick Depailler's day.*'

Cue 'The Chain', in full, memorable expression.

12

RELUCTANT RELATIONSHIP

The BBC continued to take excerpts from occasional Grands Prix but pressure to televise all of the races live, and in their entirety, was coming from fans as well as F1 itself. The emergence of Bernie Ecclestone as the de facto head of F1 on the commercial side led to some hard bargaining. Instead of television companies cherry-picking races to suit themselves and more or less holding organizers to ransom, Ecclestone had turned the tables. Not only would broadcasters lose the ability to do what they pleased, it was all or nothing if F1 was to be included on their schedules.

'I became [BBC] head of sport in '81,' recalled Jonathan Martin. 'The live coverage fitted very well with *Sunday Grandstand*, which we started and were able to put on BBC2. All the European Grands Prix fell beautifully into the time slot.

'Most live sports commentary on television was a one-man job with summarizers coming in at an appropriate moment. These days, there's three or four and it becomes a conversation rather than a commentary. Sometimes they're so busy chatting among themselves and I'm shouting at the screen: "Tell me who he is!" or "Tell me about what I'm seeing right now!" Back then it was clear that, if we were going to do a Grand Prix live for ninety minutes or two hours, or whatever, Murray would need a break [Martin had in fact decided in 1980, prior to becoming head of sport, that the BBC coverage could do with a second voice, even when showing edited highlights in *Grand*

Prix]. I was obviously aware that James Hunt, having retired from racing in 1979, might be available. I'd seen him interviewed a lot. He was articulate with a very, very good broadcasting voice, easy to understand, a good vocabulary – all the things you look for with, of course, the "I've been there, I've got the T-shirt" knowledge.

'Barrie Gill, the motoring journalist, made the initial approach on our behalf and I ended up negotiating a contract with Peter Hunt, who was James's brother and more or less his agent. Peter was unlike James; when you first met him, you thought he might be a librarian or an accountant. I spent many a whole day with those two, which was a bit of a pain for me, because I had other things to do. But James enjoyed the challenge of having a discussion about his contract. He knew that the BBC only had a certain amount of money. We spent hours gossiping about this, that and the other. He was a wonderful man to talk to, a very interesting chap.

'We reached agreement but, while I felt James was the ideal choice in one respect, I didn't know how it would work with Murray. When you're putting a partnership together, you can never tell how it's going to turn out. Also, I didn't know whether James would just do it for two or three races and say he wanted to go off and do something else. But I obviously hoped that James and Murray would get on.'

The news that he was to have Hunt as a broadcasting partner came as a surprise to Walker on two counts: first, he did not feel the need for a co-commentator; and second, James Hunt was the last person he would have nominated if pushed to make a choice. Murray's underlying feeling was that this was the prelude to the BBC showing him the door when, in fact, nothing could have been further from the truth.

'I didn't understand any of it at the time,' Murray said in 2013. 'I thought, with what I hope was due modesty, that I had been doing a reasonable job. I'd had no complaints and this seemed to me to be a vote of no confidence – a vote of no confidence aggravated by the

choice of James Hunt. My thoughts were: He may be a world champion racing driver, and a very good world champion racing driver, but
what on earth does he know about commentating? And, what's more,
I didn't particularly like him as a person. I was old enough to be his
father. My views on life were diametrically opposed to his. I was a
pretty plonking straightforward up-and-down bloke and here I was
with this booze-swilling, cigarette-smoking, womanizing, drug-taking
chap who I associated with rudeness and being objectionable. I was
pretty wary about it.

'I was immediately recalling some of the things I'd seen. There
used to be a series called the Tarmac Championship in which all cat-
egories of cars, in races anywhere in the world, competed. Tarmac
being a big international conglomerate, they milked this as much as
they could. At the end of the season, they had a gigantic dinner party
in somewhere like the Dorchester or Grosvenor House. They brought
in people from the West Indies; all their big buyers were there. It was
a very, very posh affair with the main award presented by Prince
Michael [of Kent]. James wandered in about an hour late, dressed in a
T-shirt, jeans – and he'd actually got a pair of trainers on for a change.
There was a collective gasp of astonishment and horror. But it wouldn't
occur to him to be embarrassed.

'On another occasion, I was at a terribly up-market black tie event
at the Sporting Club in Monte Carlo. And James appeared in a purple
Marks and Spencer corduroy jacket and a pair of denims. He talked
quite happily to everybody, and everybody talked quite happily to
James. If I'd forgotten to bring a dinner jacket, or couldn't find one, I
simply wouldn't have gone. But not James. Of course, this had absolutely no reflection on how he might be as a commentator. But it was
what came with it that was bothering me more when Jonathan told
me the news about my new partner.'

Hunt had been given an audition of sorts when, several weeks after his retirement from racing, he was a guest in the commentary box during the 1979 British Grand Prix at Silverstone. The James and Murray partnership would have its first proper trial with live coverage of the International Trophy at Silverstone on 20 April 1980. It would be a difficult start.

This permanent feature on the British racing calendar had seen better days, particularly when the majority of F1 teams would use the International Trophy as a form of test session between Grands Prix. An expanding Grand Prix schedule led to an increasing lack of interest in non-championship races. In 1980, the International Trophy would be a round of the Aurora F1 Championship – effectively a British series for second-hand F1 cars. A slim entry of fourteen cars (bolstered by F2 machinery) gave a lacklustre foretaste of what was to come.

At the end of thirty-five laps, Walker declared, in his usual genuinely enthusiastic way, that it had been an interesting race. Hunt had no hesitation in offering an alternative view. 'It was a load of rubbish' was his succinct summary.

'It hadn't been a great race,' Murray admitted later. 'But I always held the view that there's no such thing as a dull Formula 1 race. For me, there was always something interesting and exciting if you knew where to look for it. I was genuinely shocked when James said what he did.'

The former champion was backed up by *Autosport* correspondent Marcus Pye when compiling his report. 'There was little memorable about this,' wrote Pye. 'The weather was bitterly cold, the action dreary. Sunday's event was a sad reflection of the former glory enjoyed by the BRDC International Trophy. This race was the worst yet!' The 'Letters' page of the weekly magazine was filled with similar sentiments, many correspondents praising Hunt. 'I feel sure', wrote I. S. Millward from Cheshire, 'the Beeb will be the first to slap James Hunt's wrists for his outspoken comments about this race, but he was quite right.' H. Croft from Sussex wrote: 'James Hunt summed it up quite well [when he said] "A load of rubbish".'

Far from admonishing Hunt, Jonathan Martin was quietly delighted: this was exactly why he had persuaded the BBC's then head of sport Alan Hart to pay an estimated £30,000 a year (about £120,000 today), for such forthright and authoritative views. If Murray remained unconvinced about the choice of broadcasting partner, his opinion would not be ameliorated when they got down to serious business a month later at Monaco.

Prior to this, James had been the victim of his own excess. While attending a Marlboro ski party in the Swiss resort of Verbier, Hunt had taken full advantage of the hospitality while watching a team of acrobatic skiers. It was while trying to emulate the experts on a snowboard that an over-ambitious back flip resulted in a heavy fall. Oblivious to most things, including detached ligaments in his left knee, James tried to carry on and only succeeded in exacerbating the damage. Doctors at the local hospital would declare it to be the worst ligament injury of the many they had seen. After a lengthy operation and remaining in traction for several days, Hunt was determined to have his life return to as close to normal as possible, even if that meant lying on the floor of the commentary box at Silverstone because his leg was in plaster for most of its length.

Getting around Silverstone on crutches would be one thing; doing the same at Monaco during a Grand Prix weekend was quite another. James eased the inconvenience and continuing pain with plenty of what he referred to as 'lunchtime self-administered anaesthetic'. This did not bode well for commentating on a Grand Prix due to start at 3 p.m. on the Sunday.

Team player that he was, Walker had stayed in the same hotel and socialized with his broadcasting colleagues. Hunt, as would become the norm, had made his own arrangements and was nowhere to be seen on race day. Just as Murray was thinking – and quietly hoping – James would be a no-show, he appeared as the cars were forming on the grid.

Walker's worst fears about the wisdom of Jonathan Martin's appointment were immediately endorsed by the dishevelled state of his so-called professional partner, a shoeless Hunt presenting himself unshaven (not yet the cult feature it was to become) and wearing a dirty T-shirt and frayed shorts while clutching a bottle of rosé, most of which, judging by his list to starboard, he appeared to have consumed. Plonking himself down on the fold-up chair at the kerbside table, James then stuck his plastered leg in Murray's lap and asked who was on pole.

It was more than likely that Hunt knew the answer, but this was an outward sign of an inner conflict. Since becoming world champion in 1976, James had never enjoyed the celebrity status. In truth he wished to get away from racing and the limelight, and yet here he was, in the public eye once more thanks to a decision of his own making.

His contributions that day would be nothing like as informed as they would become – or as lucid, thanks, in part, to dispatching a companion to find another bottle of wine. And rather than trying to extract the microphone from Walker – as would become the norm – the situation on this occasion was the reverse.

'I remember he sat there like a sullen lump,' recalled Murray. 'James didn't, or wouldn't – or couldn't! – say anything unless I physically put my hand on his shoulder and asked what he thought. I remember thinking, This will not do. I don't remember if I said anything to Jonathan after that exhibition. But I certainly felt like doing so. It all seems amusing now, but I can assure you that was not the case at the time, particularly as I was – quite wrongly as it turned out – harbouring the belief that the BBC was planning to call time on my commentary.'

'I didn't know anything about Murray's feelings – not until I read his autobiography [*Unless I'm Very Much Mistaken*, published in 2002],' said Martin. 'He thought maybe he was going to be edged out, but never told me that. And I didn't pick up on it. When I read about it, I thought, My gosh, poor old Murray! James was not a commentator, as such. He would not have had the discipline to name the running order or time the gaps; that was completely not James. So, to read about Murray's thoughts was a surprise.

'Similarly, he never relayed many of his early thoughts about James. He occasionally said "Get him here a bit earlier", or something like that. He might have seethed internally. But he never came to me, banged on the desk and said he'd had enough. Nothing like that. That was not in Murray's character. He was not a grumbler; he just got on with things. But I could understand why he would get upset: James did have a habit of leaving things to the last minute.

'The only other commentator I've known who would deliberately arrive late was David Coleman. When I was directing *Match of the Day* in the seventies and we needed a rehearsal of the opening, David would not arrive until ten minutes before the off. That was his adrenalin rush. James, I think, did it partly out of a childish desire to wind Murray up. Murray would have his detailed notes and research stuck all over the commentary box wall and James would show up and pretend he didn't know what was going on. He'd arrive and ask: "Anyone got the starting grid?" It was to give the impression he'd done no homework. But, of course, he'd been spending time in the Marlboro hospitality unit and finding out all the gossip, stuff that would be very useful in his commentary – a different sort of knowledge to the detail Murray had in his head. That was the beauty of that partnership. It was pretty obvious they were different people. I was happy with the way it was working out and felt confident it would be OK.'

13

MOMENTOUS MONACO

'Doing the highlights [*Grand Prix*] programme was pretty hard work,' Murray admitted when reflecting in 2013. 'I'd get back from wherever the race was on the Saturday night, check into a hotel – usually the Kensington Hilton – then, the next morning, go to Television Centre and we'd cover the race from there, talking about the pictures coming in as if we were there.

'Having actually been at the race track in the previous few days was a help; you felt confident enough to speak with some authority about anything going on, either on the track or something you could see in the background. "And THERE you can see the new medical centre, which they were still finishing off on Thursday morning." You could say that with confidence because you had actually seen the chap with his paintbrush on the Thursday morning. But being in London was never the same as actually being at the track on race day.

'I couldn't even go to practice for what they called the "flyaway" races in places such as Brazil, Argentina and South Africa. But we would try and give the impression that we were there and, generally, this worked. We had help from Mike Doodson or Joe Saward, journalist colleagues who would be at the track, keeping a lap chart and being at the end of a phone line with the producer. So, if they told the producer it was starting to rain, I would get a note passed to me to that effect. I'd immediately say: "And now it's starting to rain. This is going to make things interesting!"'

'Putting on this act of suggesting – without actually saying – that we were there was blown apart one year when we were covering the South African Grand Prix. James had pretty strong views – as he had on many things – on apartheid, which was a controversial subject in South Africa at the time. The race is going on and he suddenly launches into an attack on the evils of apartheid and the shortcomings of the South African government. These may have been his personal opinions but it was pretty strong stuff for the BBC to be putting out on a sports programme. Or any programme, come to that. The producer didn't take long to pass James a note, which said "TALK ABOUT THE RACE!", with "THE RACE" heavily underlined. So, James finishes his sentence and then says: "Anyway, thank God we're not there!" Thank you for that, James!'

There was no question, however, that the BBC team was, as usual, present for the actual race in Monaco in 1982, even if Walker and Hunt struggled at times to identify the leader. For a Grand Prix with a long record of incidents through the years, this one rewrote the script in a major way.

The result had seemed a foregone conclusion for much of the race, so much so that Murray felt secure in predicting an easy win for Alain Prost as the final laps beckoned. The Renault driver had led a processional race since quarter distance and was comfortably ahead of Riccardo Patrese's Brabham-Ford.

'*As Prost goes into the tunnel, he's now on his way to his sixth Grand Prix victory in two years,*' says Murray. '*Three wins last year. Two wins this year in South Africa and Brazil . . .*'

At which point the yellow Renault turns sharp right and spears into the crash barrier, Prost having been caught out by the effect of a light shower falling on a track coated in oil and rubber. Now the fun really begins. Walker's commentary tells all. Or, most of it.

'*AND THERE GOES PROST – OFF! MY goodness, what about*

Patrese now? That tells you how wet it is. Is Patrese going to see it? Yes, he is. Patrese is through . . . what an incredible development. Riccardo Patrese takes the lead on the seventy-fourth lap out of seventy-six . . . and HE is on his way to his first Grand Prix victory.

'*And into lap seventy-five, the penultimate lap, goes the new race leader. In second place now is Didier Pironi in the Ferrari, in third place is Andrea de Cesaris* [Alfa Romeo]*; in fourth place, and he's been lapped, is Derek Daly* [Williams-Ford]*; in fifth place, Nigel Mansell* [Lotus-Ford]*.*'

James Hunt takes over.

'*Riccardo Patrese now has all the pressure off and he only has to cruise round. AND HE'S SLIDING! AND HE'S LOST IT! Dear, oh dear, oh dear. Can he keep the engine running cos he can still win the race if he can just get going again? It's obviously getting very slippery out there. There goes Pironi through into the lead.*'

Having consulted Mike Doodson's lap chart, Walker takes up the story.

'*Didier Pironi leads, and Patrese is stalled . . . Well, incredible . . . And Riccar—Didier Pironi is on his way to HIS second Grand Prix win this year and the third in his career . . .*

'*Now, Pironi is about to start his last lap – or are they stopping the race? It's tremendous, there's an enormous electric atmosphere here. And Pironi is going through. One lap. He's been given the signal. One lap to go and he's now behind the new third-place man, Derek Daly. Well, Daly in his second race for Williams is going to finish third. Who could possibly have forecast that earlier on?*

'*And there goes Patrese. Patrese is on the move again – very fast, but no hope of catching Pironi, who goes into the tunnel for the las—Is that Pironi stationary? IT IS! My goodness! The third leader in two laps . . . And that's de Cesaris's car* [stationary]*. De Cesaris would have taken the lead when Pironi – so that means to say that Derek Daly could win this race. Patre— well, Patrese could win. Now then, if he's push-started, he will be disqualified.*

'*Well, de Cesaris out; Patrese could still win. And now, there's Daly coasting to a standstill! This is UNBELIEVABLE.*'

Hunt: '*We've got this ridiculous situation where we're all sitting about at the finish line waiting for a winner to come past – and we don't seem to be getting one!*'

Walker: '*We're just hoping Riccardo Patrese comes in because, if he doesn't, heaven knows who is going to be the winner. The winner would be Nigel Mansell . . . Well, Prost led and went out. Patrese led and went out. Pironi led and went out. De Cesaris led and went out. And now Patrese is coming in to win, without a doubt.*

'*There is the man – who could have said this? – who is going to win the Monaco Grand Prix despite having spun off . . . He takes the chequered flag and wins, certainly the most eventful, exciting, momentous Grand Prix I have EVER seen.*'

At that moment, it would have been reasonable to expect a summary from Hunt. Two years into their commentary relationship, however, Murray had learned that the end of the race signalled James's immediate departure – or, as Walker put it more succinctly in his autobiography, 'it was as though the chequered flag was connected to a spring in his arse'. Keen to avoid the crowds and make good his escape, Hunt would usually have arranged a lift out of the circuit and on to the airport. Murray, meanwhile, would be gathering up his notes and preparing to visit the paddock to discover the background stories to the race, the better to inform columns he would write for various newspapers and magazines.

These pieces would be carefully crafted in longhand. In the coming years he would have many a tale to tell, not least during Prost's battles for the championship with Nelson Piquet in 1983 and Niki Lauda in 1984. The latter was settled at the final race in Portugal, the McLaren team-mates running head-to-head. The Estoril circuit was a demanding one – for drivers and television producers alike.

Roger Moody had been transferred by Jonathan Martin from the BBC's sports production team to F1 when the *Grand Prix* highlights programme was instigated. That led to Moody's role as producer when live transmissions began from the race track.

'It could sometimes get very stressful at the end of a race,' said Moody. 'In Portugal in 1984 we had the added pressure of it being the championship finale between Prost and Lauda. One was going to become world champion and we needed to interview them. We had to wrap up our live commentary and dash from the commentary boxes, which at Estoril were located at the back of the grandstand opposite the pits.

'In those days, there were no proper interview facilities. We would have what was known as a Unilateral slot – usually no more than fifteen minutes – to have access to the host broadcaster's lines, get the interview done and send it back, in our case to Television Centre in London. You had to get to the camera position for that allotted time.

'In Portugal, I had to grab Murray, rush down several flights of stairs and head for a pedestrian tunnel beneath the track. The problem was that it would be full of people as they left the paddock and headed for the exit. Murray and I battled through there and fought our way to the back of the pits and a little room that I had arranged. The cameraman and sound engineer were waiting for us – but Lauda and Prost [were] some distance down the pit lane. I told Murray to get ready while I had to find and more or less frogmarch these two superstars, with the world's press on our heels and trying to follow us into the little room. It was extremely stressful both physically and mentally but, throughout, Murray would remain perfectly calm and get the job done. He could cope with anything.'

Moody would have been helped by Prost and Lauda being amicable team-mates. That would not be the case a few years later when Ayrton Senna joined McLaren and began increasingly tense in-house contests with Prost. The BBC commentary box, meanwhile, had an edginess of its own – a feature that had quickly become evident to the BBC F1 team's latest recruits.

Steve Rider had joined in 1985. His principal role may have been as a replacement for Harry Carpenter as presenter of the network's *Sportsnight* programme, but Rider was keen to diversify. Having presented sports programmes, he had got to know Murray over the years and shared his enthusiasm for motor sport.

'It was while working at Anglia Television that I first became involved in motor sport,' said Rider. 'Anglia was a big motor sport area in terms of off-road activity and everything that was going on at the Snetterton race track [in Norfolk]. In 1978, I was particularly fortunate because we had Lotus, about to become the F1 world champions, just down the road. We managed to get a fairly decent relationship with [Lotus boss] Colin Chapman.

'As far as I was concerned, Murray was always the sort of voice that you would really relate to in terms of professional broadcasting of the sport. When I joined the BBC, I had this vision that you would walk into a room and there would be Richie Benaud here, John Motson over there and David Coleman doing his preparation in another corner. But I quickly discovered that you never ended up meeting any of these great commentating legends unless you were closely identified with their sports. As far as Murray was concerned, I never dared approach him. The first time I met him, I think, was at the launch of the Beatrice [Team Haas] F1 team in 1985. We clearly had an affinity with motor sport and hit it off quite rapidly after that.

'Along the way, I witnessed Murray's working relationship with James. I thought, to be honest, it was poisonous at times.

'I recall one occasion at the British Grand Prix at Silverstone. I had been on the grid, doing what you might now call pre-Martin Brundle grid stuff; it was very amateurish by comparison. The commentary box was on top of the Shell Tower on the outside of the final corner, Woodcote, and overlooking the start/finish straight.

'As soon as the cars leave the grid, I leg it towards the back of the tower and as I start to climb the iron external staircase I hear footsteps behind me. Don't forget, the cars are on their way to the grid and about to start the race. I look round to see James – with a pint of lager in each hand. "Hi Steve," he says. "Tell me something. Have we any cricket on after this?" When I replied that we had, James said: "Well, that's good. If cricket is on, I'll stay and watch it. If there's no cricket, I might try and get out of here a few laps before the end of the race."

'James carries on into the commentary box and slams down a pint of lager – all over Murray's carefully coloured and handwritten information sheets. You could see the look of absolute fury on Murray's face, even while he's talking in his usual animated way. He must have been filling in now for about four and a half minutes. James then plonked himself down – and immediately contradicted every single word Murray was saying. It wasn't cosy. But it was dynamic, and you have to say there was a wonderful edge to it. I don't think there's any other commentary partnership that was as recognizable or as distinctive as theirs.'

Mark Wilkin would, at times, have the unenviable job of keeping control in the commentary box after joining the F1 team as producer. But first he had to learn more about the sport, and the man in charge of F1.

'The first race I ever went to was the San Marino Grand Prix in April 1989,' said Wilkin. 'I happened to be working on a European Cup semi-final the night before at the San Siro stadium in Milan. Because I was desperate to go to a race, I drove down with the team when they arrived at Milan airport the next morning.

'It was on this journey when I heard what you might call my first "Murrayism". We were on the motorway, heading towards Imola, when Murray suddenly said: "Hang on a second! We're near that place where they make the cheese, aren't we?" I said: "Cheese?" He said: "Yeah, the place they make the cheese, you know..." We went through as many Italian cheeses as we could: mascarpone, Gorgonzola, mozzarella, Parmesan. And then he suddenly said: "That's it! Parma! Parma!" "Parma *ham*, Murray?" "Oh ..."

'I got the lay of the land that weekend and ended up producing every race for the rest of the 1989 season – starting with Monaco. We used one of those Page & Moy trips to get there and stayed at the Balmoral hotel. Once we had dumped our bags, I said to Murray that I'd like to walk round the circuit. Being Murray, he was delighted to show me around. He had all the stories: "This is the bit where this happened. And this is where Senna hit the wall when he was leading the race last year." It was just like a dream come true, being shown round Monaco by Murray Walker. His enthusiasm for everything associated with motor racing and this race was incredible.

'Apart from all of that, there was a very interesting moment during the walk. I'd only just been made a producer, so I was about as junior as you could get. I'd been told: "There's a chap called Bernie Ecclestone who runs the show. We're having a row with him at the moment and it's a bit of a mess; lawyers are involved. Whatever happens, do *not* engage with him. He might challenge you on something, but this is way beyond your pay scale, so steer clear."

'I'd no intention of meeting Bernie; I didn't even know what he looked like. So, walking around the circuit, we had just reached the swimming pool when a black Mercedes with tinted windows drove past and stopped about 10 metres further on. A rear passenger window glides down and a hand comes out, with a crooked finger beckoning us. Murray says: "That's Bernie! I'd better go and see what he wants." He rushes over, the door opens, Murray jumps in the car, and it moves off. I'm thinking: What's going on? We've got this huge problem with

Bernie Ecclestone. He surely can't be kidnapping Murray? I've only just got here and already I've lost our star performer! About 100 metres further on, the car stops and Murray gets out. I go running over to find out what has been going on.

'Murray was holding a small pad of tissue paper, and he seemed lost for words. Inside was a gold lapel pin in the shape of an old BBC Reithian-style eight-sided table microphone. Apparently, some of these had been made way back when the BBC was inaugurated. Bernie had been in a jeweller's in Hatton Garden and spotted one. So, in the middle of all this "I hate the BBC" stuff, he had bought this pin because, he said, it made him think of Murray. I thought that said a lot about them both, actually. Murray, as you might imagine, was absolutely thrilled.'

'I was pole-axed,' admitted Murray. 'When I stumbled through what I hoped was a very sincere thank you, Bernie waved away my thanks by saying: "Well, you *are* the BBC, aren't you?" I really didn't have an answer for that.

'I'd be the first to admit that Bernie has his faults,' Walker went on. 'But, as far as I'm concerned, he has done an absolutely enormous amount for Formula 1. If it wasn't for Bernie, the sport would not have a worldwide profile which nations vie with each other to host. I considered myself very fortunate to be a part of that even if there were times when you didn't know what Bernie was going to do next.'

The previous year's race had been a case in point. The 1988 Monaco Grand Prix had marked the tenth anniversary of the *Grand Prix* programme. To signify the occasion, the BBC crew had brought a large cake, the plan being to have Ecclestone and team bosses such as Colin Chapman, Ken Tyrrell and Ron Dennis form a semi-circle around Murray while he did the honours with a cake knife. It was agreed, when the cutting was complete, that the assembled company would shout 'Happy Birthday, *Grand Prix*!' Walker suspected something was afoot when he saw Bernie move among his mates, having a quiet word with each of them. With the camera rolling, Murray made his introduction and began cutting. As he finished and looked up expectantly, the audience shouted as one: 'BOLLOCKS!'

Ecclestone had tried, but failed, to qualify as a driver for the 1958 Monaco Grand Prix at the wheel of his Connaught. Realizing his skills lay elsewhere, he had become involved with driver management, first with Stuart Lewis-Evans in the late fifties and later with Jochen Rindt, the 1970 world champion. Both had died of injuries received in F1 cars. Ecclestone then turned his hand to team ownership when he bought Brabham in 1971, a move that opened his eyes to the financial opportunities available if the teams united and got their act together. Murray had chosen the *Grand Prix* celebration in Monaco in 1988 as a suitable occasion to interview Ecclestone about his influential role in the sport.

'Bernie, it's some seventeen years since you bought McLaren. You've had some good times and bad times. What do you remember best?'

'I don't remember buying McLaren,' Ecclestone replied.

'Oh . . .'

14

FRICTION AND FRIENDSHIP

When Mark Wilkin began producing F1 programmes at Monaco in 1989, Walker and Hunt had been working together for nine years. The relationship may have improved since James's slovenly start at the same circuit, but Wilkin was to discover on occasion that there was still some way to go. The cause of one particularly tense moment had its roots in an important policy introduced by Jonathan Martin at the very beginning of the Murray and James partnership.

'There weren't many commentary teams at the time [1980],' said Martin. 'We had one for athletics. But that was rather different because they were covering different disciplines in the sport. David Coleman would be doing the track, Norris McWhirter would commentate on hurdles and Ron Pickering would be doing field events. My thinking with Murray and James was that the last thing you want is people talking over each other because, if you have two open microphones, you can't hear what either is saying. So, with F1, we had a potential situation of one who doesn't ever like to stop talking, and the other who wants desperately to get in. I thought the best solution would be one microphone between them. In any case, it was a bit easier because we were using lip microphones, which you held to your mouth, rather than the type you clip on the commentator's shirt or is part of their headset.

'Although Murray and James were crammed pretty close together in most commentary boxes, the potential problem was a geographic one. Murray was always on his feet; he never sat down. It was a physical job as far as he was concerned. James preferred to sit, which suited his more laid-back style.

'Having one mic worked. Occasionally, Murray and James both wanted to speak. I wouldn't say they had a battle for the microphone. Normally, in those circumstances, one would tap his colleague on the shoulder and sort of point at the screen. Murray was a very affable man, what I would call an old-fashioned gentleman. It's presumptuous of me to say whether somebody has manners or doesn't have manners. But Murray was of the generation who thought it was right to behave properly.'

Walker's sense of decorum generally held true, even in the most trying of circumstances. There was one occasion, however, when Hunt pushed beyond the boundary of acceptable behaviour. Wilkin saw it happen.

'Jonathan's idea of having an expert in the commentary box as a summarizer was a good one,' said Wilkin. 'It was a novel concept in the early eighties whereas now, if you look at the Sky cricket commentary box for example, if you haven't captained England, you don't get a look-in. Back then, Murray had a role; James had a role; they were very different – but that's what made it work.

'As time went by, however, it reached the stage where they both obviously believed that they ought to do most of the talking. And what they had to say was *way* more interesting than anything the other had to say. Jonathan's decision to give them just one microphone meant it was physically handed from one to the other. Having hold of the mic was like nine-tenths of the law at that point.

'James had a sort of laconic style; he would often have his feet propped up on the desk. He'd sometimes ask to have another sport on a different monitor because he was just as interested in the Test match, or the tennis, or whatever else was going on. So, he would sit there and eventually he'd put his hand out, which would mean "I've got something to say". And if Murray ignored him, he would lift his hand a bit higher, close to Murray's eyeline. And if that didn't work, he'd wave his hand to indicate "Come on! Come on! I've really got something to say."

'It came to a head during the European Grand Prix at Donington in [April] 1993. This was a very dramatic race: run in the rain; lots going on; Senna overtaking four cars to lead at the end of the first lap; loads of pit stops. At one point, James stood up – which was unheard of – and yanked the microphone from Murray's hand. There was this unseemly tussle. Then Murray drew his fist back. At that moment, I dived in between them. I couldn't speak because the microphone was live, so I just wagged my finger at Murray. They fell back from the brink. All was well.

'We discussed it quite a lot after the race. I thought that discussing commentary was a good thing to do. Why are you commentating? Who are you commentating for? What information are you trying to get over? What's it like watching a race without commentary? We tried to come up with rules. James would concur but occasionally he would jump up and down and say: "Tell Murray, I do the replays! Tell him!" It was things like that. But, overall, it worked really well even though they were very different.'

Hunt's role as a former driver, race winner and world champion brought valuable insight to the commentary. Being outspoken, however, sometimes meant the expounding of marginal views on a driver's behaviour that were seemingly driven by personal animosity. Riccardo Patrese was a case in point.

James's naked dislike of Patrese stemmed from a serious accident at the start of the 1978 Italian Grand Prix. Hunt had been involved and blamed Patrese for cutting across, barging into his McLaren and triggering the multi-car collision that eventually took the life of the popular Swedish driver Ronnie Peterson. Despite vehemently claiming his innocence (subsequently proved by an aerial photograph), Patrese became a scapegoat. While other drivers would later express regret about their part in a kangaroo court that had Patrese banned from the next Grand Prix, Hunt would continue to believe in the Italian's guilt – a view he would express on air at the slightest excuse.

'The business between James and Patrese was a falling out that couldn't be repaired,' said Wilkin. 'Murray always wanted to play the opposite side of that argument. There was one occasion in the commentary box in South Africa in 1993 when James is going all out against Patrese, Murray is defending him, and James keeps coming back. Eventually, I said: "Right! That's it. Stop! Stop!" They both wanted to have the last word; they were like children. Afterwards, they sort of acknowledged that. Then James would say: "But he's still a lousy driver!"'

Walker would occasionally use Hunt's blatant bias to his advantage. 'If the race was proving to be a bit dull and not very entertaining, I only had to say something complimentary about Patrese,' said Murray. 'James would immediately gesture to have the microphone and then spew vitriol over a bloke who had long since been established as innocent. What made it even worse from my point of view was that Riccardo was an amiable, likeable sort of chap. He didn't deserve the criticism that James would heap upon him at any and every opportunity. And it wasn't just Patrese. James wasn't very complimentary about Nigel Mansell. As for [Jean-Pierre] Jarier ... James once said: "The problem with Jarier is he's a French wally, always has been and always will be."'

The difference of opinion over Patrese and others contributed to Murray being more reluctant than he might have been to accept having James alongside in the commentary box.

'My attitude,' said Walker, 'was that I was extremely lucky to be in the situation where literally millions of people worldwide were depending on me – depending on us – to inform them entertainingly and excitingly about the thing that was dearest to their hearts. And I deeply resented the fact that this chap was not putting his all into it. [But] I don't want to give the impression that we couldn't stand the sight of each other. James always had enormous charm. Well, most of the time.

'James could have outbursts of temper that were really, really frightening. I was in the commentary box at Adelaide one year and one of the technicians did something that irritated James. He turned on this bloke and screamed at him using the most foul language; a great torrent of it. This bloke had only done some terribly trivial thing and I was really shocked at that. But when he was in a good mood and in a communicative mood – and the further he got away from his driving career the better he became – he was an absolutely delightful bloke to be with.

'I went to his house in Wimbledon once. He had a manservant called Winston, who he appeared to be helping out because Winston had got himself into some sort of difficulty. As for the house, it was furnished as if James had gone round all the second-hand shops in Wimbledon, loaded what he'd bought into a cannon and fired it at the house. That was one of the – I wouldn't call it endearing – characteristics of James. He just didn't care what people thought about him. That, in turn, meant there was absolutely no animosity between us. None at all. We always got on, but what I didn't do in the beginning was respect him.'

Respect, or the disappointing lack of it, created an inner conflict for Walker. 'Murray was wrestling with this,' said Wilkin. 'He had a huge problem because James was a racing driver – a Formula 1 driver – so he was therefore up on a pedestal. Not only that, James was also a world champion. So, he was on an even higher pedestal. And yet this hero was not living up to the sort of expectation that Murray had of how such people should behave. The drug taking, the drinking, the womanizing, arriving in the commentary box drunk — all of these things offended Murray. And yet he had to put these two completely opposite views together. Which he did.

'Yes, it's true that Murray did rather resent James not knowing stuff, plus the fact that quite often James hadn't seen what happened in practice,' continued Wilkin. 'But he did realize that what James brought to the commentary wasn't an in-depth analysis of what happened in Friday practice, it was a real understanding of what was going on inside a racing car, and James had this tremendous ability to communicate that.'

Hunt, for his part, was learning to appreciate the difficulties involved in being a broadcaster. He was aware of criticism in the UK media about mistakes made by Walker during commentary and sprang to his colleague's defence during an interview with the author about another matter. Completely unprompted, James said: 'I want to say this about Murray. People criticize him for getting things wrong. It's bloody difficult to get it right. I certainly get confused from time to time. Why people insist on criticizing, I don't know. If they know the driver is Prost and not Piquet, then why write in about it if they know in the first place? So what? Murray is loved in Australia, for instance. All he ever hears in this country is criticism. He's a tremendous enthusiast and does a hell of a lot for the image of the sport.'

Walker admitted to being surprised and touched by Hunt's support. All of which would contribute to an increasing willingness to make their relationship work better in the commentary box. That would be important in 1989 and 1990 as they found themselves describing a relationship that clearly was not working on the race track.

15

PROST V. SENNA

Along with everyone else in F1, Murray had become aware of increasing tension as Ayrton Senna, into his second season with McLaren in 1989, was very keen to put one over his team-mate, Alain Prost, who was widely considered to be the best driver of that era. Senna's view was that if he could beat the Frenchman, there could be no argument about who was the greatest.

As Senna took his first title in 1988, the season had been harmonious enough until the Portuguese Grand Prix in September when Senna eased Prost against the pit wall at more than 175mph in an attempt to prevent his team-mate making a pass. The relationship deteriorated further two races into 1989 when, according to Prost, Senna broke a private agreement between the two over who should win the San Marino Grand Prix. By the time they had reached the season's penultimate race in Japan, the affiliation had become toxic, made worse for Senna thanks to Prost leading the championship.

Senna needed to win at Suzuka, come what may. Prost, claiming he had endured enough of his team-mate's intimidatory tactics, made it clear he was determined to hold his ground. Such a statement from the normally mild-mannered Frenchman was a portent of troubled times ahead. Walker and Hunt prepared for a lively couple of hours as the cars rolled on to the grid – Senna on pole, with Prost sharing the front row.

'*And they get away very quickly indeed*,' says Murray as the green light comes on. '*A beautiful start by Alain Prost, who goes into the lead.*'

The positions remain the same through the pit stops, Prost seeming to have the measure of Senna on this testing, old-school circuit.

Lap 40

Walker: '*Look at that! Ayrton Senna right with Alain Prost. This is Senna's opportunity to take the lead and his World Championship chance at the same time.*'

There is no attempt by Senna to overtake.

Lap 41

Walker: '*And now, for the first time, we see the two McLarens absolutely together. Now it's going to be really enthralling because Alain Prost can see the McLaren-Honda of Ayrton Senna big in his mirrors.*'

Hunt: '*And now we have another ingredient – which is probably not such a good one. Believe you me, we have very, very high emotions running in both those cockpits. It wouldn't be unreasonable to say that they hate each other. On that basis, to be racing at those speeds, as a further and rather unnecessary dimension, to have any emotional feelings of antipathy towards each other is not good. But that is the situation. It almost makes the pressure much greater for Prost with his lead. His dislike of Senna makes him much more twitchy; much more inclined, if possible, to make a mistake. It's not a good pressure to have.*'

Walker: '*And look! LOOK! Senna's going through . . . no, Prost holds him off. It's going to be constant attack, attack, attack! Because Senna has got everything to gain and nothing to lose. And Prost has got everything to lose if Senna gets past him. If Senna can get past him, it will keep his World Championship hopes alive down to Australia in two weeks' time.*'

Lap 42

Walker: '*Down the finishing straight at 190 miles an hour. What a fantastic scrap. Here is the excitement.* [On-board shot over Senna's right shoulder, showing the Brazilian constantly working the wheel and the manual gearbox, his iconic yellow crash helmet bobbing in and out of shot.] *And we are right with it – a master stroke to have the cameras on board the McLarens.*'

Lap 43

Hunt: '*Particularly exciting for our viewers in Australia because, depending on this, whether they host the deciding race in the World Championship . . . They will be cheering like mad for Ayrton Senna with the tremendously dramatic race we're getting here . . . We're having a helluva good time here, just watching the race – and Senna threatening a little bit.*

'*But remember,*' continues Hunt, '*this is a narrow track; the cars are fairly equally matched on power . . . Senna will have the added knowledge that Prost only needs to take them both out of the race to win the World Championship. Whether Prost is going to do it or not – because I think it's highly unlikely – but Senna must always allow for that possibility in his thinking, even if he believes Prost wouldn't do a thing like that . . . he can't afford to go very close to Prost looking for a way past, just in case Prost does something silly like that.*'

Lap 46

Walker: '*We're riding with Senna now. Prost is in his sights; the World Championship chance is in his sights. It's a fifty-three-lap race. Prost has got ENORMOUS pressure on him. So, in a way, has Senna because Senna knows that if he can't get up with Prost, and take his opportunity to get past, he will not repeat his World Championship* [of 1988].'

Lap 47

Hunt: '*Prost, still defending. Ayrton Senna is now the man upon whom the onus rests. Has he got something up his sleeve, or will he try – it looks to me he has no obvious answer – will he try something desperate? He has shown himself capable of doing that. Prost is making sure that Senna will have to do something like that because he's going slowly into the corners, getting early on the power – and Senna is closer than ever before.*'

Walker: '*This is Alain Prost's 150th Grand Prix. He has had experience of just about every situation – including this one. The situation of being in the lead with* [the] *second-place man treading on his rear wheels, almost. And having to resist that pressure, keep his racing line, not go wide, not leave an opportunity with a door open, through which Senna would be LIKE A FLASH.'*

The leaders approach the final chicane at more than 180mph. Senna aims for the inside.

Walker: '*THIS IS THE OPPORTUNITY SENNA'S LOOKING FOR! AND HE'S GOING THROUGH!* [The two cars collide and come to a halt, locked together.] *OUT! Oh, my goodness! This is fantastic! They meet. This is what we were fearing might happen during the race.* [Prost begins to climb from his car; Senna beckons marshals to come to his aid.] *And that means to say that Prost has won the World Championship. Alain Prost, world champion of 1989.*

'*Here's a* [overhead] *replay. Now, let's look. Senna comes up to try and go through on the inside. Prost moves across; takes them both out.*'

Hunt: '*Yes, well, Senna went for a gap that wasn't there. You could see quite clearly that Prost was already turning into the corner . . .*'

And so began a long-lasting debate, albeit one partially cut short by officials when it was deemed that Senna, who got going again and went on to cross the line first, had rejoined illegally and was denied the win, thereby ensuring Prost was champion.

The anger felt by Senna would simmer for twelve months, the return to Japan in 1990 bringing the same two drivers into contention for the title. The difference this time was that Prost had moved to Ferrari and, in the reverse of 1989, it was Senna who had come to Suzuka with a points advantage.

The febrile atmosphere was intensified when Senna, having won pole, was refused permission to move the prime starting position to the cleaner side of the track, leaving that advantage to Prost. The stage was set for a dramatic Murray Walker commentary. This time, however, it would be much briefer than in 1989.

Walker: '*And the hot news from Suzuka is that Ayrton Senna – and there he is – is starting from the right-hand side of the grid, much to his annoyance. The right-hand side is pole position, and the track is dirty there. Senna asked for pole position to be changed to the left. His request was refused. And the result is that Alain Prost, starting from second on the grid on the left-hand side, is actually going to have a start advantage at a circuit where passing is virtually impossible – except at the notorious chicane where Alain Prost and Ayrton Senna, both in McLarens, collided. And we all know what happened subsequently. Ayrton Senna went on to win the race, only to be disqualified.*

'*We are waiting for the start of this fifty-three-lap race. On the left* [from the camera angle looking back towards the grid] *is Ayrton Senna. On the right is Alain Prost . . . The grid is clear . . . The lights – GO! And Senna sprints away – BUT ALAIN PROST TAKES THE LEAD! It's happened! Alain Prost has taken the advantage – SENNA IS TRYING TO GO THROUGH ON THE INSIDE, AND IT'S HAPPENED IMMEDIATELY! THIS IS AMAZING! SENNA GOES OFF* [in a cloud of dust] *AT THE FIRST CORNER! But, what has happened to Prost? HE HAS GONE OFF TOO! Well, that is amazing! But I fear, absolutely . . . predictable.*'

Hunt: '*Well, that makes Ayrton Senna world champion this year. With Alain Prost not finishing the race quite clearly, he's out of his car, stuck in the gravel pit. That, I'm afraid to say, is the end of this year's Drivers' World Championship in favour of Ayrton Senna.*'

The fact was not lost on Mark Wilkin that both Japanese commentaries – and those in between during the twelve-month period – had worked very well for the BBC team (if not Prost and Senna in every case). 'It was about finding the right balance,' said Wilkin. 'Murray and I did talk about limiting James's involvement. In other words, I said to Murray, let's not get into what happened during practice on Friday; don't go there because you know James won't be able to offer much. We need to concentrate on the here and now; that's where he really scores.

'Saying that, there had been amusing moments because of Murray's initial unease. He would make copious notes and write them out incredibly neatly – a mass of information which he liked to have to hand. There were times when I saw James attempting to read the notes and Murray shielding them, just like you might do at school! His attitude seemed to be: "You're not looking at my notes; why should I make you look good?"

'But it had begun to dawn on Murray that they were a double act that worked well. This process had actually started before I arrived and it only got better. At the same time, James went through a personal change – also very much for the better.'

Hunt had hit rock bottom in 1988. Bouts of depression had not been helped by a divorce that, in part, had been brought on by the effects of his frequently decadent lifestyle. When the net result – aggravated by a poor investment costing in the region of £200,000 – resulted in a bank balance reading red rather than black, James accepted he had no alternative but to pick himself up by the bootstraps. Abandoning alcohol and cigarettes and other substances, he resolved to get fit again. With his Mercedes on bricks, it suited Hunt to cycle wherever he could. John Hogan, the head of Marlboro's motor sport division and a good friend of James, witnessed the change at first hand.

'Initially I had no idea he was in such trouble,' said Hogan. 'I always thought he was suffering from a hangover when, in fact, he was actually a depressive. He was under terrible pressure for all sorts of reasons, some financial. Then he just turned it all around through nothing more than sheer willpower. It was amazing to see but not really a surprise if you knew James and what he was capable of. He had enormous strength of character and this is when it really paid off. He cut back on everything: the booze, the drugs, the cigarettes, even the womanizing. His focus was phenomenal, which tells you how bad he had been when he couldn't get out of it initially.'

Hunt set about becoming established in the media, writing columns for newspapers and, of course, continuing his broadcasting with greater enthusiasm than before.

'He became much sharper and he knew a lot more about everything that was going on,' said Wilkin. 'The commentaries developed and changed because of that. He took much more of an interest. He was a changed man. The partnership with Murray was working extremely well. No one ever expected it to end the way it did.'

16

A TRULY SHOCKING LOSS

The Canadian Grand Prix was the seventh round of the 1993 F1 World Championship. Murray and James had covered the previous race live from Monaco, but since Montreal was a so-called 'flyaway' event they would commentate on the feed being relayed to the BBC Television Centre in west London. Hunt had cycled the 6 miles from his home in Wimbledon on Sunday morning.

'He was riding his bike everywhere,' recalled Murray. 'He seemed as fit as a fiddle because he had stopped smoking; he was back into sport again. We'd been having dinner at one of the races – Imola, I think – and I had said to him: "What are you having to drink, James?" He said: "I'll have an orange juice." When I said "Orange juice? What happened to the wine?" he replied: "I think I've had my fair share, Murray." Which was a masterpiece of understatement! As a result of all that, he became an altogether nicer person to deal with. I don't want to give the wrong impression, James was basically a very nice, friendly, cheerful, outgoing bloke, but with all the adulation that he got and his natural temperament, he could be bloody arrogant and impossible. But he lost all that and got stupefyingly fit.

'When he arrived at Shepherd's Bush that day, he looked pretty scruffy. I jokingly said I hoped he wasn't going to speak to his public dressed like that. In all seriousness, he replied that he wasn't and went off to change into a fresh set of clothes he'd brought with him in the basket on the handlebars of his bike.

'He seemed to be in good form; he was always in good form, but he was very upbeat, and that seemed to be in keeping with the way his life had changed gear. We were talking about the Canadian Grand Prix, which had become one of the few long-haul races we had yet to do live. CBC [Canadian Broadcasting Corporation] took the BBC commentary through the rest of the year but, of course, they did their own race in Montreal. James seemed to think, for whatever reason, that we would be in Canada the next year and he was very much looking forward to it. He really meant it.

'We did the commentary as usual; it went perfectly well. James then phoned Gerald Donaldson, who was ghosting his newspaper column. That done, we went on our way, James cycling back to Wimbledon, and I went home to Hampshire.

'On the Tuesday morning [15 June 1993], I was doing a job when Elizabeth [Murray's wife] phoned me. She said, "Brace yourself. I've got some bad news." My mother was ninety-six at the time and I thought it must be her. "No," she said. "James has died." I said: "James who?" When she said "James Hunt" I simply could not believe it and said something silly like you tend to do on these occasions: "But I was with him on Sunday, and he was perfectly OK." It was a truly dreadful shock – not just for me, of course, but for millions around the world. He was only forty-five.'

Hunt had died of a massive heart attack in the early hours of the morning. Having played snooker at home with a friend, James had retired, complaining of feeling unwell. He never made it into bed. His distraught family held a private funeral on 21 June.

Murray's thoughts led tributes spread across four pages of the next issue of *Autosport*.

'Two days after the hammer blow of James's death, I still cannot really grasp it,' wrote Murray. 'It's very hard for me to accept that he isn't breezily going to appear in the box for the French Grand Prix to commentate in that laid-back and authoritative style that won him a place of affection and respect in the hearts of millions of Formula 1 enthusiasts all over the world.

'Ours was an unusual partnership. It would be difficult to find two people who were a greater contrast in terms of personality and attitudes, but in spite of it, or maybe because of it, the chemistry was right and it seemed to work. It wasn't easy for either of us, though! There are very few top sportsmen who can talk fluently, entertainingly and with authority about what they do so well. James was certainly one of them. He had an unerring ability to read a race, forecast tactics and explain the action. Plus the courage and conviction to criticize and correct. That takes guts, for it often leads to angry reactions from irate and biased viewers (and me!).

'You couldn't find a more cheerful and friendly chap with less side or self-importance. People loved his warmth, his openness, his honesty . . . to say that I will sadly miss him is a masterpiece of understatement. So, I am sure, will you.'

The BBC produced a twenty-minute tribute made up of interviews with key players in Hunt's racing life and a narration by Walker. In the closing sequence, filmed in his garden, Murray speaks quietly to camera about the global effect of James's passing, before concluding, 'It's left an enormous hole in my life . . . and I really am going to miss him very much indeed.' The pause is a poignant one. For someone noted for the ability to hold it together, Murray chokes slightly and comes close to breaking down. The depth of affection is unmistakable.

Murray was correct when he said the shock and distress would affect huge numbers of people. On 29 September 1993, St James's Church in Piccadilly was chosen for a memorial service attended by relatives and six hundred friends from James's life. Murray gave the address.

'We're here today to remember and to honour James as a very

special person, who in different ways has been part of the life of each and every one of us,' said Murray. 'To his family, he was a loving son, brother, father. To the motor racing world of which he was such an outstanding part, he was a great competitor, a forceful team-mate, a determined and gifted rival. And to millions of Formula 1 fans all over the world, from Adelaide to Andover, who listened to the authoritative and witty television commentaries he gave, his was the voice that made sense out of an involved and complicated sport. And to me, he was a respected and admired colleague, whose wit and wisdom added immeasurably to our joint efforts to communicate the sport that meant so much to both of us.

'Quite apart from his talents, his success, his commanding presence and his natural dignity, he was an immensely likeable, warm, different kind of human being. One who made wherever he was a livelier and more stimulating and enjoyable place to be, because James didn't think like other people. He didn't act like other people. He refused to conform to the rules that govern most of us. And he had the presence and the charm to get away with it.

'I bet almost everybody here could tell a story about something that James did or said and they'd tell it with affection and warmth, to emphasize that he was no ordinary person.'

Murray went on to describe events at their first commentaries together on the 'rubbish' Aurora F1 race at Silverstone, followed by the nonchalant Grand Prix debut at Monaco 'when he stuck his leg [in a plaster cast] on my lap and sailed into the comments that were to endear him to his vast following for thirteen years'.

Detailing Hunt's racing career, which had gone from 'virtual obscurity to world champion in an incredibly short time', Murray pointed out that James raced in an era when it was possible 'both to succeed and enjoy yourself. And he did both to the full. And then he matured to pass on his experience and his knowledge to his successors and an enormous audience, by means of that commanding voice, presence and his natural authority.'

Murray then touched upon the effect James's death had had on the public. 'I have had dozens and dozens of truly moving letters,' he said. 'They tell me that the writers felt they had lost a real and valued personal friend, whose warmth and humour had enriched their lives and whose experience, knowledge and outspokenness had kindled and developed their intense interest in Grand Prix racing.

'Now, if my theory is correct, it's not difficult to see why. They saw James as a character, which he certainly was. They saw him as his own man, which he most certainly was. They saw him as having a bright, breezy, lively personality, which he did. And they loved his irreverence and his provocative comments. Because James, anywhere and everywhere, was never reluctant to speak his mind. An incredibly clear-thinking and analytical mind, which may sometimes have produced words his targets didn't like – I didn't like some of them – but which he always was ready to defend to their faces with logic and eloquence that usually won them over. "I'm just off to have it out with so and so about last week," he'd say. And then you'd see him calmly justify his case in the paddock, when most people would have laid low and hoped it would go away. But then he would always apologize if he felt he'd been wrong. Apropos of which, I have never known a public figure of his magnitude, his very considerable magnitude, who was as unaffected by his success and as self-effacing as James was.'

Murray described how James had felt the pressure of being a superstar because he was essentially a private man and didn't enjoy the ceaseless adulation.

'So, a paragon of humanity?' asked Murray. 'Nothing to criticize? No weak points? Well of course there were, and thank heavens too. None of us is perfect. There are people here who could write a book about James's escapades. And an immensely readable best seller it would be too. But when the adrenalin was running high, he could be a fearsome chap. I've seen him fell a rival competitor who angered him. I've seen him do the same to a marshal who incurred his wrath. And I certainly won't forget the tongue-lashing that an unfortunate [broadcasting] technician got in Australia when a communication failure made James look silly.

'James could charm the birds out of the trees but sadly he wasn't spared hard times in recent years. Personal and financial problems had made things very tough indeed for him. But you'd never have known it. He was unfailingly cheerful and remained the kind, courteous and helpful English gentleman he had always been. And he industriously knuckled down to getting out of the trouble he was in.

'In his job as a racing consultant, he passed on his hard-won knowledge and expertise to the new generation of drivers. Ask his friend and mentor John Hogan. Ask [F1 drivers] Johnny Herbert and Mika Häkkinen.

'In his job as a TV commentator, he was a friend and talented contributor to his colleagues. Ask Jonathan Martin, the BBC's head of sport. Ask Mark Wilkin, the producer of *Grand Prix*. Ask me.

'And in his new job as a journalist, he was a very welcome and lively addition to the press room. One who had shown the same dedicated determination to succeed as he had at the last three Grands Prix of 1976, where quite outstanding drives against the odds won him his World Championship.

'It seems hardly conceivable that we're no longer going to enjoy his ebullient presence and it hasn't somehow been a ghastly dream. They say the gods take those they love early; in which case we can only console ourselves with the knowledge that forty-five years of James's life contained at least as much as ninety of anybody else's.

'His loved ones, motor racing, his countless friends and all those who admired him from afar are infinitely the poorer for his passing.'

Murray's address had followed four readings from family members and friends. 'James's brother, Peter, had asked me to deliver the address,' recalled Murray. 'I was honoured to do so. The great and the good of motor sport were there and it was a truly moving, warm and cheerful occasion, which we all felt James would have wanted. Like all of us, James was a mixture. I was the first to admit that we'd had our moments but, at heart, he was an endearing, good and honest man. He was a one-off. Who would replace him in the commentary box? That was a question which was difficult, not to say impossible, to answer.'

In the meantime, Murray had discovered a useful distraction on the other side of the Atlantic.

17

A DIFFERENT WORLD

'I 'll make no bones about it: I was at my happiest when a British driver was winning.'

Murray was referring to tongue-in-cheek claims, usually made in Australia, that he was president of the Nigel Mansell fan club. 'I always tried to be objective and not favour one team or the other,' he said. 'But, yes, there were occasions when I'm sure my style of commentary resulted in my true emotions coming to the surface. Nigel Mansell's incredible exploits – and there were many – would have been a good example.'

Both born in the West Midlands – albeit thirty years apart – Walker and Mansell had a link that grew into friendship and mutual admiration when Nigel began to make his name in motor sport. It had been a slow start, Mansell taking part in seventy-one Grands Prix before winning his first on an emotional afternoon at Brands Hatch in October 1985. Then the floodgates opened, Nigel's association with Williams putting him in contention for the championship, albeit one that ended spectacularly in Australia a year later – the 'Colossally, that's Mansell!' tyre failure at 180mph part and parcel of the drama that seemed to accompany Nigel wherever he went.

Murray would add to the sense of theatre in Austria in 1987. After winning the race, Mansell's biggest concern was where to place an ice pack first. A sudden decision to have a wisdom tooth extracted the day before practice led to a throbbing jaw that was not ideal for the

bumps of a very fast Österreichring track. The pain was eased somewhat by victory, though when it eventually came the man with the
chequered flag failed to see Mansell as he crossed the line. The organ-
izational ineptitude continued when the open-top jeep taking the first
three finishers from parc fermé to the podium drove under an iron
gantry just as Nigel stood up, and he received a hefty blow to the forehead. Podium ceremony complete, Nigel sat down to an interview
with Murray.

'Nigel,' said Walker, 'first of all, would you slowly and carefully take
your hat off? You've got an enormous bump on your head; can you let
them see it?'

Mansell removed his Goodyear cap to reveal a livid lump, high on
his forehead.

'Right up there,' said Murray, taking the microphone in his right
hand and using his left index finger to poke the large bump – quite
hard. As Nigel recoiled, Murray said: 'Oh, I'm sorry!' And then pressed
on with questions about the race.

Walker's sense of anticipation matched the keen expectation of the
British media when Mansell signed for Ferrari in 1989 and won his
very first Grand Prix with the iconic Italian team. What seemed a
marriage made in heaven gradually turned sour, to the point where
Nigel announced his intention to retire at the end of 1991 – and then
decided to rejoin Williams. It was a blessing not just for Walker and the
BBC but also for Mansell himself since he had returned just as Williams was on the point of developing what has since been regarded as
one of the most sophisticated F1 cars ever made. Murray had the
pleasure of commentating on the 1992 Hungarian Grand Prix as
Nigel crossed the line to become world champion.

'Nigel was a fantastically popular world champion,' said Murray.
'He was a man of the people, a real showman who knew how to work
the crowd. He could be difficult at times but that was outweighed, in

my view, by the excitement and drama he delivered on the race track. Away from the circuit, I found him to be kind and generous; he and his charming wife Rosanne are lovely people. Nigel has always been a true friend to me.'

'I would echo that,' said Nigel. 'Murray was a very dear friend. During my time with Williams we did a lot of work with one of the sponsors and Murray used to host those events. I spent a lot of time with him over the years and we got to know each other very, very well. There were a lot of very amusing moments.

'When Murray interviewed me after I won the World Championship, he called me Nigel Manson. When I pointed out that he seemed to be connecting me with a murderer [Charles Manson], he said: "Oh, sorry! I've just been reading this book about Manson ..."

'On another occasion, we did the most fantastic interview together in Rio. It was off the cuff, about twenty minutes long – in the Brazilian heat – but that didn't matter because it had been brilliant. Murray came back a couple of hours later and said: "The interview was fantastic, Nigel. But can we do it again? I forgot to switch the sound on."'

'I got back to the BBC unit and that's when we discovered the engineer hadn't turned on the mic,' admitted Murray. 'There was nothing for it but to go back to Nigel and own up! I do recall that interview. It was one of those occasions when it flowed without the need to refer to scripted questions. I must admit I was sorry at the end of 1992 when Nigel left Williams and F1 and went off in a bit of a huff to IndyCar racing in the United States. I obviously wanted to follow his progress but I didn't have strong feelings about motor racing in the States, particularly on the ovals which tended to dominate the series. I couldn't see where the skill was in that.'

Walker's one-eyed view was about to change, courtesy of Nick Goozée, the general manager at Penske Racing, one of the foremost teams in American motor sport. Goozée had begun his racing experience with Brabham in 1963 and it would be a happy coincidence for Murray that Goozée and the Penske operation were based in Poole, about forty minutes from Walker's home in Hampshire.

'Murray was obviously very familiar as a BBC commentator,' said Goozée. 'I happened to catch him being interviewed on BBC Radio as a consequence of Mansell leaving Williams. It was soon apparent that Murray wasn't particularly well informed about IndyCar racing. So, I wrote to the BBC and suggested if they were going to ask people like Murray Walker to comment on IndyCar racing, they ought to educate him. I said they should send him to see me. It was done tongue in cheek, and I thought no more about it.

'A couple of weeks after that, I've got Murray Walker on the phone. He came down to Poole, we had a pub lunch, and got on really well. Our relationship went on from there. But it was different to most because, for the majority of people, their relationship with Murray was motor sport-based. Ours covered a much broader base. Saying that, we obviously did cover motor racing. I took him to Indy [the Indianapolis 500] in 1993, where he saw Mansell race, and I took him to Nazareth in 1994 so he could see a one-mile oval. It's fair to say it changed his perception of IndyCar racing.'

'If I hadn't seen the Indianapolis Motor Speedway, I wouldn't have believed it,' said Murray. 'I wandered around the place with my jaw hanging slack, marvelling at its unrivalled facilities, the lavish hospitality rooms and enormous tiered grandstands, the wonderful Hall of Fame museum, and the eighteen-hole championship golf course contained within the perimeter. But most of all I was struck by the fabled Gasoline Alley with team garages steeped in history.

'For the race, I had one of the best vantage points at the whole circuit: a front-row seat in the Penske Penthouse Box high above the track on turn one. When the race began with the traditional rolling start, the incredible sensation of speed, noise, colour and aggression as they blasted away below me was something I'd never experienced before. Quite incredible.'

Subsequently, most of the time Goozée and Murray spent together was away from motor sport.

'We had a number of holidays together,' Goozée recalled. 'There were two in Europe, one of which was a visit to the World War One battlefields. Then we had a trip from the site of the Normandy Landings to try and recreate some of the journey that he took [in his tank] towards Berlin.

'We had many meals together over the years. During these times, apart from chatting about motor racing, we tried not to have a relationship that was based entirely on the sport. Between the two of us, we had a lot of respite from motor sport and I think that's what gave the relationship its strength.

'We didn't get into deep things. We just talked, generally, about a lot of his trips. He used to send me postcards from where he was in the world when he and Elizabeth went on one of his many cruises, which he had a passion for. Of course, he was very well travelled and there were certain parts of the world, specifically Australia and Malaysia, that he loved. Once, when he was between the Malaysian and the Japanese Grands Prix, we flew out and met him at Langkawi. I remember I had to cut my trip short because of something that was developing back in England. But it was wonderful, nonetheless.

'He was naturally curious about a lot of things. I never heard him express a strong opinion. Whatever opinions he had, they were always courteous opinions. He would listen to what other people might have to say on a certain topic, nod slightly, and then move on to something else.

'He loved to see people doing really well. He was utterly fair in his praise and appreciation of everyone. And very careful to be non-critical about the people he could have been critical about. I never heard him – ever – say a bad word about anyone, even some of the people he found difficult to be in their company.

'Much has been made of Murray's relationship with James [Hunt]. Murray gave me a copy of James's biography and he wrote a very long eulogy in it. He knew that I was probably one of the very last people, by default, to speak to James. In 1993, Penske had a really good season of racing and BBC's *Top Gear* wanted to do a feature about this little team in deepest Dorset, if you like, conquering the world of IndyCars. Jeremy Clarkson came down, and the interview was set up and completed. They were due to go from me to James Hunt and do an interview, but they were running late. This was before mobile phones, so they asked me if I could contact James and let him know they had run out of time and they would call and make another appointment. I didn't know James that well. We had raced against him [when Penske Racing was] in Formula 1 [from 1974 to 1976]. Things were very different in those days because the various teams often spent time together. So, we had a brief chat, I passed on the message. James died that night.

'Murray was aware of this, and my background with James, and he knew I would be interested in the James Hunt biography [by Gerald Donaldson, which received universal praise for the quality of the writing and the author's pin-sharp portrait of a complex and colourful character he had got to know extremely well as the ghost-writer of Hunt's columns]. The handwritten eulogy by Murray in my copy was, I felt, very revealing. It said: "Nick, I saw James at his best and his worst as a driver, a commentator and a person, so feel qualified to pronounce Gerry Donaldson's book a wonderfully perceptive and understanding analysis. I hope you enjoy it. Murray." When James suddenly passed away, I was in no doubt that, despite their obvious differences, Murray would miss him.'

18

IMOLA '94

There was much to look forward to as the BBC F1 team left their hotel in Ravenna on Thursday 28 April 1994 and headed for Imola. The San Marino Grand Prix would be the third race of a season that, so far, had generated plenty of interest.

Michael Schumacher, the young upstart, had won for Benetton in Brazil and Japan (the Pacific Grand Prix in mid-April). Ayrton Senna, the three-time world champion, was in trouble. During his previous ten seasons, Senna had never failed to score in one of the first two races; on seven occasions, he already had at least one win to his name by the time he arrived at the third round. A fat zero on the points table was a stark indication that the move by the Brazilian star from McLaren to Williams was nothing short of disastrous. Senna urgently needed to turn things around this weekend. If nothing else, Imola would be a pleasant and satisfying place to do it.

The Emilia-Romagna region was welcoming in the spring sunshine, the first race of the European season allowing teams the convenience of bringing copious equipment by road rather than having to cope with the limited resources made necessary by air travel to the long-haul events.

The BBC crew was no exception, Imola marking the introduction of more elaborate production through the use of their own roving camera – an addition that would prove to be an enormous blessing come Sunday afternoon. Mark Wilkin would be overseeing this, along with additional team members. Jonathan Palmer had stepped into the void left by the much-missed James Hunt, Palmer having previously worked for the BBC team in the pit lane. Steve Rider had come to Imola to act as presenter and, when necessary, interviewer. 'We had used Jonathan as a pit lane reporter and he seemed a logical choice when it came to replacing James,' said Wilkin. 'Steve was with us at Imola, which was important because this would be the first race where we'd brought a truck with a satellite dish on the roof and a live camera in the pit lane. So, we needed a bigger team to deal with all of these things.'

If Imola was to be a landmark event in a positive way for the BBC F1 crew, it would also turn out to be a catastrophic race weekend for F1. Trouble started during first practice on Friday when Rubens Barrichello lost control of his Jordan, rode along the top of a tyre barrier and landed upside down on the track. When the Brazilian escaped with a cut lip and broken nose, the accident was seen as one of those unfortunate things that happen in motor racing. Another crash the following day would not be dismissed so lightly.

Roland Ratzenberger, in his first season of F1 and attempting to qualify his Simtek-Ford, slammed into a concrete wall at high speed. The session was brought to an immediate halt. It was clear from the television images, as doctors urgently attempted resuscitation, that the thirty-three-year-old Austrian was in a bad way. As qualifying eventually continued, the worst-case scenario was unthinkable. It had been twelve years since a driver had lost his life during a Grand Prix meeting, and eight years since a death during testing.

Rather than follow up qualifying with his usual summary and enthusiastic prediction for the race, a grim-faced Murray Walker did a piece to camera. Standing in the pit lane, speaking slowly and deliberately, he began:

'*Here at Imola, at the conclusion of this afternoon's final qualifying session for tomorrow's San Marino Grand Prix, I sadly have to report that the news is bad. Twenty minutes into the one-hour session, the very popular Austrian driver Roland Ratzenberger unaccountably went off the circuit at some 190 miles an hour, straight into a concrete barrier at the side of the track. His car disintegrated and, by the time it had stopped, Roland was not only very clearly unconscious, but even more clearly, in a very sick condition indeed. Now, the medical facilities here are superb and Professor Sid Watkins, the FIA's doctor in charge, were on the scene immediately, applying cardiac massage and other resuscitation techniques. Ratzenberger was taken to Bologna hospital by helicopter, and we have just had the very sad news that he has succumbed to his injuries.*

'This confirms the fact that nobody had any doubt of: that Grand Prix racing is a dangerous sport. It now requires the drivers who had qualified for tomorrow's event to examine themselves and decide what they want to do about it. Gerhard Berger, an Austrian fellow countryman of Roland Ratzenberger, has just issued a very moving statement to the media in the press centre, the gist of which is: "I had to decide, not whether I was going out to complete practice this afternoon, but whether I was going to race tomorrow. I think that if I did not race tomorrow, it would not help Roland, so I am going to race."

'I suspect, believe and hope that the other drivers will adopt a similar attitude. But, whatever, it is a tragic start to the European Grand Prix season of 1994.'

Continuing to digest this terrible news, the paddock remained subdued on race morning as F1 followed the dictum of keeping the show on the road. Nerves were set on edge once more when a start-line collision sent wheels and bodywork flying in all directions, some of it clearing the fencing and injuring several spectators. The safety car, a relative novelty to F1, was dispatched to control the field while debris was cleared. Senna had led from pole position with Schumacher glued to the tail of the Williams. The field completed four laps at a crawl before being released again.

Schumacher continued to hound Senna for another lap before they headed once more towards Tamburello, a long, fast left-hander. At 193mph, Senna's Williams failed to follow the racing line, veered right and ran into the wall lining the outside of the corner. The car careered off the concrete barrier and came to a halt. Apart from a missing right-front wheel and suspension, the Williams looked largely undamaged. As had become the way of improved safety in F1, the driver was expected to undo his belts, climb from the cockpit, dust himself down and curse his luck. Senna remaining motionless in the car gave the first hint that all was not well. But Walker and Palmer had no more idea than anyone else about the reason for the accident – or its outcome.

'In previous years, I had seen three drivers do the same thing at the same place and come to little harm,' recalled Murray. 'I had immediately thought: Wow! That's a big one! But when I saw Professor Sid Watkins leading the medical team at the scene, serious doubts began to creep in – particularly as we were being served up some disturbing pictures by the host broadcaster.

'It was very difficult because on the one hand you can't say: "Don't worry, folks, I've seen three people go off there in identical circumstances and they were all right, and I'm sure he will be." Because that was clearly not the case. But nor could you say for obvious reasons: "My God, this is terrible. I fear it's terminal." First of all, you don't say things like that, and secondly, I didn't know that it was. So, you just have to walk the tightrope between the two. That was probably one of the lowest moments of my motor sport career. At the time, as I began to fear the worst, I became very grateful the BBC had our own camera unit in place for the first time.'

Murray's hunch had been correct. Despite not having a broken bone in his body (the driver's safety cell having done its job), Senna had received a grievous injury to his forehead when part of the front suspension, torn off with the wheel by the impact, had penetrated the visor on his helmet. One look inside Senna's visor had told Professor Watkins all he didn't want to know about his very good friend. The watching world, fortunately, had no indication of such unthinkable detail as the Italian TV helicopter relayed pictures from overhead.

'As Murray was pointing out, we'd had accidents at this spot before,' said Wilkin. 'In 1989, when Berger crashed his Ferrari and it caught fire, *Grandstand* realized the implications could be severe and cut to the snooker. [Berger, in fact, would walk away with minor burns to his hands.] London would have done that again with Senna but, in this instance, we had our live cameras for the first time. So they stayed with us all the way through, because I could guarantee that we wouldn't show any pictures that could be upsetting. I simply cut to my camera; our guy was in the pits and he would pan up and down the pit lane for however long was necessary. I would record the incoming feed and, as soon as we had a minute of something that was usable without the graphic close-ups, we would play that in. And then cut to our camera again and do another minute in the pit lane while we found someone to give an expert opinion.

'That meant Murray was live all the way through, which was obviously a huge test for him. But having Dr Jonathan Palmer next to him was a really good thing [Palmer had trained as a physician at London's Guy's Hospital]. As it happens, we had talked about how best to deal with such a scenario the night before. This had come up because, when Ratzenberger had his massive accident, we weren't live, but Eurosport were. I believe it got to the point where one of their commentators rang and asked the Eurosport controllers to take them off air because there were so many ghastly images of Roland's car. And they were told: "No, keep commentating, keep commentating." So, we had a feel for what we were doing because of the very specific conversation the night before.

'Murray and Jonathan had to toe that very difficult line between not being overly positive and being all gloom and doom. As we received more information, I'd feed things to Murray. It became clear that it was looking more and more serious. We tried to keep the tone as low as possible without saying any more. I thought Murray was brilliant. He kept up a constant stream of thoughts all the way through without ever once diving into anything that he shouldn't have done. It was a huge moment for all of us.'

Palmer had been working in the commentary box for less than a year but, during that time, the former F1 driver had become familiar with Murray's traits.

'In many ways, Murray was quite a complex character, which is something viewers might not have been able to appreciate,' said Palmer. 'He was unfailingly courteous and would always answer any questions you may have had. But he never went out of his way to say: "Look, come and sit down, Jonathan. Let me tell you how it all goes." It was very much a case of Murray getting on with doing his bit and expecting you to do yours. He was quite possessive of the microphone. I had the impression that, if I wasn't there, he simply would have carried on quite happily. It was as if having somebody alongside was, at times, quite useful to him; at other times, it was a distraction. At Imola, it was the former.

'Murray had an extraordinary ability to be able to change from an excited delivery, that sometimes came close to hysteria, to very mellow, profound tones with the gravitas you need when bad things happen. And, of course, nothing would ever be as bad as Ayrton Senna dying at Imola.

'You were dealing with a combination of disbelief mixed with the awful reality you were seeing on the screen. The way Murray handled it was so impressive; his slow, deliberate, careful delivery was awesome. Because of my medical background, as well as having raced, I was able to add some reasonably sensible information about the trackside procedures while at the same time giving Murray a chance to catch his thoughts. There's a limit to what you can say continuously.'

Steve Rider was called upon more than he'd envisaged to use his presenting skills once the news of Senna's death had been confirmed after the race had finished.

'Following Ratzenberger's accident the previous day, the mood had been understandably glum,' said Rider. 'When Senna crashed, we were in the fortunate position of having, for the first time, an extra visual source. It meant poor Murray wasn't stuck with the pictures from Italian television, which were particularly intrusive. Nonetheless, it's a really tricky job in circumstances like that. Murray handled it superbly. It soon became clear what the outcome was, and you just had to use discretion over how it was going to be delivered. We gave the bad news at the end of the race. And then Murray immediately was in demand.'

Senna's death was a major story. Standing on top of the BBC's truck, with the Imola paddock behind him, Murray had to comment live into the BBC's evening news programme.

'*This is the blackest day for Grand Prix racing that I can remember in the many, many years that I've been covering the sport. We've had fatalities before and in a sport that is dangerous and where the drivers know it in their heart of hearts, and although they never expect it to happen to them, for there to be two fatalities on successive days is quite appalling. And that one of them should be arguably the greatest driver who has ever lived in the history of Grand Prix racing, makes it doubly so. Ayrton Senna was a great personality not only as a driver, but as a man. He was a very successful businessman, he was supreme in almost every way in the sport, and to say that his loss is tragic is a masterpiece of understatement.*'

When the newsreader asked where Grand Prix racing stood after the loss of two drivers in twenty-four hours, Murray replied: '*Well, everybody is shocked and stunned here and it is very easy to make emotional judgements. Without wishing to sound callous, I have to say that this sort of thing has happened before; it will happen again. Motor racing is dangerous and the important thing is drivers should not take spectators with them. They enter the sport knowing what the risks are. I don't agree with the suggestions that the Imola circuit is dangerous ... I honestly do think that this is just a hideous chain of circumstances, coincidences, which have all come together.'*

'It was interesting watching him do this,' said Rider. 'Very slow, very deliberate. Always very thoughtful. Although Murray didn't fancy himself as a sort of down-the-lens broadcaster, he did some good stuff down the years. When it came to tragedy in the sport, Murray had his own way of dealing with it.

'Anyone with a motor sport connection who came through the fifties, sixties and seventies would have been either completely put off by the sport or, while not being completely inured to the dangers, have a way of dealing with the darker side of things that happen in motor sport. That's not to say he was flippant or offhand, but he had a way of handling it, containing it and moving on. For a commentator that's absolutely vital because you cannot drag the audience down with you. You've got to respond and offer a context. And Murray could do that.'

'We had thought we'd be easing in the new unit gently that weekend – so much for that!' said Wilkin. 'But we were so pleased to have it. Murray was obviously in huge demand. With the story leading the news, they came straight to Murray for his thoughts. Through his earpiece, he could hear the newsreader doing the headlines – and then over to him. "This is the blackest day ..." and off he went. He didn't know what he was going to say, but as all good communicators do, he found a way. He never knew what his first words were going to be; he didn't have an opening script. A lot of people write their opening lines and then they get into ad-libbing. Murray never did that. And he didn't need to do it that night, despite it being such a big moment.'

Left: A proud Murray poses with his father after Graham Walker had finished second in the 1931 250cc TT.

Below: Murray, in his Lieutenant of the Royal Scots Greys uniform, with the family golden retriever, Judy.

Right: Murray was amazed when, while he was close to the German border in the Second World War, his father turned up as a reporter.

Top: Murray cut his broadcasting teeth with BBC Radio in the 1950s.

Above: On his feet and going for it. Murray at Suzuka, in one of the more spacious F1 commentary boxes.

Left: Ready to do a piece to camera in the paddock in Mexico, 1986.

Above: The working relationship with James Hunt got off to a tricky start, but had settled into an iconic broadcasting partnership by the time they reached the 1986 German Grand Prix at Hockenheim (**right**).

Left and above: Martin Brundle worked with Murray as an F1 driver and then as a highly acclaimed co-commentator.

Above: Maximizing the 1992 French Grand Prix media day by interviewing the reigning world champion, Ayrton Senna, at Magny-Cours.

Right: Louise Goodman and Andy Parr (dark-blue shirt) look on as Murray addresses his many fans at Silverstone.

Above: Nigel Mansell attempts to distract his good friend Murray in full flow.

Above: Michael Schumacher struggles w a 'Murrayism' during the 'Farewell' part Indianapolis in September 2001.

Above: Murray and Damon Hill enjoyed a close relationship that embraced advice on driving a vintage car and making a pizza advert (**right**).

Below: The Best of British. Murray interviews Lewis Hamilton and Jenson Button (world champions in 2008 and 2009) at Silverstone in 2010.

Left: *F1 Racing* found that putting Murray Walker on the covers of their monthly magazines created best-selling issues.

Below: Bernie Ecclestone was never in any doubt about the massive contribution Murray made towards the popularity of Formula 1.

Above: Damon Hill, Steve Rider and Neil Duncanson (**right**) played varied but significant roles in the life of Murray Walker.

Above: Suzi Perry and Murray shared a love of motorcycles.

Above: Perched between Jacques Villeneuve (**left**) and Damon Hill, Murray enjoys a tumultuous reception at Silverstone prior to his last British Grand Prix commentary for the BBC in 1996.

Right and below: Flying Farewell. Tony Jardine raises a toast to Murray on his final 'Stoddy Air' flight from a European Grand Prix in September 2001.

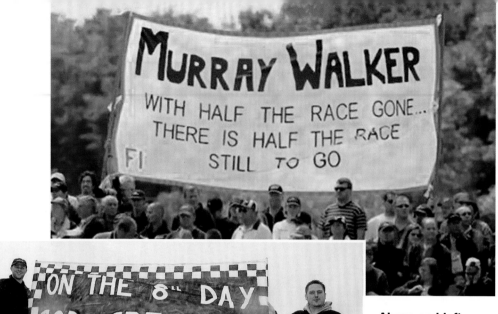

Above and left: Murray's fans made clear their affection in 2001 throughout arguably the longest retirement party in history.

Below: Returning to his radio roots. One last shout for Murray as guest commentator, with the author, on BBC Radio 5 Live's coverage of the 2007 European Grand Prix at the Nürburgring.

'After Murray had done all that, he came and joined me,' said Rider. 'We scrapped the planned *Grand Prix* programme for that evening and we did a live special, finishing probably around about half past nine that night. Everyone was absolutely knackered. We climbed into the hire car and headed back to Ravenna, which was about forty minutes away. We were numb; emotionally drained. Everyone was lost in their own thoughts. Nobody said a word. We'd been going about half an hour when Murray, who was sitting in the back, suddenly piped up: "What lap did Alesi come in for tyres? Was it 17 or 18?" Everyone just burst out laughing. He was busy writing his column. It was a job to be done; his way of coping.

'We then went to the only Italian restaurant that was open in Ravenna. We got through quite a few bottles of wine, and then Murray got on a slot racing machine. They had a couple of those, and we had half an hour of just being silly buggers. It was the only way that you can end a day like that. Murray was brilliant throughout.'

'I think in some ways Murray handled it better than all of us because he had been there before,' said Wilkin. 'All the experiences that he had had in Grand Prix racing through the years – and during the war, particularly – all the racing drivers and people he'd known that had died. He was able to compartmentalize it. The rest of us had never needed to work out how to do that. But he did. And that's not to say he was cold and callous and didn't care at all. Quite the reverse. This was just Murray's way of coping. He'd been an absolute rock that weekend. Quite extraordinary.'

19

THE BOY DAMON

As a repercussion of Senna's death, Damon Hill found himself hurled into the limelight – a place he had neither expected to be nor, in truth, wanted to be at this stage in his career. Having enjoyed his first full season as number two to Alain Prost at Williams in 1993, Hill had been looking forward to learning even more when Senna replaced the Frenchman, who had announced his retirement.

That plan had begun to unravel when the 1994 Williams-Renault turned out to be so difficult to drive that not even Senna's exceptional skill set could overcome the car's shortcomings. Now, three races into the season, Hill was having not only to cope with this car's unpredictable handling but also to shoulder the responsibilities of being lead driver for a team that had won the championship for the previous two seasons.

As things stood going into the next Grand Prix at Monaco, Hill would be lucky to win a race, never mind the title. Then he multiplied the pressure when, as the only Williams entry in Monte Carlo, he got himself involved in a collision on the first lap. As he made a lonely and disconsolate walk back to a sullen reception in the Williams pit, it was not the moment for Damon to reflect that his father had won this race no fewer than five times.

Murray knew all about Graham Hill's victories in the Principality. In the days when socializing was part and parcel of F1 life, Murray had become good friends with Graham and his wife Bette, and approved wholeheartedly when their teenage son began racing motorcycles.

Before that, however, Murray had shared the agony felt in November 1975 when Graham died, along with five members of his racing team, in a light-aircraft accident. (It was later discovered that documentation and insurances relating to the aircraft had not been in order.) Murray admitted to an affinity for Damon born from the fact that, in his view, he was the son of a man he saw as a national hero, a father and a champion whose passing he still mourned.

'Damon was just fourteen at the time,' said Murray. 'That's a difficult time for any child. He unexpectedly finds himself the only man in the house [Damon had two sisters]. And the family, who had been extremely wealthy and the centre of attraction, were suddenly cast into the wilderness and financially broken. It makes my respect for Damon even greater.'

Murray was effectively linking Damon's progress as a driver with that of Graham, winner of fourteen Grands Prix and a two-time world champion. As Damon made his first difficult steps into Formula 1, the attraction for Murray went beyond that of a broadcaster following a young British hopeful; in this case, it was as close to fatherly interest as it was ever likely to be, particularly when Murray knew Hill had endured a very tough time.

'I think that was typical of Murray's generation,' said Damon. 'In some ways, I was seen as a footnote to Graham Hill. Friends of my dad were interested to see how I was going to cope with the challenges of growing up. People of that older generation were much more conscious of the legacy of my dad. I was aware of that. But it was paternal in the same way that we all are when we look at younger people now. There is a concern for them but, at the same time, we have to let them do their own thing. We can see pitfalls coming up and they invariably fall into them. But you can't interfere. Thinking back, there was quite a bit of that with Murray and me.'

Walker could see several traps looming in the road ahead as Hill tried to deal with the responsibility being thrust upon him by Williams, Renault and the world at large. A win for Damon in the Spanish Grand Prix was an impressive and timely tonic for the team but it did little to counter the relentless march by Benetton as Schumacher generally had the edge.

By the time they reached the penultimate round at Suzuka in Japan, Hill had won at Silverstone and elsewhere but was behind on points and needed to win the race to stay in championship contention. When the Japanese Grand Prix was stopped (due to a marshal having been injured by a wayward car in wet conditions), then restarted, it was decreed that the result would be decided on the aggregate times from the two parts of the race. Schumacher had 8.6 seconds in hand (his lead over Hill when the race was red-flagged). Schumacher and Benetton then made an extra pit stop for tyres and the German driver dropped back, handing Hill the lead on aggregate. If Schumacher could close down Hill's lead on the road, he would win without having to physically overtake the Williams. As far as Hill was concerned, the equation was simple: he had to push himself to the limit in truly atrocious conditions against an unseen rival and hope he had done enough.

To complicate matters further, Damon was having to race the full distance with the same wet-weather tyre, his mechanics having been unable to remove the right-rear wheel during a pit stop for fresh rubber. If Hill failed to win this race, his championship was as good as over. If he left the road, his reputation would be in tatters. It was pressure like Damon had never known before.

Walker is commentating on the outcome of the final 3.6-mile lap.

'*The gap* [aggregate lead held by Hill] *was 4.2 seconds. Here is Michael Schumacher approaching the start of his last lap. The gap as he goes across the line is . . . 2.45 seconds! On the previous lap, Schumacher took 1.8 seconds out of Damon Hill's lead. It's going to be something like half a second or a second if they keep up the pace that they're doing now. WOW!*

'*Two point four seconds it was. But Michael Schumacher was lapping 1.8 seconds faster on the previous lap. The two team bosses, Frank Williams and Flavio Briatore, are consumed with excitement – as I AM.*

'*Now ... Hill is approaching the chicane. This is the last time and I'm looking for the chequered flag now for Damon Hill to come home, completing his race distance – but has he completed it, when he does so, as the winner of the Japanese Grand Prix and close the World Championship gap between himself and Michael Schumacher to one point as they go into Australia? Or will it have increased to nine points? We'll have the answer very soon ...*

'*Damon Hill takes the chequered flag. BUT ... we wait for Michael Schumacher. Aggregate time, I remind you, is what matters. HERE is Schumacher! He's got somebody* [a backmarker] *in front of him. Is he going to be delayed?*

'*THREE POINT THREE SIX SECONDS! Damon – Hill – wins – the – Japanese Grand Prix! And ...* [Murray briefly chokes with emotion] *takes his sixth win of the year to close the championship gap between himself and Michael Schumacher.*'

The result in Japan ensured an exciting conclusion to the championship, made all the better for Murray since it would be staged in Adelaide, one of his favourite venues in F1, and helped by the fact that Nigel Mansell had been drafted into the Williams team for the final three races.

The Australian Grand Prix would live up to its billing, with Mansell taking pole position, followed by Schumacher and Hill, the first three covered by just over half a second. Walker and Palmer prepared themselves for an eventful race commentary.

Lap 36

Jonathan Palmer is discussing Gerhard Berger's race strategy following a pit stop for the Ferrari driver. The director suddenly switches to an on-board shot from Schumacher's car as he recovers from running wide and hitting the wall with his right-front wheel.

'*Schumacher's off!*' shouts Palmer, seconds before Walker jumps in.

'*Yes! And* . . . [the shot switches to a trackside camera showing Hill going for the inside on the approach to the next corner, the two cars colliding] *Oh! Oh! Out goes Schumacher! The German is out of the Australian Grand Prix – and Damon Hill only has to keep going to be world champion of 1994 – but can he keep going? Because he hit Schumacher's car, and if Damon Hill has to retire – you see smoke pouring off a wheel – that will mean that Schumacher will be world champion. What an INCREDIBLE development! Now, you can see Damon Hill's right-front wheel is canting over. He's got a puncture on the front left.*'

'*Yes,*' says Palmer, '*and I think, hopefully* . . . *No! He's bent his wishbone as well. You can see on the on-board camera he's got a bent left-front suspension. What needs to happen now – clearly, Schumacher is out – the question is can they repair Hill's car? Can he get out and can he get into the top six and get two points – he needs a fifth* [place]. *But it's not looking good.*'

A re-run of the incident, taken from on board Schumacher's car, shows the Benetton running wide on the grass verge, hitting the wall, regaining the track, and moving to the left, Michael checking his right-hand mirror. Then he starts to turn towards the next right-hand corner as the left-front wheel of Hill's Williams comes alongside. Contact is made, the Benetton being tipped on to its left-hand wheels before thumping back on to the track and careering into the tyre wall on the outside of the corner.

'*Now that's bad from Schumacher,*' says Palmer. '*Schumacher should have known his car was damaged, Damon had the line; I'm afraid that is a fundamental mistake, I believe, from Michael Schumacher at a real moment of crisis.*'

The producer then shows a replay from a trackside camera, prompting Walker to come in.

'*There will be people who say, of course – as we see this replay of Schumacher going into the wall – that that was a desperate manoeuvre by*

Schumacher to stop Damon Hill winning the championship. Into the wall he [Schumacher] *goes. Now the question is, can Damon Hill get in and have his car repaired?* [The producer returns to live coverage, showing Hill arriving in the Williams pit.] *You see the front-left wheel is locked up. Nigel Mansell is going to go through in the lead, but he was fifty-four seconds behind the leaders. Damon, obviously, extremely worried. The question is, how long is it going to take them to repair whatever damage there was?* [A stopwatch graphic appears on the screen.] *You see, he's been in the pits for about sixteen seconds now. And Mansell has gone through. Berger has gone through. Alesi* [Ferrari] *has gone through. Häkkinen* [McLaren] *has gone through.'*

Palmer comments on a cockpit shot of Hill slowly shaking his head, indicating he believes his race – and the championship – is run. The camera zooms in on Patrick Head (Williams' technical director) vainly trying to pull straight the bent suspension arm as Jonathan underlines the bad news that it will be impossible to either change the component in time, or strengthen it. A re-run of the incident as seen from a camera on board Hill's car prompts Jonathan to reiterate his view that Schumacher was at fault. Murray switches to a less controversial tack.

'*No responsible team is going to send Damon Hill out with a bent wishbone. They won't be able to replace it.* [The picture returns to a live image of Hill, sitting helplessly in the cockpit of his Williams.] *You can tell, even by seeing his eyes, how bitterly disappointed he is. The World Championship has literally been torn from his hands.* [Shot of a helmetless Schumacher standing behind the trackside fence.] *Michael Schumacher doesn't know this, of course. He's standing behind the wall, waiting for Damon Hill to come round but, such has been the gap, he must know by now that the Englishman is either in trouble, or out. Meantime, as the Williams team discuss with each other what to do, Nigel Mansell – there he is! – is in the lead of the Australian Grand Prix . . .'*

Mansell's thirty-first and final Grand Prix win would provide

Murray with some uplifting consolation during the remainder of a race that had been completely deflated. But there could be no getting away from the disappointment felt for his boy, Damon.

'Apart from the routine interview, I can't recall if I had much of a conversation with Murray immediately after that race,' said Hill. 'My mind was still reeling – particularly after I had seen a video showing the incident with Schumacher. I had watched in amazement when I saw Michael hit the wall. Because his car had been obscured around the corner before we touched, I hadn't realized his was fatally damaged. I remember thinking: They can't let him get away with that. But they did. The result stood. Michael had won his first F1 World Championship.

'Racing had changed a bit since my dad's day; no more gentleman racers. Saying that, Murray was old school and, to his credit, remained that way. I got the sense that there was an element that he kind of wanted to put an arm around me a little bit when I was going through the painful bits. But he never did because he was so professional; quite stiff upper lip in the old-fashioned way.

'He was of that era – typically British, stoic and understated. It may sound odd to say that Murray was understated at sport because, in his own lovely way, he was overstated with so many things in his commentary. But, away from that, he was modest and unobtrusive. If you asked him, for instance, about driving a tank through Germany during the war, he'd play it down. But you knew there was a lot more to it than that. He was typical of that dry British culture with a wry take on things; you know, the sort of situation where, if a bomb went off, they'd say: "Oh dear. What was that loud noise?"'

There were about to be explosions of a different kind within the Williams team in 1995 as the chance of a championship for Hill seemed further away than ever.

20

LOST FOR WORDS

'*A*nd into the pit lane – *OOHH! MY GOODNESS! David Coulthard smashes himself out of the Australian Gra—I have NEVER seen that before. He comes into the pit lane and into the wall and blows his chance of winning for Williams.*'

That line from Murray Walker's commentary during the Australian Grand Prix summed up the Williams team's season in 1995. Having joined Hill the previous year (alternating occasionally with Nigel Mansell), David Coulthard had begun to establish himself as a threat to his slightly more experienced team-mate by winning the 1995 Portuguese Grand Prix. The growing internal conflict between the two drivers had done little to ease a tension within Williams that had been exacerbated by Michael Schumacher romping to a second successive title and helping Benetton deny Williams the Constructors' Championship for the first time in four years.

The season had started brightly enough as Hill won two races and actually led the World Championship for the first time in his career. Then Williams began to fade. Hill drove into the back of Schumacher while trying to regain the lead (following a pit stop) at Silverstone; he spun in Germany and misjudged his braking at Monza, hitting the back of Schumacher once more. Coulthard's extraordinary attack on the pit wall in Adelaide would have been the last straw for Williams but for one thing: Hill had arrived for the final race a changed man. Putting all his woes behind him, a more positive mindset led to his domination of the Australian Grand Prix and set him up for a renewed attack on the championship the following year.

The good news for Hill in 1996 was that Schumacher had joined Ferrari at a time when the Italian team would be out of serious contention thanks to starting a rebuilding process. The bad news was that Coulthard had been replaced by Jacques Villeneuve, a precocious young Canadian who could see no reason why he shouldn't continue the momentum that came with winning the Indianapolis 500 and the IndyCar Championship in 1995. Villeneuve laid down his intention by claiming pole position for the first race in Melbourne, with Hill starting alongside.

The Williams pair were in a race of their own, no quarter being asked or given. Villeneuve had led from the start but Hill saw his chance when the planned pit stops took place just after half-distance, Villeneuve having come in first, Hill making a faster stop two laps later. Murray Walker rose to the occasion – not that he needed much prompting.

'*And Damon Hill takes the lead – and stays ahead of Jacques Villeneuve. Look! You can't be much closer than that! Villeneuve realizes that, now – HE'S GOT TO GO FOR IT. Damon Hill's tyres are not as warm as Villeneuve's are – there's not a lot of difference in it – AND VILLENEUVE FIGHTS! FIGHTS! FIGHTS! AND RETAKES THE LEAD! FANTASTIC! ABSOLUTELY IN-CREDIBLE!*'

One lap later: '*The gloves are off. They're team-mates – AND OFF GOES VILLENEUVE! AND HE GETS ON THE COURSE, BACK IN FRONT OF HILL! And he manages to block his team-mate. That was Damon's opportunity; he wasn't able to take it. Now, Hill can push very hard indeed – AND HE'S TRYING TO TAKE HIM ON THE OUTSIDE. HE nearly goes off on the inside of the corner. SEN-SATIONAL SCRAP! And remember, this is for THE LEAD between team-mates!*'

Villeneuve's off-course incident would cost him, the trip across the kerb damaging an oil pipe and forcing a cruise home in second place. The win made a good start to Hill's championship campaign, and it continued that way with five more victories. Then a surge by Villeneuve ensured this was by no means a done deal for Damon. As if this was not enough pressure with three races to go, Frank Williams revealed that he would not be requiring Hill's services in 1997.

'The pressure on Damon was really telling,' said Murray. 'I remember doing an interview with him at that time and he was as tense as a violin string. He also had to cope with Villeneuve, who was not at all bad at the mind games. We sat down – I think Damon was doing six hours a day in the gym; his cheeks were sunken. I said: "Are you all right? You look a bit peaky." "What did you say that for?" he exploded, and got up and stormed off.

'I gave him a little time to simmer down before going up to him and saying I'd obviously said something that had offended him but that it was unintentional, and I was sorry. He said not to worry because, before we sat down, he had just been interviewed by a foreign journalist, who had asked Damon: "What would you give to have your father back for just one hour?" I mean, poor bloke. Damon was having enough to cope with without an insensitive question like that. Quite incredible. It was a shame these things had happened because we had gone quite some way earlier in the summer to help Damon relax – in a rather unusual way.

'Damon wanted to lighten his image – that was one reason for doing a pizza advert together. Damon told me he knew he had this serious, beetle-browed, uncommunicative look. But he wasn't like that really. I knew him as an extremely nice, good-humoured, bright, well-educated, thoughtful and personable sort of chap. I had been sorry to see him overwrought and highly strung at times. Doing the commercial was the perfect antidote to all that.

'The Pizza Hut chain had wanted to boost sales of their new Stuffed Crust Pizza with Pepperoni, and, of course, with my background in advertising, I understood exactly what they wanted and felt completely at home with this. They were using a top agency, Abbott Mead Vickers. When I saw the script, I loved it immediately. They reproduced a Pizza Hut restaurant in a studio and it took two days – and a great many takes – to get it right.'

The clever idea of linking Walker and Hill revolved around Murray commentating on everything from their arrival ('*IT'S GO! And Damon Hill leads into the first bend!*'), bumping into Damon ('*There's been a shunt! IT'S HILL!*') and choosing from the menu ('*Hill orders a Pizza Hut Pepperoni! A cheese-stuffed crust!*') through to the arrival of the food ('*Mmmm! And Hill's going for it! He's spun his pizza through 180 degrees!*') and Walker finishing first ('*And Hill finishes second! Again!*'). At which point an exasperated Hill grabs Walker by the lapels ('*HE'S LOST IT! HE'S OUT OF CONTROL!*'). It was a brilliant concept, beautifully executed by the main characters. The subsequent success of the commercial was such that Australia went so far as to introduce the Stuffed Crust with Pepperoni to their menu in order to be able to run the advert.

'It was good fun to do,' said Damon. 'It had come at a time when I wanted to relax a bit more and show that I could enjoy a laugh at my own expense. I thought the commercial was very funny; it made people smile. But I have to say, when the director said I had to grab Murray by the lapels and shake him, at the time that seemed like a very unnatural thing to want to do to someone I respected, someone who I felt was senior to me. Murray really bought into it because, as an actor – which he was – he knew exactly what he was doing. I was not an actor and I'm still a rubbish actor.

'They had to work hard to make it look convincing. But it's good looking back because it was time spent in a studio and a complete change to everything else that was going on in racing. There were certain aspects that took a bit of getting used to – such as chewing on some deep-crust pizza and then spitting into a bucket that stank of pizza at the end of the day. And poor Murray must have caught the garlic on my breath as well.'

There was a seriously bad taste in Hill's mouth on the weekend of the Italian Grand Prix in September 1996 when Frank Williams dropped his impending redundancy bombshell. Adding to the pressure, if Damon could win at Monza, the championship would be his. An aggressive overtaking move at the start gave him a lead that looked completely secure – until he unaccountably spun and retired. Villeneuve went on to strengthen his last-minute challenge by forcing Hill into second place and winning in Portugal.

There were nine points between them going into the final round in Japan, with Hill the favourite – on paper, at least. The Williams pair shared the front row. At the start, Hill took off like a rocket, leaving Villeneuve trailing. The result was settled when Villeneuve lost a wheel after thirty-six of the fifty-two laps. Hill could have stopped there and then but he wanted to savour the moment. Which was just as well because it gave Walker the final lap he had been waiting to commentate on for a very long time.

'*This is something many people didn't think could possibly happen today,*' says Murray, his voice beginning to crack. '*They thought Damon would drive a cautious race. But he FOUGHT. He fought from second on the grid. He passed Jacques Villeneuve. He took the lead. He stayed there. DAMON HILL EXITS THE CHICANE – AND WINS THE JAPANESE GRAND PRIX! And I've got to stop, because I've got a lump in my throat.*'

After a brief pause, Murray resumes. '*Michael Schumacher passes Damon Hill, but ... too late. Damon Hill wins in Japan.*' Reducing his pace and volume noticeably, Murray then adds: '*I really ... am ... for once ... almost at a loss for words. I am so happy, as the majority of Britain will be. I must confess, I have a soft spot for Damon and it has been magnified as a result of his achievements here.*'

Seeing Murray's reaction to this culmination of Hill's ambition had been another interesting experience for co-commentator Jonathan Palmer. 'We know that Murray raced motorbikes,' he said, 'but the fact that he never raced a car of any description actually served him well. It meant he was always in awe of every driver, from Grand Prix winners to someone struggling at the back of the field. If he sat beside any racing driver and they took him for a quick lap of a race track in a road car, he would think they were Ayrton Senna – and he would happily admit that. It meant he had a great deal of adulation and respect for any F1 driver. But he also loved a hero – particularly a British hero. He would get hugely excited and emotional about the success of Brits, especially Nigel Mansell and Damon Hill. That's why we had that open and unashamed reaction to Damon winning the championship at Suzuka.

'Murray's sense of vocal drama was powerful. His ability to produce a feeling of huge excitement, almost a thrilling crescendo of near-disbelief over what he was seeing, was unique. And it was totally genuine. Murray understood perfectly that good commentary was about contrast. You don't just shriek from the start of the race to the chequered flag. Murray had measured tones of excitement and that made him so captivating. You could tell what was going on by listening to the tone; it was like music. His commentaries were two-dimensional in that you could be doing something else and the rising crescendo in his tone told you when you needed to start listening to what was going on. And, inevitably, it *was* worth listening to.'

It was no surprise, therefore, to learn that the 1996 Japanese Grand Prix would forever hold a place in Murray's heart, as he explained not long after the race to the journalist Adam Cooper.

'I honestly can't find the words to tell you how euphorically overjoyed I am,' said Murray. 'I like to regard Damon as a friend of mine. I've watched him and talked about him from his very earliest days in

Formula Ford, right through Formula Ford 2000, F3, F3000 and his testing with Williams. He's done incredibly well if you think of the load he's had to carry. He won it in the best possible way. I'm pleased, not so much because he won the championship, but because of the way he won it, and particularly the fact that from second on the grid he was first into the first corner. Damon drove a superb race and controlled it all the way.

'I nearly broke down at the end of it. I had to stop talking on two occasions. One was when Georgie was embracing [her husband] Damon and I said pictures speak louder than words, as indeed they did. And the other was when Damon came out on to the podium and got on to the top step as world champion. It's been a very emotional occasion for me – I think as emotional as Nigel [Mansell] winning in 1992. I'm a lucky chap because I've seen two of my mates become world champion.'

21

CHANNEL CROSSING

'We had done a big interview with Damon in Tokyo the morning after he had won the World Championship,' recalled
Mark Wilkin. 'We were flying back to put the whole tribute
programme together on the Monday night. Our route took us from
Tokyo to Hong Kong, and from there on to London.

'Just before we started the descent into Hong Kong, the stewardess
came up and said to Murray: "The captain is delighted to have you on
board and would like to offer you the chance to sit in the jump seat
as we go in to land." This was when Hong Kong was still using the old
Kai Tak airport with that amazing approach between all the buildings,
before the aircraft would bank sharply right and drop on to the run-
way. It was pretty spectacular, and I was very excited. I had got seats
on the right-hand side to make sure that I got the view.

'So, Murray had this message from the captain. And he said: "We'll
need two seats. My friend will want to come and see as well." I said:
"Murray, don't be daft, they've only got one jump seat." And he
replied: "Well, you go. Go on!" I said: "No, Murray. They don't want
me to go, they want you up there. Off you go, and enjoy."

'That was so typical of Murray. He was always very much a team
player; everything was about our team. We had an engineer called
Tony Richie. He had been with us for a long time and came to a lot
of the races. He was very quiet, very studious and conscientious, a
very good engineer. He was good fun at dinner if it was just the three

of us. But the moment anybody else came to the table, whether it was Ron Dennis or Bernie Ecclestone, or one of the British newspaper guys, Tony would clam up. If anyone asked what he did, Tony would reply: "Oh, I just twist the wires together." Murray wouldn't have any of that from Tony. I remember him saying more than once: "If you don't twist those wires together properly, Tony, nobody hears a word that I say; no one sees anything that we do. So, your job is absolutely as important as any of the rest of us." And he meant it sincerely. Murray fundamentally believed that everyone on the team, from the guy who drove the truck to every single person involved, was of equal importance. If he got an invitation to something or other – and that would happen a lot to Murray – he would immediately ask: "Can I bring the team? Can we all come?" And if he was told the invitation was only for him, he'd say: "Thank you, but I don't think I'll be able to make it." Quite amazing. A total team player.'

At the end of the 1995 season, that cohesive little BBC team had received a profound shock that threatened to blow their unity asunder – a moment none of them was likely to forget. Having enjoyed eighteen increasingly successful years with the *Grand Prix* programme, BBC's head of sport, Jonathan Martin, had been confident of extending the contract with Bernie Ecclestone and Formula 1 for at least another five years.

Martin's phone rang on 13 December. It was Ecclestone, informing the BBC that the contract would be going to ITV at the start of 1997. That was it. No debate. Not that Martin could have entered into one when he discovered that ITV had bid £60 million, a figure far in excess of anything the BBC was likely to offer – a fact that Ecclestone knew full well, and therefore he did not waste time engaging in business niceties when bluntly delivering the bad news.

'I remember where we were when we heard that the BBC had lost it,' recalled Steve Rider. 'We were in the departure lounge at

Heathrow, on our way to interview Michael Schumacher for a documentary that was going out in eight days' time – and we hadn't got an interview with Michael Schumacher! So, this trip was quite urgent. The only chance we had to do it was late afternoon during a test at Estoril. And then the flight got delayed.

'The Christmas party was going on, back at the office. They had left one person manning the office and he'd been watching Ceefax. He rang Mark Wilkin, who was with me, and said: "I don't know whether I've got this wrong, but something's just come up on Ceefax saying that ITV have taken Formula 1 from the BBC." Mark immediately made some calls – and confirmed the worst. That just made our day.

'We thought the reaction to this was going to be very interesting when we finally got to Estoril – our interview had been rearranged for 7 a.m. the following morning. Sure enough, the press guys come straight to us. But they only had one question: "What on earth is going to happen to Murray?" That really did say a lot about Murray. Not that any of us on the team needed reminding – well, not at that particular moment!'

Murray was giving the impression he had no more of a clue than anyone else. By the time the 1996 British Grand Prix came round seven months later, many of the national newspapers carried features written around the possibility of this being his last F1 commentary from Silverstone.

In an interview with Mary Riddell in *The Times*, Murray indicated that he, among many others, was being considered by ITV. 'Anyone who has any pretensions is seeing that the stumbling block that has existed for so long – that's me – is now potentially out of the way,' said Murray. 'So, they're whanging in their applications. I've got nothing to prove. If they want me, they will ask. And if they don't, I've had a bloody good innings. I've done it for nearly fifty years and I'd rather go out with dignity than scrabble and grovel around, even though I do passionately want to go on.'

It may have been the same story in the *Telegraph*, the *Guardian* and the rest, but Murray knew more than he was perhaps prepared to admit.

The political world of sports broadcasting had been constantly shifting beneath the surface. ITV may have won the contract, but the actual F1 content and output would be handled under contract by an independent production company – of which more than a few had their eye on such a high-profile prize.

'When ITV won the F1 contract, they then put the production out to tender,' said Rider. 'My dear old company, Anglia, rang me and said they fancied having a go at this. I said I was up for that. We had a number of meetings with various people and the bid became quite decent when a company called Chrysalis got involved.'

Established by Neil Duncanson, Chrysalis Sport had gained motor sport experience through producing two years of IndyCar for ITV when Nigel Mansell was racing in the American series. Having successfully dealt with football, rugby and basketball, F1 was an irresistible challenge.

'IndyCar had given us a taste for motor sport,' said Duncanson. 'At the time, ITV didn't actually have a head of sport, or a sports department per se. When they acquired these rights, it was done by a bunch of execs at ITV, who didn't really know too much about sport. So, they thought: Bloody hell! What are we going to do now? We'd better put this out to tender. When I got a phone call saying this was going to happen, I remember thinking we were well up for this. We were still regarded as the bright new things back then. I'd been a bit of a motor sport fan, but that was about it. I knew next to nothing about Formula 1. We knew there was one of the in-house ITV companies thinking they were going to get it. So, we pitched what we thought was a winning bid.

'We were coming in afresh. Because we were changing everything, we thought we needed some consistency. The only person that we wanted to keep from the BBC was Murray. That was a no-brainer. Frankly, there wasn't another commentator who came close. It wasn't like football, where there are so many different commentators. This was Formula 1; there was only one voice; that was Murray Walker. So, we had to have him.'

The bidding process was in full swing at the time of the British Grand Prix in July. Speculation was swirling around the Silverstone paddock – a hotbed of gossip at the best of times.

'I knew that we had to have Murray as part of our bid,' said Rider. 'Just to be sure, I'd double-checked that he was willing to come on board and that everything was OK. "Yes, yes, dear boy," he had assured me. But when we were together at Silverstone, I began to have my suspicions. We'd be walking through the paddock and Murray would be waving and saying hello to various people – and wishing them luck. "That's Jim," he'd say. "You know, he's the producer from such-and-such company. I might have signed something with him as well." It became clear that Murray had agreed to be part of every bid! Quite rightly, he was taking no chances by covering all bases with every company in the bidding process. And good luck to him. We just had to make sure that our bid was the successful one.'

In the meantime, there was a job to be done. As Murray kept his options open with regard to his future prospects, the one certainty was that this would be his last home Grand Prix as a commentator for the BBC. Bernie Ecclestone, ever the opportunist, but with a benevolent eye for the man who had done much to spread F1's popularity, pulled Murray aside on the Saturday.

'He said to me, since this is your last race with the BBC, I want you to go round in Damon's car tomorrow,' Murray recalled. 'I thought this was a typical Bernie wind-up! If he thought I was going to try and drive Damon's Williams in front of ninety thousand people, he had another think coming. Don't be daft, he said. I mean the drivers' parade; I want you to go with Damon. Be ready after the drivers' briefing.'

The surprise didn't end there. When Murray duly presented himself by the fleet of open-topped cars, waiting in line on the starting grid, he was nonplussed when the drivers emerged and, rather than climb into the cars bearing their names in readiness for the lap in front of the fans, they formed a circle round Murray. Michael Schumacher, the reigning world champion, then stepped forward and presented Murray with a magnum of champagne, signed by all the drivers.

'I was enormously touched by all of this,' said Murray, 'from the huge gesture by Bernie – he was not known for interfering with the carefully planned programme on race day – to the very kind thought by the drivers; although I did suspect that Bernie had prompted them! Then, to climb on to the back of the Rolls-Royce with Damon and Jacques [Villeneuve] and experience the enormous reaction they get every race from the crowd was quite incredible.'

Murray, typically, was playing down the fact that much of the crowd reaction was for him as well as the two Williams drivers. This was being witnessed first-hand in the open-topped car by BBC cameraman Andy Parr, new to the F1 team in 1996.

'Everyone thought this was going to be Murray's last Silverstone race,' said Parr. 'We didn't know at that time whether he'd go to ITV. So, I'm in the car, trying to balance on the dashboard and keep as low as possible while pointing backwards, with Murray in between Damon and Jacques. It was just insane. It was novel for me as well as Murray. I hadn't realized the crowd would be so close to the track. Drivers' parades are filmed all the time now but, back then, this was something very new. The noise was incredible, absolutely incredible, because don't forget, there was no engine noise drowning it all out. And as far as I could tell, nearly all of this was for Murray. I knew he was very popular, but this really brought it home.'

Just over a month before, Murray had received recognition of a different kind when appointed an OBE in the Queen's Birthday Honours. 'I have been incredibly, gigantically lucky to do what I have been able to do,' said Murray. 'To me, this has never been a job in the normally accepted sense of the definition. So, you can imagine my feelings when I received a letter, notifying me in the strictest confidence that my name had been put forward for appointment as an Officer of the Order of the British Empire. The very title sends goosebumps through me as a flag-waving patriot, fiercely proud of his great country. It was beyond my wildest imagination that I should receive an honour such as this. I felt truly humble. The letter telling me this from the Prime Minister's Office asked me to assure them that this would be agreeable. *Agreeable?* I couldn't get pen to paper fast enough! It was a source of immense pride for my mother – then aged ninety-nine – but, of course, I obviously wished my father had still been with us.'

On 12 December 1996, Murray had what he described as 'probably the most important single occasion of my life' when he put on his best suit, old school tie and broadest smile to visit Buckingham Palace and receive the OBE. During a brief conversation, Her Majesty asked Murray how long he had been commentating. When he replied, 'Forty-eight years, ma'am,' the Queen said: 'That *is* a long time!'

Indeed it was. And seventy-three-year-old Graeme Murray Walker OBE was not yet done.

22

SAFE PAIR OF HANDS

S peculation had ended on Monday 23 September 1996 when it was revealed that Murray Walker would be ITV's main F1 commentator. The announcement was made by MACH1, a trading name devised from a coalition of the Meridian and Anglia ITV channels, plus Chrysalis, Neil Duncanson's production company that, a few days before, had won the five-year contract. Having secured their key player, MACH1 would continue to put together the rest of the broadcasting team, with particular focus on the commentator to accompany Murray.

Martin Brundle was mentioned in various speculative media reports. But the man himself was not so sure – primarily because he was, first and foremost, a racing driver. Martin had just completed his eleventh full season of F1, Jordan having been one of several different teams the Englishman had raced for across 158 Grands Prix. Still chasing that elusive and much deserved first win, the thirty-seven-year-old continued to have his eye on racing F1 cars rather than talking about them.

Brundle did, however, have a brief experience of broadcasting – thanks to the extracurricular activities of James Hunt. Much to the alarm of the BBC team, James had failed to turn up on race day for the 1989 Belgian Grand Prix at Spa-Francorchamps.

'James was not to be seen, five minutes before the race, five minutes into the race, twenty-five minutes into the race – nothing,' recalled Murray. 'I was doing it alone and Mark [Wilkin] was getting anybody who had retired from the race to come to the commentary box. James never turned up. He apologized afterwards. He said: "I'm terribly sorry I wasn't there. I was in bed with a stomach complaint." And I thought – it's the first time I've ever heard it called that! But the point is, this was when Martin Brundle did his first talk on TV and the first occasion when we started to discover how good he was.'

'I was driving for Brabham in 1989,' said Brundle. 'The car was quick at times, but unreliable. Spa was one of several retirements. When that happens you just want to get away from the race track as soon as possible, but on this occasion I was out quite early in the race and I got dragged up to the BBC box to help Murray out and comment on what was going on in the race.

'One of the problems with Spa is the horrendous traffic after the race. I remember sitting there thinking: I need to get out of here. As soon as I could, I slipped away. When I spoke to my manager the next day, he said: "Why did you stop? It was going so well. Were you crazy? You should have stayed up there." I have to admit I found it interesting that I got quite a lot of nice feedback.

'My next experience behind the microphone was in 1995. I was driving for Ligier, and Tom Walkinshaw [team boss] had done a deal to have Mugen engines and sponsors from Japan, and they wanted the Japanese driver Aguri Suzuki. Tom wasn't so keen on having Suzuki in the car all the time, so I had this sort of share drive with him. When I wasn't racing, I used to commentate on qualifying for the Eurosport channel with Ben Edwards and John Watson. On race days, I'd been asked by Mark Wilkin to join Murray and Jonathan [Palmer] in the BBC box.'

'I wanted Martin to do the whole race when possible,' said Wilkin. 'We'd have a team of three, with a microphone each. I think Jonathan was more put out, but Murray liked having Martin's influence there.

It was very clear that Martin was a natural communicator and Murray enjoyed having people alongside that knew what they were talking about. Typical Murray: he recognized that the success of the programme wasn't down to him. It was about everybody enjoying all of it, and it being a team. Then, of course, the BBC lost the rights at the end of 1996. But the plan had been to have Martin in the commentary box when he retired – whenever that might have been.'

'I was driving for Eddie Jordan in 1996,' said Brundle. 'I thought I'd be with Eddie again in 1997. Then this story started to come out – which was probably planted by Eddie – that I would be going to the commentary box for the new ITV production.'

It suited Neil Duncanson to run with the 'Brundle goes to ITV' story because it matched the ambitions of MACH1 very well. 'Having Murray on board, I wanted to bring Martin in,' he said. 'But that didn't happen until quite late, mainly because Martin believed he would be driving in 1997. As professional sports people tend to do after being consumed by a particular sport all of their lives, Martin still saw himself as a driver, not a broadcaster. Everyone else had told us he wouldn't be driving. Even Eddie Jordan told me that would be the case – but Eddie hadn't told Martin! So, we'd make our proposal to Martin and he'd say: "Well, you know, that sounds very interesting. But, look, I might well be driving next year ..." "Um, don't think so, Martin ..."'

On Monday 27 January 1997, Brundle was part of a seven-strong team announced by ITV. Simon Taylor (formerly BBC Radio) and Tony Jardine (former BBC pit lane reporter) would offer analysis from a studio on site at each Grand Prix; pit lane reporting would be handled by Louise Goodman (ex-Jordan press officer) and James Allen (former *Autosport* news editor), with the seasoned ITV sports presenter Jim Rosenthal hosting a package that promised to give 'more interviews, analysis, expert opinion and humour'. A publicity photograph showed the ITV team ranged around a Williams F1 car and incongruously holding white crash helmets, perhaps suggesting they expected flak from an F1 audience nurtured by the BBC and unaccustomed to adverts interrupting their viewing. It was promising to be a particularly difficult role for Rosenthal, despite his vast experience in broadcasting.

'When I got the F1 assignment, it was a bit of a rush job,' said Rosenthal. 'Steve Rider had been lined up, but they came to me in early January and said I had the job and it was starting in less than two months' time. From that moment on, my house sounded like a bloody race track as I went through videos of every Grand Prix known to man.

'I was obviously very aware of Murray, but I didn't know him personally. I rang Murray and said: "Sorry you've got me doing this. I'm a bit hesitant in asking [for help]." He said he'd be delighted to help. "You'll be absolutely fine," he said. "If you need anything, I'll be here twenty-four/seven." That was phenomenal; such a comfort to me, it really was. Murray was hugely supportive.'

If Rosenthal was at home in the wider world of broadcasting, it was completely new territory for Louise Goodman. 'I didn't grow up in a massively motor sport family,' she said, 'but we did watch the Grands Prix and, when I got interested in the sport, it was at the time of Murray and James, that absolutely iconic partnership. When I began working in the F1 paddock doing sponsorship coordination with some of the F1 teams, I remember the great Murray Walker coming up and saying: "Hello, dear. Just wanted to say hello – I'm Murray Walker." And you think: Oh my God, why is Murray Walker introducing himself to little old me? You're glancing over your shoulder to see if he's actually talking to someone else. But that was so Murray. He had time for everybody in the paddock, and it wasn't as if he forced himself to make time; that was just the way it was with Murray.

'The step into broadcasting was obviously a very big one for me – as it was in different ways for the ITV F1 team. We had said we're changing everything; we're going to have ad breaks; we're not going to have "The Chain"; we're going to have a bunch of different people; we're going to have a woman on the crew; we're going to have this, we're going to have that. But then to say we'd got Murray Walker meant everyone could feel they were in a totally safe pair of hands. That's the bit that fans cared about, the bit that made them think "Formula 1". Having Murray on board meant exactly the same thing to everyone on our team. It was like: we'll be OK, Murray's on board.'

James Allen needed no introduction to Murray. Having grown up in a motor sport family – his father had won his class at Le Mans in 1961 – James had met Murray several times, a relationship that moved on to a more professional basis when Allen began working in F1 in 1990. 'I was with the Brabham team in a communications role, which brought me into contact with journalists and broadcasters,' he said. 'I had quite a bit of engagement with Murray and always found him very straightforward, very easy to deal with, and very serious about the sport. But there was a great humour and warmth that went with his massive passion for motor racing. I understood that enthusiasm because it came from the same place as mine – as it does if you grow up in a racing family. I always got on really well with him. And then we were thrown in together at ITV, which was hugely exciting.

'Apart from knowing him, I would be working with a legendary broadcaster who was enormously popular with the audience. But Murray did not stand back, take the plaudits and do little else. He really bought into this new era. Before the whole thing went live, he would regularly travel up from his home in Hampshire and become really involved in the production meetings when we covered how we were going to manage everything from the ad breaks to features to taking comments from the pit lane and the studio.

'It had been a complete no-brainer for ITV to take Murray,' Allen continued. 'In fact, I think the production company [MACH1] felt the BBC had never really made enough of Murray; they had undervalued him because, as a public broadcaster, they had such an embarrassment of riches they didn't really treat any of the people as stars. ITV, on the other hand, perhaps being more commercially minded, realized they'd got a red-hot star in Murray Walker. They marketed the sport and Murray in such a way that he was front and centre in the adverts and promos leading up to our first Grand Prix in the spring of 1997.'

Hyping up the forthcoming show would be one thing; presenting the first Grand Prix live quite another. The buck stopped on Neil Duncanson's desk.

'We were understandably nervous about the whole thing,' said Duncanson. 'There was so much at stake for MACH1, for ITV, for everyone involved. We had twenty-three hours, or however long the flight took, to think about this on the way to Melbourne. Murray was on our flight – and we just weren't ready for what happened when we landed. It was like travelling with someone like Bono. We'd never seen anything like it. Getting Murray out of the airport felt to us what it must have been like trying to get Jimi Hendrix out of Woodstock. It was absolutely extraordinary.'

'I knew about Murray's status as an F1 guru, but this was a real eye-opener,' said Rosenthal. 'This mob descended on Murray and they wanted his thoughts on winter testing times; favourites for the race; the Melbourne circuit. What about this? What about that? He was firing back answers with great gusto, happy to share his enthusiasm and knowledge. I could barely remember my own address. He was seventy-three years of age! I thought it was remarkable that he could do that after a long flight.'

The Australian Grand Prix in Melbourne's Albert Park felt like the start of a new term for F1 personnel as they gathered in such large numbers for the first time in five months. The ITV crew, in their unfamiliar uniforms, were conspicuous as the new intake for the class of '97.

'We spent the next few days getting ourselves sorted out; there was obviously a massive amount to do,' said Duncanson. 'Everyone wished us well, but you could feel there was a lot of pressure. We were aware that people were saying it was going to be rubbish, the BBC had done it so well – real rose-tinted stuff. We were putting commercial breaks into the races, which no one liked – even us. The tension builds, and by race morning I have to admit we're all pretty nervous.

'We went down for breakfast on the Sunday morning, and no one's speaking. We just sat there. Stomachs knotted. Not really feeling like eating. You could read the thoughts: Bloody hell, hope this is going to be OK; what will people think? Murray walks into the breakfast room and notices that nobody is saying a word. So, he wanders over to the breakfast buffet and he starts commentating. "What will Murray have? Hmmm! Murray's looking at all the cereals. There's cornflakes. Look at that! There's muesli. No! Murray's not going to have cereal. He's going for porridge. Incredible!" We're sitting watching all this as he assembles his breakfast, talking all the way. By the time he reaches the table, we're in hysterics. Completely broke the tension. We were ready to roll.'

23

A TALK IN THE PARK

'It was the most nerve-racking broadcast I've ever done,' said Rosenthal. 'I felt like I'd been slung off the top board. It's the only time I've ever not slept before a broadcast. I walked from the hotel across Albert Park to begin preparations in the paddock and wondered: What have I done here?

'I felt a tremendous sense of reassurance knowing Murray was on the team. Even before I knew I was going to have anything to do with the F1 contract, I remember saying to ITV that they had to have Murray Walker on board if they wanted any form of credibility. I said he would be the biggest passport to success that we could possibly have; if we don't get him, we really will be in murky waters. It was good for all sides when the deal was done with Murray because we gave him a bit of star treatment and properly looked after him.

'Murray and I had quite a few discussions. He told me how he prepared for a broadcast by doing exercises and so on. Seeing him doing his stretches and breathing routine was a bit like a 100-metre sprinter going through his preparations. In its own way there was something reassuring about this because, in the back of your mind, there was the thought that the British public do not like change – and here was the most famous voice in motor sport getting ready to perform on our stage.

'Nonetheless, we were venturing into new territory with things such as adverts – which was just about the only aspect of all of this that

I was used to. One of our deputies had flown in that morning and he had a copy of the previous day's *Guardian* newspaper. There was an article on ITV taking up F1 coverage and it more or less said Jim Rosenthal's career was going to crash and burn at the first corner. When I asked our man why he was showing me this, he said he thought I'd want to be aware of it!'

Regardless of the *Guardian's* gratuitous comment, Rosenthal's reputation as a broadcaster was at stake. Brundle was not so bothered – mainly because he had yet to see himself as a television presenter.

'I didn't really want to do the commentary because I still thought I ought to be an F1 driver,' said Brundle. 'I felt like I'd been double-shuffled a little bit and I was a little bit dismissive of the whole thing – which is laughable now when I look back.

'Before coming to Australia, we'd had a pre-season production meeting in London. We were staying in a hotel somewhere and Murray and I went out to dinner, just the two of us. I said to him: "Right, Murray, what do I need to know about broadcasting?" He replied: "I can't tell you anything about Formula 1, Martin; you know more than I do." "Yes, Murray. But I don't know this broadcasting business." And he said: "I'll tell you one thing, and one thing only. Always remember, we're only here to inform and entertain. And that's it." I've lived by that ever since. Inform the viewer; entertain the viewer; leave them to make their own mind up. I'll always remember that conversation in a dodgy little Italian restaurant somewhere in north London. That was all Murray had to tell me. But he was absolutely right.'

Like it or not, Brundle found himself in a commentary booth overlooking the start/finish straight rather than climbing into a Formula 1 car in the pits opposite. The ITV broadcast began on the Saturday with coverage of qualifying. Despite Rosenthal's understandable reservations, there was not a hint of nerves as he appeared on screen for the first time following an inventive title sequence showing sponsorship by Texaco and playing a new theme tune by Jamiroquai. With 'The Chain' and BBC images banished, the familiar mellow voice said: '*Do not adjust your sets. This is Formula 1 on ITV. I am Jim Rosenthal . . .*'

Following a scene-set with shots from Melbourne and Albert Park, Rosenthal introduced the ITV team – Taylor, Jardine, Allen and Goodman – before bringing on Walker and Brundle. '*Formula 1 without Murray Walker,*' said Rosenthal, '*doesn't bear thinking about.*' Then came a run through the teams and drivers for 1997 before Murray, standing outside the commentary box with parkland in the background, said his first words: '*Thanks, Jim. Every Grand Prix season is special for me, but this one is especially special because, alongside me, my friend Martin Brundle. And it's all going to be different: different teams; different engines; different cars; different drivers – and changes of drivers.*'

After further chat, interviews, forecasts and theories, Rosenthal finally said: '*OK, settle back and enjoy the first qualifying session of 1997 in the company of Martin Brundle* [pause] *and the one and only – Murray Walker.*'

'*Formula 1 – 1997 – starts here – and now – at Albert Park, in Melbourne,*' said the instantly recognizable voice. '*A gurrreat place for the race, says the advertising – and they're not kidding.*'

ITV and Formula 1 were truly up and running. Murray and Martin followed progress as twenty-four drivers spent an hour on track attempting to find a clear lap and record their best time. With Jacques Villeneuve appearing to be completely unchallenged in the Williams, Brundle and Walker focused on Damon Hill as the reigning champion struggled to make progress in his new surroundings at Arrows, and at one stage seemed unlikely to set a time fast enough to qualify within the acceptable lap time limit.

With a few minutes remaining, Martin is commenting on Hill's predicament when Murray crashes in with his first outburst of 1997:

'*HERE IS A SENSATION! THAT MAN, HEINZ-HARALD FRENTZEN* [Hill's replacement at Williams] *HAS PULLED IT OUT OF THE BAG! With a very determined last lap to move up on to the FRONT ROW of the grid with Jacques Villeneuve.*' The fact that the German driver is a massive 1.7 seconds slower than his team-mate does nothing to interrupt Murray in full flow. '*WHAT AN INCREDIBLE AUSTRALIAN GRAND PRIX WE ARE GOING TO SEE TOMORROW!*'

As the session ends with Murray going through the grid positions, the camera switches to Michael Schumacher climbing from his Ferrari (which Brundle speculates has run out of fuel) and walking slowly round the car, parked by the side of the track.

'*And Ralf Schumacher,*' says Murray, '*doesn't really look to me as though he has run out of gas. What do you think now?*'

'*I think that's Michael actually,*' says Martin, in one of the many gentle corrections he will make – an increasingly entertaining aspect of a partnership that is due to last for five seasons.

That particular factual nudge was critical. It would be Walker's first indication that Martin was not there to score points off his more experienced colleague but, rather, to work in the spirit of cooperation for the good of a product that meant so much to Murray. The gradual growth of trust would continue the following day through a Grand Prix that would have the added bonus of a British driver, David Coulthard, winning for McLaren-Mercedes.

'Murray was just tremendous during our first commentary together,' said Brundle. 'He was so full of energy. He was genuinely into it and excited. His hands would go in and out, the finger jabbing at the screen as he shouted, "Look at that!" He was very demonstrative inside the commentary box. I didn't find it competitive at all; I found it energizing.

'Perhaps one of the smartest things I did was stand up during commentary – because that's what Murray did. He liked to open his diaphragm and talk. He would lean forward with his headphones on and his lip microphone, and go right up to the monitor, oblivious to anyone else in the commentary box, to the point where you might feel excluded.

'I didn't want to say that much. If you're with somebody who can always have something exciting and interesting to say, you stand back and look at the bigger picture of what's going on in the race. It gives you time to check the timing screen and see that [Mika] Häkkinen or [Jean] Alesi, or whoever, is recovering from a problem. He's sixteenth and you're thinking: Look at that pace – he's going to be on the podium. You can spot those little nuggets that all add up and contribute to the overall story.

'I was obviously aware that Murray had been through a relatively bruising experience with James [Hunt]. I recalled images from the commentary box of James sitting down and Murray standing up; it was very clear that they weren't working together as a team. I wanted to communicate with Murray about the race and hopefully let him realize that we were working together and I wasn't there to trip him up or try and appear to be clever. He was a bit uncertain at first but he quite quickly relaxed, which helped build up trust between us.

'The expression I would come to use most over time was "I think you'll find, Murray ..." when perhaps he had said something that wasn't entirely accurate. Once he realized I was actually his ally, it just took off. I was happy to come in with the one-liners and the experience, while he did the colour. I was trying to follow the simple code of putting the viewer in the car, or on the pit wall or occasionally in the pit lane. But nothing more. That's what made it work.'

Having worked with Martin before, Murray was not unduly worried about how the partnership would work out. 'I knew that we had always got on extremely well,' he said. 'Not only was Martin a very decent sort of chap, he was perfect for the job because he was articulate and could talk with the experience gained not only as a racing driver in Formula 1, but also as a world sports car champion. I'd worked with a lot of co-commentators: Graham Hill, Barry Sheene, Jonathan Palmer and, of course, James Hunt. But I was to find that working with Martin Brundle was very different for very good reasons. He had been on every level bar the top one on the F1 podium; he had won Le Mans. He knew what he was talking about, knew just how to say it, and he'd got a great sense of humour.

'I never had any problem. It was Martin that had a problem with me. I shudder now, looking back, because when the races started, I was so obsessed with what was going on that Martin used to say he could have walked out of the commentary box and I wouldn't have noticed. The problem was that I had been doing it for so long, I tended to be very dominant. But it did make a difference having Martin standing beside me rather than sitting beneath my eyeline. And, like me, Martin was very much a team player. I liked that.'

Reports the following week claimed 3.9 million in the UK had watched the re-run of the race, while 873,000 had got up early on the Sunday morning to watch it live. The letters page in the next issue of *Autosport* carried a predominantly positive reaction, one correspondent saying the commentary was of a 'commendably high standard; less so, the studio discussion'. Adam Parsons, motor sport correspondent of the *Sunday Times*, made a prescient observation when he wrote: 'Brundle provided the sort of acerbic insight lost to the BBC after the death of James Hunt.'

Contrary to the prickly prediction in the *Guardian*, far from crashing and burning at the first corner, Rosenthal had completed the distance calmly and with polished professionalism. 'I can't deny I was relieved to sign off without a major mishap,' he said. 'As soon as we had finished, Murray came straight up, put his arm round me and said:

"Absolutely brilliant." He was just being very, very kind. But that was typical of the support he would give everyone, all the way through.'

'Jim did a terrific job,' said Duncanson. 'It was a hard gig for him because he wasn't a Formula 1 guy. But he was an excellent journalist, and an outstanding live presenter. All told, with Martin, Louise, Tony, James and Simon, we had a cracking little team.

'The original plan had been to have Steve Rider come over from the BBC and join us. It nearly happened, but Brian Barwick [head of sport production at the BBC] threatened him with everything under the sun and Steve didn't come. Then, as a supreme irony, it was Brian who left the BBC to join ITV as controller of sport!'

This switch in 1998 would give the network's F1 coverage even more impetus thanks to the colourful influence of this self-styled 'raggedy-arsed kid from Liverpool'. Before then, however, Murray had to make a difficult decision over the end of a long-standing liaison that had nothing to do with F1.

24

BETTER THAN BEING THERE

Five days before Murray's thirty-fifth birthday in October 1958, the final round of the inaugural British Saloon Car Championship had taken place in teeming rain at Brands Hatch. Murray may have been in the throes of negotiating an important advertising career move to Masius & Ferguson but it's a fair bet that, if not present at the Kent circuit, he would have been fully aware of the event's significance.

The British Racing and Sports Car Club, a leading light at the time in motor sport organization, had dreamed up a saloon car championship for, to quote the prospectus, 'the competitor who wants to race the ordinary family car, to do so throughout an entire season against evenly matched opposition'. This broad regulatory brush had allowed a plethora of showroom-specification saloon cars to take part in nine rounds spread across seven British race tracks.

The championship had been whittled down to a battle between Tommy Sopwith's Jaguar 3.4 and the more sedate – if just as energetically driven – Austin A105 Westminster of Jack Sears, each having accumulated points through wins in their individual classes. They finished the final race on the same number of points.

In the event of such a scenario, it had been suggested that the title should be decided by the toss of a coin – an outcome that appealed to neither of two such competitive racers. In a clever piece of marketing strategy – of which Murray would have been proud – Marcus

Chambers, the competitions manager at BMC (British Motor Corporation), offered the use of two identical BMC-prepared Riley 1.5
saloons (a nippy little car, the equivalent of today's 'hot hatch') for a
shoot-out. To ensure fairness, Sopwith and Sears would race for five
laps, swap cars, and do another five-lap race, the result being decided
on aggregate times. Jack Sears became the first British touring car
champion by 1.8 seconds.

Thirty years later, the championship still existed but, not surprisingly, a great deal had changed. Now known as the British Touring Car
Championship (BTCC), the series was sponsored by Dunlop and
fielded modified and highly tuned versions of, among others, the
BMW M3, Ford Sierra RS500, Ford Escort RS Turbo and Toyota Cor-
olla GT. The appeal to spectators was no less than it had been in 1958.

The championship's potential had not been lost on Steve Rider. As
a presenter on *Grandstand*, Rider was aware of the BBC's need to
expand motor sport coverage that, until now, had been haphazard
thanks to a limitation imposed by contracts with some (but not all) of
the leading British race tracks. It meant the BBC had been duty-
bound to cover races, sometimes of little consequence, while being
unable to televise more tasty events on tracks with which they had no
contractual ties. With these agreements expiring, Rider – along with
Murray and ex-racing driver Tiff Needell – could see a promising
alternative.

'The editor of *Grandstand* was a pioneering, free-thinking guy
called John Philips,' said Rider. 'We said to him that the ending of
these circuit contracts was a cue for the BBC to at least have a look at
being able to deliver more editorially sound coverage of British motor
sport. We highlighted the British Rally Championship and, in terms
of circuit racing, the British Touring Car Championship and the British Formula 3 Championship. There was clearly no way that the BBC
could cover every single round of these competitions, certainly not in

live terms with outside broadcasts. It was agreed that if another method could be established, financed and delivered, then the BBC would create the time within their programmes to transmit it.

'So, off we went to try and come up with a budget. The production method was easier to establish in that we would do what is known as a post-produced format. This amounted to several cameras recording remotely to generate coverage, which would then be edited over the next few days, and commentary added. Which, of course, is where Murray would not only come in by providing what amounted to a musical score, but also in being very useful when setting up this touring car package.

'Before we could get going, however, things got a bit bloody. I had been working with BHP, a production company run by Barrie Hinchcliffe, a brilliant guy who knew everything – and everyone – in this end of the industry. We had to move quickly, and the obvious assumption was to use BHP. In truth, it should have been put out to tender.

'Very early on, we were challenged for the contract by Brian Kreisky, a feisty individual who had been operating in motor sport film for some time. The contract then had to be sorted out, which meant a formal tender. One of the requirements was that the coverage had to be in the BBC's style. That could only mean one thing when it came to commentary: we signed Murray to our bid. Kreisky put in his bid with no commentator allocated. With Murray on board, it was game, set and match. We owed him one for that.'

As a fan of touring car racing, and given the promise provided by the turbocharged, flame-spitting Ford Sierras, Murray was up for the challenge. It would add considerably to a routine that was already occupied by coverage of sixteen Grands Prix.

'In the early days, I used to go to Silverstone and Brands Hatch to watch what was then the British Saloon Car Championship,' said Murray. 'I'd always loved seeing top drivers, people like Mike

Hawthorn [1958 Formula 1 world champion] and Tommy Sopwith driving the wheels off Mk II Jaguars against Jack Sears and Jeff Uren in, believe it or not, an Austin Westminster and a Ford Zephyr. All sorts of unlikely cars won the championship, from an Austin A40 to an enormous Ford Galaxy. I was more than happy to get involved with Steve and the BBC to cover the championship in its latest form.

'I went to as many BTCC races as I could and immersed myself in the championship. It didn't matter that some of the Grands Prix clashed with the BTCC because, of course, the touring cars were being filmed and then edited. BHP had cameras trackside, outside and inside the cars; they filmed interviews, covered the prize-giving and just about everything that moved. At the end of every race there was miles of tape for some very clever people at BHP to edit down to thirty minutes. It meant there was half an hour of non-stop drama and excitement, and I had to talk through every second of it. There would be no lulls like there would when covering a race live. It was crash-bang-wallop from the start and into passing moves, collisions, door-handle to door-handle stuff. It was absolutely fabulous. I would sit at an editing machine and study every inch, working out the race story before even thinking about what the words might be. It was long-winded and labour-intensive. But it worked wonderfully.'

For Rider and the production team at BHP, it was as much fun to watch the master at work as it was to listen to the end result. 'Dubbing the commentary and fitting it into his Grand Prix schedule was always a bit of a challenge,' said Rider. 'We were not only covering the BTCC, but the F3 races as well. We were probably talking about twenty races that we would require Murray to dub. Being concerned that he could do all of this alongside his Grand Prix commitments, I said: "Rest assured, Murray, we can knock it off in half a day." And Murray said: "No. I never knock anything off in half a day." It was a two-day job for Murray. He would come up from Hampshire, take an initial look at the material, then check himself into a very nice hotel in London and come back the next day, ready to perform.

'One of the problems he had to cope with was that drivers in the championship got to know that Murray would be dubbing the commentary three days later. So, he would have to spend much of the first day fielding calls from drivers saying: "You know that sequence where I had a collision with Steve Soper? Well, when you get to that, please bear in mind this is what really happened." Or: "Murray, I wouldn't mind if you ignore the bit where I lost it on the first lap."

'Once he had dealt with all of that, Murray would sit there and compose this commentary, virtually frame by frame. It would take him five or six hours. You left him alone and gave him cups of coffee. Then, at about four o'clock in the afternoon, he would come into the dubbing theatre and just say: "I'm ready." And that would be the cue for everyone – the editor, the secretary, the accountant, the tea-maker – to stop what they were doing and take a seat as if this was a theatrical performance. Murray is about to dub!

'He would get behind the glass, and he would go for it. Jab! Jab! Jabbing at the screen, talking at full noise all the time. He would probably do it in about three or four sections. The thing that struck you was that, even though he was dubbing, he made it sound like he was there, doing it live. To do something as scripted and as pre-prepared as that and yet maintain an air of spontaneity about it is very difficult indeed. In many ways, it was indeed pure theatre.

'It took an awful lot out of him, and at the end of it he would sit down. But nobody would leave. He would come out from behind the glass and say: "Right. Now we'll listen to all that back." Everyone would sit there while we went through it from the start. Murray was exactly the same listening to the commentary as he was when delivering it. At certain points he'd be up on his feet jabbing at the screen. It was absolutely wonderful. You could sell tickets for it!

'When you listened carefully, you could appreciate Murray's advertising background. You would hear all sorts of mischievous, clearly pre-rehearsed lines in which he'd refer to a car company's buzzy marketing slogan – "The car in front is a Toyota", that sort of thing. And you can imagine what he said when a Volvo overtook a BMW M3 around the outside. His script was clearly aimed at the marketing departments. He was absolutely terrific.'

Jonathan Ashman had more than a passing interest in one of Britain's premier motor racing championships. As marketing and events director at the RAC Motor Sports Association, he knew how important the BBC coverage would be and was on hand on occasions to witness the recording. 'Murray always made it sound as though he was doing a live commentary,' he said. 'When recording, his draft script sometimes didn't exactly fit the pictures, so he would stop and re-record that piece. The astounding thing with Murray was that he could start the re-recording in the middle of a sentence and do it at full blast. When you listened to the final version, nobody would ever realize that he had stopped and started again. That's unbelievably difficult to do and showed that he was the ultimate professional.'

A selling point for everyone involved with the BTCC was the complete absence of a dull race in the entire season. Or, at least, that was the effect of the Walker treatment. Even those deeply involved – drivers such as John Cleland, BTCC champion in 1989 and 1995 – would often do a double-take when watching the BBC output. 'I would sit down on the Saturday afternoon,' said Cleland, 'and watch a race I had competed in the previous weekend, fully knowing it was the most boring race I think I'd ever taken part in. I'm watching this, and I'm listening to Murray, and the way they've cut and shut, and pushed in some in-car stuff, I'm thinking: What a phenomenal race – I wish I'd been there! Because it sounded much more exciting than when I was in it!'

Dubbing also gave Murray the opportunity to exploit his wry sense of humour. During one particularly energetic battle involving Cleland, the Scotsman had given his opponent the finger after their cars had exchanged paintwork. '*And John Cleland,*' said Murray, '*is letting everyone know he's going for first place!*'

It was this, and more, that established the BTCC series as one of the most popular in terms of not only the BBC's viewing figures but also the increased numbers passing through the circuit gates.

'I'd go as far as suggesting,' said Rider, 'that Murray helped establish that championship on television as much as anything he ever did for Formula 1. His dubbing technique provided a warm, familiar voice as much as a commentary. It was a distinctive piece of work every week that really made the event live.

'But, in the end, he sort of ran out of steam. I think a lot of people would have done that even sooner; it was such a hectic, all-consuming couple of days, added to everything else he was doing. Then, once the BBC gave way to ITV in terms of Formula 1, the pressure on Murray became that much greater. Eventually he said: "Sadly, I can't do all of this any more." We had nine years together with the BTCC, and they had all been brilliant. In 1998 we had to manage without him.'

25

COMMERCIAL DIVIDE

TV's newly appointed controller of sport in 1998, Brian Barwick, knew Murray Walker of old. Having joined BBC Sport in 1979, Barwick had witnessed the gradual growth of Grand Prix racing on the network, even though his main interest had been football.

'I worked on *Sportsnight* and *Match of the Day*, which meant I was also connected with *Ski Sunday* and *Grand Prix*,' said Barwick. 'This was in the days of David Coleman, Peter O'Sullevan, Harry Carpenter, Peter Alliss and so on. Murray fitted in perfectly because his was another voice that made sports alive for people. I arrived in the middle of this as a raggedy-arsed kid from Liverpool and was completely blown away.

'The BBC at that time was considered to be a powerhouse of sport but, to be honest, it probably wasn't as good a service as it could have been. I used to edit *Sunday Grandstand* and we'd show the first ten laps of the Italian Grand Prix, then go to cricket in Canterbury, knowing thousands of F1 fans would be throwing bloody cushions at the television. And then we'd go to swimming from Blackpool! It wasn't ideal.

'With the arrival of *Grand Prix*, F1 had become a must-see. We then capped off what had become our final year of F1 in 1996 with Damon Hill becoming world champion. The switch to ITV was heartbreaking for Jonathan Martin because he loved motor racing and he'd helped create this F1 brand on television.

'In late 1997, I was approached by ITV to become their controller of sport. ITV had a different ethos. What they needed from sport was a heavyweight product at the weekend that wouldn't get in the way of big light entertainment shows and an occasional event. They focused on Champions League football, then either a European Championship or a World Cup – which they did with the BBC – the Rugby World Cup, and Formula 1 motor racing, which they paid serious money for. Most of the Grands Prix started at one o'clock in the afternoon, which wasn't interfering with top-end drama or light entertainment. It also played incredibly powerfully for the commercial market – cars, banks, watches, men's aftershave, many of the key things that ITV on occasion would struggle to get because it was seen as a channel that attracted more female viewers than male viewers through soaps and quizzes. So, F1 was solid gold in terms of the type of audience it could attract.'

Barwick watched every minute of ITV's output from the opening races of 1998 in Australia and Brazil before making a flying visit to the Argentine Grand Prix in Buenos Aires, arriving before qualifying and leaving immediately after the race the following day.

'I think that made an impression on Murray,' said Barwick. 'We had come across each other regularly at the BBC, but we hadn't really worked together. He had a fear that, because I was well known as a football man, I'd take little or no interest in Formula 1. That was never going to be the case because it was such an expensive and lucrative contract.

'I knew Neil [Duncanson] and it was no surprise that he and his team were working very hard and doing an excellent job. Neil was never going to push back on a bit of help and I was confident that I could cast an editorial eye, in addition to working with the talent [presenters] – which I always liked to do.'

Barwick had no wish to change Walker's unique style of commentary, but he felt it might be useful to discuss his handling of advertising breaks – the one area of broadcasting that was completely alien to Murray.

'Advertising breaks in live sport would always be a challenge,' Barwick observed. 'In F1, we had five breaks to get away. They would let the race settle down, and then get one away. Then try, as best they could, to miss the pit stops. But, regardless of when the ad breaks came, I noticed Murray was so excited when commentating that he found it almost impossible to accept that we were leaving the race to go somewhere else. I brought him in and said: "I'm going to improve your commentary style." He was fascinated by this because, he said, nobody had ever taken that level of interest before. I explained that, going into a break, he would say something to the effect of: "Schumacher is catching Häkkinen. This is absolutely amazing – and now you're leaving us!" I told him: "Instead of going down, you go up; I want you to drift down into the break, so that the viewer knows and accepts it's coming. A good way of doing it is to go through the top six positions at the time. And then we cut.

'I showed him a little diagram that I thought would help. It had one line rising up across the page, and another, from the same starting point, falling away. Simple. I pointed to the top one and said: "That's what you're doing now, rising in tempo just as we want to cut away. I want you to go like this [pointing to the falling line] as the countdown for the break begins." I went to a lot of the races around the world, and Murray always had this diagram pinned up in the commentary box. OK, he would usually have known I was coming, but there it was. And he did exactly as I had asked in commentary – but not every time, because that's Murray!'

There would be occasions during Murray's career with ITV when he appreciated the opportunity to gather his thoughts during an advertising break. At one particular race, however, the commercial interludes would offer little respite.

With fifteen laps remaining, the 1997 Canadian Grand Prix had been brought to a halt following a serious accident. Olivier Panis, lying seventh, had crashed while going through a flat-out curve on the back section of Circuit Gilles Villeneuve. The Frenchman's Prost-Mugen-Honda had suddenly snapped sideways at 145mph. The nose of the car hit the wall on the right, the Prost then spinning into the barrier on the left – nose first. The violence of the impact completely destroyed the front of the car. It is not an exaggeration to say that Panis was fortunate to escape with two broken legs.

'The car was in a shocking mess, really bad,' said Duncanson. 'We'd no way of knowing how Panis was – but it didn't look good. Murray would obviously have been thinking of Imola 1994 and Senna, who had appeared to have suffered very little injury, and yet we know what happened. Murray went into full funeral mode, and I had to pull him back out of that. Which he did. I had no idea how much longer we would be staying on air. There seemed a good chance the race would be restarted, so I told Murray and Martin to just keep talking. The organizers eventually decided not to start again because the race had passed three-quarter distance. But, by that stage, Murray and Martin must have been talking for a good thirty-five to forty minutes. We had nowhere else to go. Murray was fabulous. Live TV was like falling off a log for him because he had so much experience, right back to his days on radio when you had to keep talking, no matter what.'

The 1998 season would also have its fair share of collisions, albeit with happier outcomes. The Belgian Grand Prix, run in heavy rain, had enough incidents for an entire year of motor racing.

Trouble began seconds after the start as the field accelerated downhill. David Coulthard, having started from the front row alongside his McLaren team-mate, Mika Häkkinen, suddenly flicked sideways, struck a wall and spun into the middle of the pack. Wheels, wings and bits of bodywork flew in all directions as thirteen cars cannoned into each other. His enthusiasm at maximum revs from the start, Murray had been bracing himself for an incident – but nothing on this level.

'*YES! YES! It's go! . . . Häkkinen gets away well. Look at Eddie Irvine* [Ferrari] *coming up on the inside! Villeneuve* [Williams-Mecachrome] *goes up into second position . . . Schumacher* [Ferrari] *is down into about sixth position. Bad start by the Ferraris . . . AND INTO THE WALL! Who was that? It's Coulthard! David Coulthard into the wall! They'll stop the race! They'll stop the race! OH! THIS IS TERRIBLE! OH, THIS IS QUITE APPALLING. This is THE worst start for a Grand Prix that I have – ever – seen – in – the – WHOLE – of – my – life.*'

The 1998 season had boiled down to a fight between Häkkinen and Schumacher and both (along with Coulthard in the back-up McLaren) were able to take the restart. The pressure of trying to win the championship for Ferrari for the first time since 1979 began to build on Schumacher as he took the lead in wet conditions that were even worse than before.

On lap 24, Schumacher prepared to lap Coulthard, who was running at the back of the field. Coulthard duly moved to the edge of the track. Schumacher, failing to see the McLaren lost in its own spray, smashed into Coulthard's car and tore off the Ferrari's right-front wheel.

'*But let us not forget,*' Murray was saying, seconds before, '*that David Coulthard, in these appalling conditions – OH GOD! MICHAEL SCHU-MACHER HITS DAVID COULTHARD! SCHUMACHER IS OUT OF THE BELGIAN GRAND PRIX! Maybe he should have been a bit more circumspect about trying to pass him – BUT HE IS OUT! . . . Well, what an incredible development!*'

Both drivers manage to reach the pits, where a furious Schumacher quickly evacuates the cockpit of his three-wheel Ferrari.

'*Now, what is he up to?*' asks Murray. '*He's storming down the pit lane, presumably to . . . Look at him! Look at him! He's saying: "I'm going to the stewards."* . . . *He's going to Coulthard! He's going to have it out with David Coulthard! This is a bit like Nigel Mansell and Ayrton Senna* [a collision at the same circuit in 1987] *when Nigel got him by the throat* [it was Senna who grabbed Mansell]. *James! What's the news?'*

James Allen was on hand to describe a thunder-faced Schumacher being dragged away by the Ferrari team manager. It had been an eventful race for ITV's pit lane reporter for reasons beyond the obvious turmoil on the track. 'I had also been on the spot when we had that first-lap pile-up,' Allen said. 'As they were clearing the cars away, we talked about who might and might not be able to restart. We had covered more or less everything and the conversation went back to Murray and Martin in the commentary box. I could see it was going to take a while for the race to get going again and we were in for a very long afternoon. So, I took the opportunity of nipping into a nearby Portaloo.

'I was wearing a fire suit, which was mandatory if you were working in the pit lane. I won't go into the mechanics of what you need to do to have a pee when wearing one of these things but suffice to say that the pack with the battery, transmitter and microphone was quite heavy and arranged on a leather belt. At the very moment when this was no longer attached to me, Murray, without any notice, suddenly threw to me. He had a habit of doing that occasionally, and I should have been ready for it because there wasn't much else happening on track. So, I'm scrabbling around in this tiny plastic Portaloo, struggling to get the microphone. I found something to say – I can't remember what – but that was one moment when I definitely didn't want to hear the voice of Murray Walker!'

The 1998 championship battle went to the wire in Japan. It was a dramatic race, the story being as much about Häkkinen winning the title for the first time as Schumacher and Ferrari losing it for the second year in succession.

'The race overran,' said Barwick. 'It hadn't finished, the championship wasn't decided, and we were out of time. They were about to take
it off air and go to cartoons, or something. I didn't know the mechanics of ITV as well as I had at the BBC, but I managed to find the
number of somebody significant and just went bloody bonkers down
the phone. "We're three laps from the end! Do you realize ... et cetera,
et cetera!" I managed to keep it on air, and then had to field a load of
complaints the following day from the advertising boys because somebody could have sold more Sindy dolls. Welcome, F1, to commercial
television.'

26

ON THE ROAD

Mika Häkkinen winning the championship in 1998 had interesting repercussions for Walker and Brundle. It meant a trip to the Arctic Circle as ITV filmed an F1 Christmas Special with a Scandinavian theme in recognition of the Finnish driver's first world title. Production would be in the hands of Rupert Bush, who had been part of the MACH1 team from the outset.

'I had been in IndyCar racing in the 1980s, working for a production company doing shows for ESPN and ABC,' said Bush. 'The noticeable thing, even then, was that the name Murray Walker was big in North America. Motor racing people knew all about him. I later returned to the UK and started working for Chrysalis. When they won the F1 contract, I happened to be in the right place at the right time. Working with Murray would turn out to be one of the highlights of the job.

'The thing about Murray was that, regardless of his status, he was absolutely disarming in the way that he treated everybody as a complete equal. He saw himself as part of a team. Murray brought a terrific amount of personality and character into our operation right from the start. He wanted to be involved in everything. Some broadcasting talent can be very precious about being asked to do things. Murray was never like that; he was an absolute 100 per cent collaborator. That trip to the Arctic with Martin was a case in point. It was hilarious.

'We had a number of set pieces we wanted to film. But we only had four hours of daylight. For the opening to the show, we were in the forest and the plan was to have Martin driving a Ski-Doo with Murray on the back. It's half past nine in the morning, the cameras are ready, they come into frame through the trees – and you can't see a thing. It's still dark! We had to hang around and finally got the job done.

'At one point we were in a car park that had a line marking the Arctic Circle. Murray spent about half an hour on the Ski-Doo, going back and forth, crossing in and out of the Arctic Circle and saying "Fantastic! This is great!" just like a kid!

'We had other dramas, like having Murray and Martin sitting for ages in the freezing cold, pretending they were ice fishing. Or taking for ever to set up a log fire in a hut – and then we got smoked out. But there were never any histrionics from Murray; he loved it.

'When it came to the business end of production, Murray would be totally focused. We'd have written the running orders, the scripts, and so on. Murray would meticulously read every word of the script, make small changes, add his notations, prepare his links, learn everything and be ready to go. It was like that every time.'

Bush had become more familiar with Murray's methods thanks to the introduction of *Murray & Martin's F1 Special* in 1998. 'It started part way through the season as one fifteen-minute show,' Bush recalled. 'It went out at around five o'clock on the Saturday afternoon of a Grand Prix weekend. Murray and Martin would talk about what had happened in qualifying and throw forward to the race. We were more or less making it up as we went along. ITV got more interested, and it developed into a fully fledged half-hour show, making more and more use of the Murray'n'Martin brand.

'We would produce half the content before qualifying. Then, straight after, we would scramble together the final fifteen minutes based on what had happened during qualifying. We would shoot stuff on the fly. Unlike today, we had to edit everything in a linear fashion: you had the whole show on a piece of tape and played it out live. I would be trying to hit a twenty-eight-minute target of time and I'd have a certain amount of time left to fill near the end. I'd say: "OK, Murray, I need a minute forty-three [seconds] on tyres." And he'd say: "All right, give me a minute." Off he'd go, write some notes, come back, get himself settled and say: "OK, I'm ready." We would shoot a piece on tyres, and it would come out exactly one minute forty-three. And it would be one take.

'Every single time, Murray would come into the truck and watch the show go out. At the end of every show, he would always say: "Well done." He was such a champion of everybody. There was a fantastic camaraderie between me, Murray and Martin, two editors and Andy Parr, the cameraman. It was one of the most enjoyable things I've ever done – largely because Murray was so easy to work with.'

Andy Parr had previous experience of Murray, having worked as an F1 cameraman with the BBC. The move across to MACH1 allowed a more inventive approach as Parr embraced the challenge provided by material needed for the *Murray & Martin* show. It also gave him an opportunity to get to know Murray better.

'I hadn't done much filming with Murray at the BBC because we didn't do features,' said Parr. 'When the *Murray & Martin* show came along, most of our efforts on site, from my point of view of shooting, went into making features. That usually meant going off with Rupert Bush to some location to film these features. Then we would return and Murray and Martin would do the presentation side of it, back at the track.

'But I do remember going with Murray into San Marino, to the actual place, to film a feature. That was great. Filming with Murray tended to be spontaneous. We shot some links, with Murray walking down the street and doing pieces to camera. We had more or less finished. As we headed back to the car, we walked past a stall selling souvenir fridge magnets. Murray tapped me on the shoulder and said: "Andy, just film this." He picked up this particularly tacky souvenir from the stall and said: "These are lovely. I could get some for you – cheap!" Then he put it down again and we walked on. It was a throwaway comment, completely spontaneous. It went in the piece. It was perfect for what we needed. Brilliant.

'Typically, too, this had been one take. It was always the same with Murray. We did many things over the years and I'd never been technically worried about anything with Murray. At times, we did really complicated items. They used to do a "Murray Meets ..." segment involving various personalities. We decided at one stage to try "Murray meets Murray" at his house. There was a fireplace with a chair either side of it. He sat on one chair and did all the questions. Then he sat on the other chair and gave all the answers. Cut together, it was Murray interviewing Murray. It was a technically challenging thing to do – but it wasn't difficult for him at all. He just took it in his stride. In fact, he loved the experience of doing something like that. He would always do whatever you asked; he trusted you. No matter how ridiculous your request may have seemed, he would do it because he knew there was a reason behind your apparent madness! We spent a really nice afternoon filming that. There were no airs or graces with Murray – completely the opposite, in fact.'

Louise Goodman could back that up following an unusual experience during a Belgian Grand Prix weekend. The rural location of the Spa-Francorchamps circuit meant F1 personnel were usually scattered far and wide, staying in a variety of hotels and boarding houses. Louise, Murray and James Allen were in a rustic establishment, noted for its good food if not its luxury accommodation. Murray, being the senior member of F1 society, got the only room with a television.

That race weekend, in 2001, coincided with a World Cup

qualifying round. Being a passionate football supporter, James was keen to see the match.

'It was that classic England v. Germany, which England won 5–1 with a Michael Owen hat-trick,' recalled James. 'You could get BBC on the television in Belgium and Murray said I could use his room after dinner. He came up at half-time and I offered to leave, but he said "Carry on", so I did. Murray proceeded to get ready for bed – Viyella pyjamas, brushing his teeth, and so on. He sat and watched the second half. It was like staying at your grandad's! There was a low beam over the bed I hadn't noticed. When the last goal went in, I shot up and banged my head on it – almost knocked myself out!'

'It was, according to James, a super-important match that had to be seen,' said Louise. 'I didn't care. And neither did Murray. But with alternative after-dinner entertainment being in short supply, I eventually joined them. I went in, and there's Murray in his pyjamas. James is perched on the end of his bed, engrossed in this football match, and I'm thinking: This is really bizarre. I'm in Murray Walker's bedroom, Murray's in his pyjamas, and I'm watching football with him!'

Allen frequently acted as Murray's driver, particularly for a Grand Prix such as Belgium where the hotel was some distance from the race track.

'Working with Murray on air was great,' said James. 'But I guess I spent the most time travelling with him. He didn't much like driving abroad and so we settled quite quickly into a rhythm where we would be on the same flight out of London. I would pick up the hire car at the other end and drive him about most – but not all – of the time. ITV had a bunch of cars going in and out of the circuit and he might return to the hotel with one of the engineers or cameramen. But, more often than not, I drove him from the airport to the hotel and then back again after the race. Over a season, that adds up to quite a few hours together.

'We would talk about all sorts of things relating to his time in advertising and his early experiences during broadcasting. But he didn't necessarily like talking about the war. I had an uncle who had been in the tank regiment in North Africa, and he never ever spoke about his experience. Murray would talk about it occasionally, but he never mentioned the grisly things that he must have seen. He did speak about human experiences, such as how being in the Army changes your priorities and outlook on life and so on.'

'I remember one occasion travelling in the hire car with Murray and James,' said Goodman. 'We were on our way into Germany – going to Hockenheim or the Nürburgring, I can't remember which one – and we were crossing a major river. Murray was telling us one of his stories and, clearly, he didn't think James and I were listening. "Pay attention, you two!" he suddenly said, half joking. "I nearly died so you two could cross this bridge!" It was one of the very few references I ever heard Murray make to the war.'

Early in his relationship with ITV, Murray would be called upon to engage in combat of a different kind.

'For the first year at least, I had what you might call a confrontational relationship with Frank Williams,' said Neil Duncanson. 'I thought Frank was an absolute gentleman but, like Murray, he could occasionally be a bit old-fashioned – which he had every right to be.

'Halfway through our first year in 1997, just as the so-called silly season is under way, people are speculating about where drivers are going for the following season. We did a little cartoon thing about what had happened so far in '97 and who might be going where at the end of it. [Heinz-Harald] Frentzen, who had replaced Damon [Hill] at Williams, had not been pulling up trees. In our cartoon, we put Frentzen at Kwik Fit. Which we all thought was hilarious. But Frank didn't.

'I got a summons to the Williams garage – I can't remember which race we were at – for Frank to express his displeasure. Thinking this probably wouldn't go well, I took Murray with me to help defuse the situation. I tried to explain to Frank that this was ITV, and we were trying to bring new audiences in; we were trying to have a bit of fun with it. Frank said: "Look, I didn't think it was very funny, and neither did Heinz-Harald." Whether that was true or not, I didn't know. But I apologized and said I was sorry he didn't find it funny. I didn't add that a lot of people did find it amusing. I asked if we could draw a line under it and move on. Frank was fine. But there was no doubt that having Murray there helped rescue the situation.

'That experience, and more, added to my personal feeling that Murray had become a bit of a second father to me because he was such a wise old fella. He was the kind of guy who knew pretty much everything there was to know. But he didn't wear it heavily. He could sit in a room and not find it necessary to shout and scream about what he knew. We were all aware of his vast experience in just about every-thing associated with F1 and what we were trying to do. When he said something, everyone listened. I used to ask him: "What do you think about this? And what about that?" He was always there to give you a bit of wise counsel. He was tremendously helpful to me, particularly in that first year, when I was both the executive producer and, at the insistence of ITV, the series editor and trying to spin all the plates.'

One subject for discussion by the ITV team during the 1998 silly season would have been the future of Damon Hill. A difficult first half with Jordan had led to speculation over the former champion's motiv-ation; questions that were answered in part by an unexpected but well-judged win in late August during the wet and eventful Belgian Grand Prix. When tasked with interviewing Hill about his future, Murray steered a firm but fair course.

'The thing about Murray was that, unlike, say, James [Hunt], he was never going to do something like call you a mobile chicane and suggest you had no place in F1,' said Hill. 'There was a kindness to him, an understanding which I think people trusted. And he did get stuff out of you. He wasn't going to pull any punches with some of the questions that he had to ask you. It was a bit like being at school and going to, not the headmaster, but the English teacher, who would say: "Now, Damon, about your homework. We've missed a few weeks. Have you any idea what you're going to do about it? You don't? Well, look, here's your detention. Now, run along." It would be as if he was putting a comforting arm around your shoulder while asking the difficult questions.'

As for Murray, tricky questions had been asked a decade before concerning his errors and slips of the tongue. By the end of the nineties, however, they had become something to be celebrated.

27

IT'S THE WAY HE TELLS IT

'I always felt Murray could make a 5 a.m. milk round on a cold morning in Peckham sound like the start of the Indianapolis 500.'

Neil Duncanson's description of Murray at work perfectly summed up a distinctive style that went beyond simply providing words to accompany television images.

'He's one of the very few guys I worked with over the years that actually added to the spectacle of the sport you were watching,' Duncanson continued. 'It wasn't Murray simply doing the driving and navigating, like most commentary teams do; he actually was able to lift it up.

'I know he polarized a few fans, but we always felt it was a small minority. From my point of view, especially in those Michael Schumacher years when that red car was winning all the races, we were getting concerned about pulling in viewers to ITV, particularly with no British driver anywhere near the front. When Schumacher was a lap and a half clear of everyone else, we'd say: "Turn it up to eleven, Murray." And off he'd go. He'd take off and give you something else to watch and listen to. He was an absolute joy.'

An occasional side effect of this dramatic increase in pace would be the emergence of what had become known as 'Murrayisms' – a euphemism for 'mistakes' in the eyes of the minority Duncanson was referring to but, for a contented majority, slips of the tongue that brought further listening pleasure. Rather than being a failing,

Murrayisms had become an acceptable part of the Murray Walker stock in trade.

'If a Murray Walker was to happen along now, they'd have his arm off,' said Duncanson. 'There aren't many commentators out there today that sell a ticket. I worked with some good ones, people like Kenneth Wolstenholme in football and Reg Gutteridge in boxing. These guys brought something extra to the broadcast, pulled people in because they felt comfortable listening to the voice as much as watching the images on the screen.

'Some might say that the Murrayisms became a little bit of a cliché. But as my old news editor used to say: "Clichés are clichés for a reason." They're also truisms, and I think most people loved them. They would be waiting for Murray to come out with another one.'

Simon Taylor covered F1 for BBC Radio 2, which later became BBC Radio 5 Live. Having gathered decades of know-how in radio, Taylor experienced televisual broadcasting when he became part of the ITV F1 studio team in 1997. After listening to him for many years, Simon was very familiar with Murray's individual style.

'Murray used to laugh off the mistakes brilliantly,' said Taylor. 'He would tell stories against himself. Saying that, I always had the feeling that, if you got him in a corner, he would admit to being concerned that he would go down in history not for the commentating that he'd done but for the mistakes he'd made. I have always said that would be grossly unjust because he let rip billions of words. And within those billions of words, there were some hilarious errors, which some people will remember most. But that's a rather unfair judgement on Murray, because he was a supreme commentator.

'He was a supreme commentator because he was very fluent. He was very graphic; he could describe brilliantly what was going on. Having done a lot of radio commentary, I can say that the technique of television commentating is completely different because you've got a picture. But Murray understood how to amplify the picture; how to tell people what they were seeing, rather than just leaving them to work it out. That was his technique, and he did it for over half a century by the end. No matter what anyone says, Murray was first and foremost an absolutely brilliant commentator.'

Respect for Murray was widespread throughout the business of commentating. Ian Titchmarsh, a lawyer by profession, has spent every spare weekend for decades providing extremely knowledgeable and entertaining commentary over public address systems at British race tracks. 'As a fan in the fifties, you were grateful to have any motor sport on the radio or television; you were just glad to hear anyone's voice,' he said. 'Raymond Baxter was the one I grew up with, followed by Murray Walker. The criticism that was regularly made of Murray was that he got things wrong. Looking at it from a commentator's point of view, I could see a change once Murray had retired from his job in advertising. He was then able to devote all his time to being a commentator, and he made far fewer mistakes; what you would call factual errors rather than over-enthusiasm. The latter was not a failing but, rather, one of his endearing characteristics, that the wrong words would come out because he was so enthusiastic.'

That was a view shared by Titchmarsh's fellow circuit commentators, as Oliver Owen, a young motor sport enthusiast, was to discover to his chagrin. 'It would have been when I was a teenager in the early eighties, at a time when Murray-bashing was all the rage,' said Owen. 'My dad was a Silverstone stalwart and used to help out the circuit commentators, Peter Scott Russell, Keith Douglas and Ian Titchmarsh, and I used to go along with him. The BBC team were upstairs in the Dunlop Tower and Murray would often pop down and talk to the circuit commentators about things. After Murray had left at one stage, I made some clever quip about Murray's cock-ups – and got a ferocious telling-off from Peter Scott Russell because they all admired

Murray's research and dedication. I went absolutely scarlet and didn't speak for the rest of the day. To make it worse, on the way home my dad told me I deserved it!'

A decade later, while commentating on F1 for Eurosport, Ben Edwards would catch glimpses of Murray at work in some of the open commentary positions used at the time. Prior to that, as a former racing driver and F1 fan, Edwards had been very aware of Walker's presence on the motor sport scene.

'It's not until you go back to old editions of *Autosport* that you remember Murray used to take a lot of stick in the correspondence columns for his gaffes,' said Edwards. 'But, as time went by, he got better, particularly after giving up his advertising job and focusing on commentary.

'I was quite young when I started in TV commentary, and it was really important to me not to make mistakes. I knew Murray could make them and people would laugh and enjoy them. I remember him talking at various dinners, and he would use these as anecdotes about himself. The audience would fall about with laughter, which I thought was brilliant. But I couldn't do that. I knew if I really messed up, I'd be kicking myself for being wrong. I couldn't deal with making mistakes all the time. Of course, I did make mistakes; we all do. But it was so important to me to try and get it right and not go down the Murray route. So that was the thing about Murray as far as I was concerned: he did it in a way that people loved, enjoyed and could celebrate. That was so very impressive to be able to do that.

'I thought the partnership with Martin [Brundle] worked particularly well,' Edwards continued. 'Martin was so good at picking up things in a very gentle way, as in: "Well, actually Murray, I think you'll find . . ." That's when a commentary pairing really works at its best. It was different with James [Hunt] because it was a lot more confrontational. James had the confidence of being a world champion and was very much his own man. I thought James was a brilliant commentator in his own right. But the combination of Murray and Martin had a really good tone to it, particularly when you consider what was going on in that commentary box!

'I saw it many times for myself when working for Eurosport and our booths were alongside each other. Murray had such incredible energy, and you began to understand where the enthusiasm and power that you'd hear through the speakers at home was actually coming from. You'd see him, on his feet, bouncing all over the place. It was incredible to watch.

'One of the things he did brilliantly – and it's something I never quite managed on the same level – was his ability to change the pace. It seemed to come naturally to him. He would sometimes back it right off and slow everything down a little bit – and then ramp back up even though nothing had happened on screen to warrant it. That was really clever. And he would keep talking throughout. You might pause – but Murray never did!'

During this unremitting flow, Murray would be consulting a handwritten information sheet in front of him, and pages of notes stuck to the commentary box walls. This had been part of the Walker routine from his early days with the BBC – a habit he stuck to religiously.

'In the early days of the BBC coverage, there would be no more than eight of us,' said Mark Wilkin. 'Murray always wanted to come with everybody but, on the night before the race, he would eat with the rigger – the guy that drove the truck – and our comms engineer. Because they were involved in the live stuff, they would be finished before we were. They ended up having this dinner every Saturday night with Murray – something which the boys thought was amazing. It worked for Murray because he wanted to have an early night and go through his notes.

'He had various sheets with different numbers, colours and so on. All done meticulously by hand. We had a cameraman who was very familiar with Excel in the days when none of us knew what Excel was. He said to Murray: "Look, I can do this sheet for you. All we'll have to do is put the results in and all the changes to numbers of wins, pole positions, whatever, will happen automatically. It will be really straightforward. And we'll print it, so you won't need to do it by hand. It'll look really nice." And Murray said: "You don't understand. Doing the sheet is how I remember everything that I do. And I know exactly where it all is. I can remember writing these facts and that helps it lodge in my head." That was it. End of discussion. This was Murray's routine when it came to facts and figures. The words, of course, would come from … who knows where! Sometimes you wondered if even Murray knew.'

Murray's vocabulary was a law unto itself, as noted by Damon Hill who gained a degree in English Literature at the Open University after retiring from racing. 'Murray's commentary was a constant source of pleasure – and at times, complete mystery!' he said. 'When he said [during the 1986 Australian Grand Prix] "Colossally, that's Mansell!" – I mean, where the hell did that come from? Another of his expressions was "cutting the atmosphere with a cricket stump". No one else but Murray could have come up with that.

'He was much loved because he provided this other dimension. I think we all understood where his Murrayisms were coming from. If you've never got so excited about something that you've got your words mixed up, then you haven't really lived, have you?

'I've been in the commentary box a few times with good commentators who know what they're doing. They have a wall of notes that would just blow my mind because I wouldn't know where to look in the heat of the moment. I look at a sheet of paper with lots of information on it and my mind just freaks out and freezes. So, I can excuse Murray the occasional slip of the tongue. In fact, I'd have been disappointed if there hadn't been one during any of his commentaries.'

Martin Brundle was witnessing these verbal faux pas at source. 'In moments of excitement – which were many – Murray's tongue was five hundred revs ahead of his brain,' said Brundle. 'The information was pouring out. Yes, he made mistakes, but only through sheer enthusiasm. It wasn't because he didn't care, or he was lazy, or he didn't know. It was just total exuberance. He was commentating on a live, fast-moving and potentially dangerous sport.

'He didn't always have the kind of information we've got available in the commentary box now – which is probably a bit too much, if the truth be known. Back in the day, it was very much as Murray saw it, with a massive top spin of energy, excitement and enthusiasm about the whole thing. He did get ahead of himself at times. But that, in my view, added to the whole Murray Walker experience.'

Steve Rider, who also worked closely with Murray in commentary, agrees with Brundle's assessment. 'Getting stuff wrong – the way he did that – was part of Murray's charm,' said Rider. 'Anywhere else, a commentator who took themselves really seriously and made the odd slip of the tongue, or the odd misjudgement, would be absolutely pilloried. But because everyone understood where Murray was coming from, and where that enthusiasm came from, it was like a different language – and you waited for it with Murray. To be honest, I wasn't too sure about the way it turned into a little bit of an industry towards the end, but it certainly gave him a very special place in the public consciousness.

'As far as the Murrayisms were concerned, he clearly never intended to do them. And I don't think, in a perfect world, he would have done them. But the reason it happened was because he was always on the balls of his feet. He stood up to commentate. He was always a physical man, and the blood would be pumping around the system. When you're on the limit, be it as a racing driver or a commentator, you're going to spin off occasionally. Murray was pent up the whole time. It was incredible to behold.

'There's also no doubt that his extraordinary pace when commentating came from the fact that he felt he had so much to share with the viewers. He was always extremely well prepared. Much of that came from going around and talking to people in the paddock. He would talk to everyone, from a tyre fitter to the truck driver and the Formula 1 driver, and make copious notes.

'He always had that stuff around him in the commentary box. But that's how it works for many commentators. You bring what you feel you need to do the job. I always thought it was a bit like revising for an exam. If you felt you'd covered the bases, then it helped you feel more confident when getting ready to broadcast. The reason Murray made mistakes was because he was completely on the limit; he didn't really leave any margin for error. But that was part of Murray Walker, an extraordinarily gifted commentator.'

Murray never read from a script when broadcasting live. He would have various thoughts in his head beforehand, but they might not end up coming out of his mouth on cue. Mark Wilkin recalled one occasion at Monaco when Murray was caught on the hop when operating on the fly.

'We would be all set to go but *Grandstand* would come over to us whenever they felt like it,' said Wilkin. 'You never knew. It could be ten minutes, eight minutes, five minutes before the race. We were using world feed pictures and whatever the world feed was on, that's what they went to.

'So, Murray's waiting, and waiting. "Stand by, Murray. Twenty seconds, ten seconds, coming to you in five, stand by, stand by – and cue." And just as they said "cue", the world feed cut to three girls sunbathing topless on a yacht. Murray would never have an opening line such as "Welcome to Monaco" written down. He would usually use whatever pictures were on the screen as the starting point. And here he had been immediately presented with three topless ladies. He said later: "I opened my mouth and about ten things went through my head, all of which I had to discard, before I finally came up with something I could use." That's where he was so good. He was brilliant at finding the right tone and the right thing to say in unexpected situations.

'Yes, there were obviously the occasions – now made famous – when he didn't necessarily say the right thing when in full flow. But he would take that in his stride too. There's one example which happened in Belgium one year.

'The commentary boxes at Spa were really narrow; they were like little telephone boxes, and you could just about fit two people shoulder to shoulder. As a matter of routine, I would book two boxes side by side, putting the commentators in one while I would sit in the other with all my kit. It meant there was a spare seat in my box, and Wattie [former Grand Prix driver John Watson] asked if he could join me. I was happy to agree and give him a pair of headphones – the type that had a mic attached – so that he could listen to commentary.

'It's not long before John's going: "Oh, Murray! You idiot. That's not Prost, that's Senna." Or stuff like: "Come on, Murray, he's gonna have to come into the pits now." This continues for most of the race. When it's all over, Murray comes out of the box and says: "I've no idea what happened. But every now and again throughout the race, this voice in my ear was saying: 'Murray, you're an idiot. That's Prost.' I realized he was right and corrected myself." It turns out I'd given Wattie headphones with the switch in the wrong position. Because this was the producer's box, it meant he was live in Murray's ears all the way through. Most commentators would understandably go mental, tear their headset off and demand to know what the effing hell is going on. But Murray said: "It was brilliant. I think I heard this voice say Senna's got to come into the pits – and he did!" That was typical Murray; he just got on with the job and stayed focused throughout despite this random voice in his headset.'

So Murray's Murrayisms were widely accepted, even welcomed, as part and parcel of his much admired work. But the day was not far off when the man himself would feel he had made one mistake too many.

28

LAST LAP

'In 2000, I made an absolutely hideous and unforgivable mistake during commentary in the German Grand Prix,' said Murray. 'Michael Schumacher was on the front row and Rubens Barrichello was eighteenth in the other Ferrari, eight rows further back on the grid. The race started and a Ferrari went off in a cloud of dust at the first corner. My brain wouldn't let me accept that it could be Schumacher who had gone off. I said: "And Barrichello has gone off!" I made a great song and dance about it and then realized it was Schumacher and, somehow, blagged my way out of it.

'The next day there was a really vicious piece in the *Daily Mail* – "Time for the old fool to go", that sort of thing. They reminded readers that I had been doing it since 1949. Sniffing blood, the appropriately named *Daily Mirror* picked up on the theme. I thought: I don't think that's fair, but there's an element of truth there. I got it wrong, and I shouldn't have got it wrong.

'As usually happens, the story died down after a couple of days, but the effect remained with me. I can't say this was the only reason I thought about stopping, but it must have played a part, even if it was subconscious. Much as I absolutely loved what I was doing, I recognized I wasn't getting any younger. The travel to nineteen Grands Prix – as it was then – was demanding. I wanted to follow Jackie Stewart's dictum of going out on top and not be regarded as a nice old chap who has seen better days and sadly doesn't know when to stop.

I'll admit pride was at stake here. I thought it was time to see Brian Barwick and continue a conversation we'd started earlier in the year.'

'Murray had come to me and asked when I thought he should finish,' said Barwick. 'I said: "When you think it's right, or when we think it's right, or when we both think it's right." When he asked who would be the person to tell him that he'd done it long enough, I said that would be me. Nobody else.

'So, he came back and asked if I remembered the earlier chat. I said I did. I also said: "I remember saying it would be me who would tell you you're going – and I'm doing that now, Murray." He got quite tearful and upset and talked about finishing at the end of that year [2000].

'I then said: "Now here's the thing, Murray. You're not going out for another year. You're going to do around 75 per cent of the races in 2001 because I want to try and break in a couple of voices to see if they can do it – because somebody has got to replace you. But you're going to have a lap of honour like nobody has ever had. You're going out in a blaze of glory, Murray. And all those mistakes you make? Forget it. People will say we'll miss him when he goes. The errors will be turned into commentary gold dust."

'I said we'd hold a press conference the following day. I got David Liddiment, who was a director of television at ITV, to join me and Murray. A lot of people turned up and we gave Murray genuine praise for all he'd done. Murray got his head together and said it was the right time and he was flattered that ITV were giving him another year. Although he would be missing a few races, he would be doing all his favourite ones.'

'Murray was always very aware of public criticism,' said Neil Duncanson. 'If, say, he had been thirty years younger and was commentating today, I don't think he would cope well with the nasty side of social media. For the incredibly bright, lovely bloke that he was, he had a very thin skin. That piece in the *Daily Mail* did hurt. He took it to heart, even though we all said to him: "What do they bloody know, Murray?" But no matter what we said, he wasn't having it.

'Brian and I had spoken endlessly about this. Murray was worried that he was going to go downhill, and people would start saying he was past it. In the end, it was ITV's contract and Brian's call. Brian didn't want Murray to sink; he wanted him to go out at the top. So, on balance, stopping was the right thing to do at the right time.

'We gave him a valedictory year. And it was incredible – the longest retirement party in history! Everywhere we went, there were parties, bashes, presentations. It was like travelling around with a rock star. And he loved it. Why would you not?'

'Brian Barwick had made the right decision,' said Murray. 'Brian is a super bloke – the best I ever worked for in television. 2001 was an absolutely magical year for me. At the British Grand Prix, I had the most emotional send-off. The RAF parachute team came down with a bloody great banner which said something like "We're going to miss you". ITV had a Murray Walker poster competition; you had to produce a banner at the Grand Prix, and there were dozens of them. It was absolutely incredible.'

The final race of the 2001 European season was at Monza. Quite a few of the British F1 teams got there with European Aviation, an ad hoc charter airline run by Paul Stoddart, who also owned the Minardi F1 team. Stoddart kept his pair of ex-Dan Air BAC 111s at Bournemouth's Hurn airport, not far from Murray's home. It was typical of Stoddart, and his fondness for Walker, that a car would be sent to pick up Murray and he would have the plane to himself as they flew to Birmingham and collected the rest of the passengers.

Louise Goodman was also a regular flyer with what was known affectionately within F1 as 'Stoddy Air'. 'We had the same crew every time,' she said. 'They knew the return journey from Italy would be

Murray's final flight with Stoddy Air. They put decals down the side
of the plane saying "Murray: Thanks for the memories". That was the
theme on T-shirts we all wore. Murray didn't know any of this and we
were all on the tarmac, forming a guard of honour, waiting for him to
arrive. Stoddy had given party poppers to everyone but, just in the
nick of time, the pilot came rushing out and said not to fire them off
because it wouldn't go down very well on an airfield! [Stoddart was
using a small airport some distance from Milan and capable of handling a BAC 111.]

'It was a typical Stoddy Air flight on the way home. A regular
occurrence on each return flight was that somebody would be selected
to swap clothes with a hostess and serve drinks to everybody. So, of
course, it only seemed right and proper that Murray should be desig-
nated to swap outfits on this trip. Murray being Murray, he fully got
into the spirit of it and had a wonderful time! As did we all. It was
absolutely hilarious.'

A more official send-off would occur at the next race, the United
States Grand Prix, which would be Murray's final television broadcast. As ever, Murray was focused on the job in hand and gave little
thought to having one or two people apologize for being 'unable to
come to the party'.

'I knew something was going on, but I didn't know what it was,'
said Murray. 'On the Friday evening, I was taken to the Paddock Club.
When we got there, I found Tony George [boss of the Indianapolis
Motor Speedway], Flavio Briatore [boss of the Renault F1 team],
Bernie Ecclestone, several drivers, mechanics – an enormous number
of people all standing round drinking champagne. Michael Schumacher was there, so I thought: Well, if whatever's happening is good
enough for Schumacher, it's good enough for me. So I went and sat
beside him.

'When Tony Jardine stood up and began to act as compere, I

realized what this was all about – especially when he started getting the drivers to come up and read from pieces of paper on which were written things I was alleged to have said!

'Then it's Michael's turn. Tony gives him a piece of paper which has on it "The boot is now on the other Schumacher" – which I'd allegedly said at one time! A bemused Michael looks at this piece of paper and says: "I don't understand. What am I supposed to do?" Tony tells him he has to say it like I say it. Michael says: "Yes, but when Murray says it, I'm in the car and I can't hear him." I said: "C'mon, Michael, we'll do it together." I put my arm round him and off we went.

'Michael came up to me afterwards and said: "Can you help me, Murray, because there's something I don't understand. This party is in your honour – but they were all making fun of you!" I said: "Well, I suppose that's our way, Michael." I'm not sure he really got the British sense of humour.

'Bernie would have noted the not-so-subtle use of it when it was Eddie Irvine's turn. I'd never felt as warmly towards Eddie as I had to most British drivers, but I was made to feel rather churlish about that when, as he recalled having to sit in technical meetings at Ferrari and review Grands Prix without commentary, Eddie said: "Jeez, Murray, I never realized how dull some of them would be without your commentary." Then he looked towards Bernie and said: "God, Bernie; we don't put on a good show!"'

Ecclestone did not need to be reminded of Murray's contribution to F1 – as Rupert Bush had discovered when putting together a video on Murray's broadcasting career. 'It was a tribute VT for Murray's retirement, a really long piece that went out on ITV,' he said. 'I needed to source archive material and found some proper gems of Murray in the Beaulieu Motor Museum, and in the BBC archives.

'One of the biggest issues we were always going to have with other archive pieces would be the cost, because Bernie charged a fortune. We would have made many historic pieces if we had been able to afford the archive, but Bernie priced it so high it was completely out of the question. You'd get maybe eight seconds, but if the clip went over, say, ten seconds, it would cost tens of thousands of pounds more.

'On this occasion, I approached him and said we wanted to make a tribute for Murray. Straight away he said all the fees were waived; there was absolutely no hesitation or discussion. That, to me, said everything about Murray and his standing in the F1 world. It was a real labour of love to put together all this incredible stuff.'

It may have been an emotional weekend for Murray, but that was nothing compared to the poignancy surrounding the event itself. The United States Grand Prix on 30 September 2001 was to be the only time in the history of F1 when the occasion was arguably more important than the actual race. This was the first major public gathering in the USA since the 9/11 atrocities nineteen days earlier. It was seen as an important step in America's struggle to return to normality. The mood throughout the race-day crowd was powerful in the sense that it was driven by a steely determination rather than the usual relaxed mayhem of enjoying a day of racing at this cathedral of speed. Formula 1 did not disappoint. Walker and Brundle would have a lively race to commentate on.

'I didn't have a lot of time to think about this being the actual last commentary for Murray,' said Martin. 'I'd done my usual grid walk and it's a very long climb from the track up to the booths high in the grandstand. As I got there, they were throwing to Murray, and we were off.

'When the race was over, he gave a short monologue, during which he thanked me. I just put my hand round his shoulder and said: "Thank you, Murray." Now, with a lot more experience, I would have had two or three sentences ready to thank him.

'When we did a feature remembering Murray in 2021, I looked at that clip and thought about what I should have done. Murray was talking to his public, to his following. He was announcing the end of the road. I was watching him come up with those words and I should have interjected and thanked him on behalf of Formula 1 and the public. It annoys me that I didn't do that. But, at the time, I thought this was Murray Walker speaking to the nations that took our broadcast. Shut up, Martin. Let him get on with it and say what he needs to say.'

This is what Murray Walker needed to say for one last time:

'*I'm a happy, smiling man because what I wanted above all else, after fifty-two years of talking about Grand Prix racing, was to go out on a high note and be euphoric about the fact that we'd just seen a great race. We've just seen a great race, in a great country, and, hopefully, it will have done something to lift the spirits of America. It's certainly lifted mine. It certainly lifted the spirits of Formula 1. And Martin, as ever, it was a joy to be working with you.*

'*So, that's it then, folks. Um, that's the last from me. All I can say is, it always has been a pleasure, and I hope you will enjoy Grand Prix racing from now on.*' There is a discernible crack in his voice before he softly adds: '*Goodbye.*'

29

PENSION POT

' was at a lunch for my wife's golf club, sitting next to a very grumpy bloke, trying to make conversation,' said Murray. 'I said: "What do you do?" He said: "I've retired, haven't I." He said he was the chairman of the Livestock Marketing Committee. "Do you miss it?" I asked. "Miss it?" he spluttered. "Of course I bloody miss it!"

'I thought: I'm not doing very well here. Never mind, press on. So I said: "What do you miss?" He said: "I miss the power. When I walked in it was 'Good morning, Mr Smith. Would you like two sugars in your coffee or one?'" So, when I asked what he did now, he said: "I hoover the house for the bloody wife!" And I thought: How pathetic. I bet you were a lousy boss too.

'People ask me if I miss it. Like that bloke, of course I bloody miss it! How else are you going to feel when you are suddenly cut adrift from something that has been the central focus of your life? If you have led a busy, interesting and stimulating life and if you've been − not that I was − a captain of industry and used to making decisions and leading people, and all of a sudden you stop because you're sixty − not for any other reason − and you are still healthy and mentally alert, then it's an absolute killer. Literally. I've seen people die through sheer boredom. I was determined that was not going to happen to me at seventy-eight.

'I'm as busy as I want to be,' he continued. 'I do stuff for the BBC F1 website; stuff for Radio 5 Live; a column in *F1 Racing* magazine;

make after-dinner speeches and give talks on cruise ships. That's the good thing. Well, they're all good, but cruising is the particularly pleasant bit.'

We were speaking over lunch at the Beaulieu Hotel in April 2013, twelve years after his retirement. Murray was as fresh-faced and spritely as ever, still flushed by the success of an autobiography that sold 560,000 copies – a truly outstanding success by any standard.

'When I stopped commentating – I don't want this to sound bigheaded – I had eight publishers come to me and say they wanted to do it,' said Murray. 'I talked to all of them and the first thing I had to decide was whether I was going to do the deal or get an agent to do the deal. I thought: If the agent does the deal, I'll have to give 20 per cent of it to him. I don't know if he will be able to do a better deal than me – but I'll try. Basically, all I had to do was to say "No" until there was just one publisher left.

'The next decision was, do I write it, or do I have a ghost-writer. I decided to have a go myself. They told me how many words – I can't remember how many, but I do remember nearly falling over at the thought of having to write that many. It can be a daunting prospect. But once I got going, it seemed to flow OK.

'One of the chapters was on my time in the Army and I wrote twenty thousand words and I sent it off to the editor; I used to send it a chapter at a time. I called and asked if it was OK and he said: "Yes, Murray, it's fine. It's a bit long." "Oh. Do you want me to cut it down a little?" "Yes, Murray, that would be good. Sharpen it up." I said: "OK. How much would you like to cut out?" "About half of it," he said. He wasn't joking, unfortunately. That's very difficult. But it's a great way to learn to be economical with words. You have to learn to do a lot of editing and adjusting. It took me about a year to do the whole book – and it went very well. I was amazed. I didn't think for one moment that people were going to be that interested in it.'

Murray had always enjoyed cruising – particularly if the cruise line paid him to go in return for entertaining the passengers with tales of his varied and interesting life.

'I don't do as many cruises as I used to,' said Murray. 'There are people now – can you believe it? – who have never heard of Ayrton Senna. Well, the same applies to me in a different and much less important way. I stopped at the end of 2001, which means it's twelve years since I did television commentary. So, for anyone to have heard me, remember what I've said and have any opinion on what I was like, they have got to have been at least ten years old in 2001. That means to say that anyone below twenty-four now will be asking: "Murray who?" Fortunately, there are people around older than that, of course, but my point is that time is continuously marching on.

'The topic I'd choose depends on the audience. If you're doing something for Cunard, for instance, and it's a long voyage, they'll want three talks. I'll do one which I call "A funny thing happened to me on my way to the race track", which is largely anecdotal. If you're doing a talk to people in these conditions, it doesn't matter whether you are a nuclear scientist or a Belgian carpenter or an F1 commentator, they don't really want to talk about whether or not we should have the atom bomb or whether one carpentry joint is better than another, they want you to make them laugh. And because you are a nuclear physicist, doesn't mean you are also a stand-up comedian.

'Over time, you find out what makes people laugh, and I have a speech that I know from experience is relevant to what I'm talking about, but makes people laugh. So, if you're talking to the United Glassblowers of Sheffield, you'll start it one way, and if you're talking to the Bideford Ford dealers, you'll start it another way and probably finish it differently. But the central part of the speech is the same.

'Then I have illustrated talks on subjects such as the Monaco Grand Prix. For years, I've done talks on cruise ships visiting the

Monaco Grand Prix, so you want to refer to that race. And in that case it's illustrated. And a third topic is on great drivers, talking about the people you know and the time Senna kept you waiting for four hours, things like that.

'People are very sniffy about cruises. But when you think about it, if you go on a holiday in Sardinia or somewhere, you virtually mooch about the hotel for a fortnight. If you are on a decent ship, you have good food, good accommodation, lots of things to do on the ship – shows, gym, cinema and so on – and you're in a hotel that goes to places. And you don't have to get off and look at Venice or wherever if you don't want to. So, to have all that – and have, in my case, some-one pay for it – seems to make a lot of sense to me!'

Murray could never be accused of failing to have an appreciation of his own value. If he had not been a commentator, he would have made a shrewd financier. Some of his former colleagues would argue that he always was the latter. Estimates of the book deal Murray negotiated vary between £850,000 and £1 million – either way, an advance that was colossal and incredible, as Murray might have said. The cost of securing his services for the day could range between £10,000 and £13,000 – a tidy sum for an eighty-four-year-old when adding up five days, multiplied by ten European Grands Prix, as Murray did when acting as ambassador for the Honda F1 team in 2008.

'He wasn't slow in coming forward when negotiating the fine detail of his contracts,' recalled Steve Rider. 'When we were doing the dubbing for the BTCC commentary, we had to swallow the bill for his choice of a very smart hotel for the overnight stay. On one occasion, Murray had done his dub and the sound assistant went into the booth to clear up. Murray wrote everything longhand on scraps of paper. The assistant turned a couple of pieces of paper over, and found Murray had written his entire script on the back of share dealing certificates.'

'Murray was always his own agent,' said Mark Wilkin. 'He knew exactly what was going on when it came to payments. But I think he fell slightly foul of his lack of an agent when it came to negotiating his overseas rights. The BBC used to hold UK rights. If other broadcasters wanted to buy the feed – this was in the 1980s; the situation changed after that – they had to negotiate with the commentators directly. When James [Hunt] started with us, he had a huge anti-apartheid stance and hated South Africa in lots of ways. He said there was absolutely no way he was going to do the commentary for South Africa unless they paid him £5,000 a race. This was his way of saying "No" because he thought there was no way in the world they'd pay. But they called his bluff. So, for five grand, James was prepared to put aside his apartheid views. Of course, he told Murray straight away. Murray had sold his rights for something like £200. He was absolutely livid!'

Being of a certain age and having lived through rationing and the financial restrictions that came with the war years in the 1940s, Murray clearly believed in the adage 'Look after the pennies and the pounds will look after themselves'.

'We were doing a shoot in Barcelona,' recalled Rupert Bush. 'It was quite busy, and we had to go through several motorway tolls to get to five or six different locations. The producer always pays, but for some reason I didn't have any cash on me. So I had to ask Murray if he wouldn't mind paying the tolls; they were only a couple of euros each time. He agreed to do this. When we got back to the hotel that evening, he gave me a sheet and said: "That's six euros seventy you owe me, Rupert. D'you want to give it to me now?" Everything had been written down meticulously on this sheet of paper, every single cent carefully recorded. I went straight to my room to get the cash – and I have to admit I was chuckling as I went.'

'I don't remember contract negotiations with Murray being very tough,' recalled Jonathan Martin. 'He knew he was working for the

BBC, we had a price, and that was it. I think he respected our relationship in the sense that [as head of BBC Sport] I would do what I
thought was fair.

'My view was that you don't have successful commentators if you
make them unhappy or resentful. I'm not saying every negotiation
ended up with them walking out with smiles on their faces, but I never
thought it was my job to screw commentators down to the ground
simply because quite a few of them didn't have anywhere else to go.

'One of the advantages of working for the BBC was that they had
status and earning ability elsewhere. I used to have a "Pillow Slips
Rule", the gist of which was you can advertise anything like a pillow
slip. But Murray, you can't advertise tyres. And Peter [Alliss], you can't
advertise golf clubs. You can't advertise anything that's related to how
you earn your living with the Beeb. That worked well. But I never did
see anyone advertise a pillow slip ...'

In Murray's case, being careful with money did not automatically
mean frugality in all things, as Roger Moody discovered during their
time together. 'As a producer, you get used to putting your hand in
your pocket – it comes with the territory,' he said. 'On one occasion,
we were at Hockenheim for the German Grand Prix. The race had
finished and we were back at our hotel in Mannheim. Murray was
returning home that night; I was staying on to Monday morning. I
suddenly realized I was out of cash. I suppose I had a credit card –
maybe I didn't in those days – but, whatever the case, I had to ask
Murray if there was any chance of lending me a few quid to tide me
over and I'd pay him back in the office next week. "Oh no," he said.
"No, no. I need this for a taxi at the other end." That was the end of
that particular discussion. I took him to Frankfurt airport and, when I
got back to the hotel, I threw the few coins I had on the bed. I had
just enough to get a burger, with nothing left for breakfast. So, yes,
Murray could be quite careful!

'On the other hand, a few years later, I moved up to management and, to all intents and purposes, I stopped being producer of *Grand Prix*. I threw a little early evening supper party at the Hilton Hotel in Shepherd's Bush. The *Grand Prix* production team was there, and Murray came along. He suddenly stood up, made a lovely little speech – which was a bit emotional, actually – and then he said: "I'd like to present you with this." It was a set of cut-glass tumblers. It was very generous. I still have these tumblers. Whenever I have a drop of Scotch, I always think of Murray and raise my glass to him.

'He was a bit of a contradiction in some ways. Yes, he was careful with his cash. But his generosity in helping people and imparting knowledge was second to none. In all the time I worked with Murray, I don't ever remember him losing his temper – and we did have some very stressful moments. I was a rank amateur compared to his vast experience in motor sport and yet his patience with me and others was unlimited. When it came to his time and his knowledge, and giving encouragement, there was no one more generous. And that's what really mattered to everyone who was fortunate enough to meet and work with such a lovely man.'

30

PUBLIC PERSONA

Murray did not attend the 2013 British Grand Prix at Silverstone. Missing an event that had been central to his life for more than sixty years was not through choice. The news had broken a few weeks before that Murray had been diagnosed with a form of lymphatic cancer – and he considered himself fortunate.

'I fell over on holiday in Germany and fractured my pelvis, which I thought was pretty rotten luck,' said Murray. 'But if it had not been for that, I would not have had all the blood tests and they would not have found out about the cancer. It was a blessing in disguise. They've caught it incredibly early. It's treatable and doctors say my condition is mild. I was really looking forward to going to Silverstone as usual, but I've really got to concentrate on getting the chemicals inside me, getting over it and getting back into form as quickly as I can.'

This being his ninetieth year seemed an irrelevance as Murray made a strong recovery. He met the disease head-on, as he had promised to do when we discussed the potential setback during its early stages. 'I don't want to hide from this; it's nothing to be ashamed of,' said Murray. When I asked if he would like me to post something on social media, asserting his genuine hopes for a positive outcome, he was happy to agree.

I wrote a brief tweet. The response was stunning. For the next twenty-four hours, the flow of messages and comments seemed never-ending, the outpouring of love and concern overwhelming. When I called Murray to explain what had happened, he sounded mystified, not just by the effect of social media, but that so many people should care so much. For anyone who had worked with Murray in the past, this would have been no surprise.

'He never seemed to realize his place in everyone's hearts and minds,' said Mark Wilkin. 'Traditionally, on the night before we left the UK for a race, Murray would come up from Hampshire and stay in a hotel at Heathrow overnight. It worked well because I would be driving past the hotel in the morning on my way to the airport. So, I'd always stop and pick him up.

'As he gets in the car, you'd say: "How are you? Did you have a good night?" "Oh, it was marvellous," he'd reply. "I got in and I went to dinner as usual. And, do you know, I was sitting on my own and this lovely couple at the next table, John and Wendy, said: 'Oh, Murray, are you eating on your own? Please do come and join us.'" There was a sort of incredulous tone to the way he said it – as if had I been sitting there on my own, John and Wendy would have invited me over as well because they were charming people being nice. People would have paid £1,000 to have dinner with Murray Walker! He never really understood that; he never, in his lovely way, fully grasped the effect he had on people.'

When Andy Parr joined the BBC F1 team as cameraman, his initial experience of Murray's widespread popularity may have been in glamorous surroundings, but the effect was to be the same wherever they went.

'My first race was Monaco,' said Parr. 'We were staying in the Balmoral Hotel and, on the first night, we went out for dinner. There were just four or five of us, including Murray of course. We started walking up the street; I've absolutely no idea whereabouts in Monaco we are, so I'm just following along. About 100 yards later, we suddenly step into Casino Square. My mind's blown by this. But Murray – who has seen it all before, of course – is just chatting away, reciting anecdotes about watching Ayrton Senna doing this and Alain Prost doing that. I'm looking at surroundings that are instantly familiar from the television pictures I've seen in the past. And Murray is standing there, telling me all this stuff. I can feel it now, the hairs on the back of my neck standing up.

'We walked down the hill, dropped in for an expensive beer at the famous Tip Top bar, and then carried on down the hill, round the hairpin and into an Italian restaurant. And all the way, you couldn't help but notice that people – loads of people – recognized Murray and wanted to have a chat. It was incessant, but he was unfailingly polite and interested in people, and took the time to talk to everybody. At the track it might be different because he had a job to do and had to get from A to B. I would often keep him company when walking back from the TV compound to the paddock. He quite liked to have someone to chat with him.

'He was always interested in the people he was with. He would remember things. He would remember the football team you supported and would ask how they were getting on even though he wasn't necessarily a football fan. That was part of his technique when talking to people. He was always very democratic; nobody was ever left out of a conversation.'

James Allen would be very impressed by Murray's sense of recall, going back more years than most people would care to remember. 'My eldest son went to Highgate, which was the same school Murray attended,' he said. 'It was the school's 450th anniversary and they asked if I could approach Murray and see if he would be willing to speak at a commemorative dinner. I said I'd ask, but I couldn't be sure because, you know, he was into his nineties then and it might be a bit much. They had a two-hundred-seat theatre and I suggested it might be better having "An Evening with Murray Walker"; that might be a better context for him. I also knew that Christian Horner [team principal at

Red Bull] lived nearby, so I said I would ask Christian if he could come and help lighten the load a little on Murray.

'Murray agreed, and Christian was fantastic, saying he would do anything for Murray. Not only that, but he arranged to have a Red Bull show car present. Everyone was super-excited and the tickets sold out almost immediately.

'Murray arrived, immaculately turned out as ever, with his BRDC tie and so on. The school regularly sent a magazine to the alumni, so Murray had been reading it over the years and was bang up to date with everything that had been going on. Everyone was delighted to see him and they showed him around.

'Murray was on a stick, still recovering from a hip injury, but he was absolutely brilliant. I'd asked the school if they could look out some pictures from when Murray was at the school during the 1930s. They produced black and white photos of him, and you could tell it was Murray – a thirteen-year-old version wearing the sort of round-rimmed spectacles they had in the 1930s.

'They put a picture of his class up on the screen behind us. We were sitting in armchairs. Murray turned himself around in his chair, took one look, got out of his seat and, with his stick, started pointing at each of the boys in turn. "Jones – Simpkins – Fotheringham – Thompson . . ." He remembered every single name in the photo. Unbelievable. And then he came to a pupil who had what sounded like a Hungarian name. Murray said: "And this fella here, Spezlasoss, on the first night in the dormitory, he went to bed wearing a hairnet. As you can imagine," he went on, "he got a bit of a pasting!" Brought the house down. He was absolutely in his element. For someone in his nineties, it was remarkable.'

Murray's sense of recall was put to good use when he went on those reflective journeys in Europe with Nick Goozée, the former Penske Racing manager. 'Wherever we went, we obviously met people that recognized him,' Goozée said. 'And he always, always found time to speak to them. He would get some ridiculous questions, but he would always handle them as if the person he was talking to was very important, and the answer he was giving was very important because he knew that person would remember, for the rest of his or her life, this brief conversation that they had with Murray Walker.

'At one stage, while going between the battlefields in the Somme, we were looking for a cup of coffee. We drove past one site with plastic chairs outside. It looked a likely place, so I told Murray to sit tight and I'd go and enquire. I walked up, and it was a husband and wife who were looking after what was known as the Irish Tower, which is where many Irish soldiers had been killed in battle. They had this little coffee shop. Nobody else was in there.

'I went back and got Murray. As soon as we walked in and the lady saw him, she said: "Ah, you're Murray Walker. Please stay there." She rushed off and brought her husband in. He had been a competitor in one of the minor TT races that Murray had commentated on. That made their day – and Murray's.

'We drove on a few miles and noticed there was an excavation taking place. We got out of the car and wandered across. It was an excavation of a German dugout, which was almost totally intact. As we were peering down at this, one of the excavators looked up and immediately said: "Are you Murray Walker? Oh! Come on down and have a look." So, whereas we would have ordinarily been ignored or dismissed, we were invited in and shown the dugout. And, of course, given Murray's military background, he was fascinated by all this.

'Those are just two very small examples of situations that happened on many occasions when we were together. As soon as anybody recognized Murray, they wanted to invite him into their little world. Interestingly, those examples cover his two very different backgrounds in the military and with bikes. There was never any doubt that motorcycle racing meant a great deal to him.'

31

GIRLS AND BIKES

Murray's study represented an automotive Aladdin's Cave, with a wide variety of memorabilia mixed with art and photographs, the room dominated by an enormous padded chair in bright blue. In pride of place above the fireplace, a dramatic drawing in charcoal depicted Graham Walker on his Rudge chasing Charlie Dodson's Sunbeam during their epic duel in the 1928 Isle of Man TT. This work by Gordon Crosby, one of the leading artists of the day, served as a reminder of not only Murray's revered father but also the love they shared for motorcycles.

'Although I will forever be connected with Formula 1,' said Murray, 'I have always had a love for bikes. Much of that stems from my father, of course, but I have to admit that probably the most exciting and mentally rewarding time I ever had was when Mike Hailwood was racing. In my view, and the view of many, many others, he was a one-off like there's never been before – with the possible exception of Valentino Rossi. Mike was a lovely bloke. He was totally laid-back. He didn't care about anything very much; he was the ultimate party animal. But he rode a motorcycle like a genius. And he won many TTs. Undoubtedly, the most exciting race I have ever seen in my entire life was the 1967 Senior TT when Mike Hailwood and Giacomo Agostini were battling for supremacy on their Honda and MV bikes respectively. It was an absolutely fantastic race.

'I started racing bikes, probably because I thought my father would want me to rather than because I passionately wanted to. I raced against the young John Surtees – well, I used to watch him disappear into the distance, and saw him again when he lapped me – and the pinnacle of my achievement was winning a 250cc heat on the old anti-clockwise grass track at Brands [Hatch]. I realized racing wasn't for me, so I switched to trials, and did rather better. So, fundamentally, I was the chap who did all the motorcycle stuff. I had the great privilege of living through and talking about a golden era of bikes and the men who rode them.

'There were so many characters. Barry Sheene was another in the Hailwood image, a lovable cockney rogue but also extremely bright. He spoke fluent Spanish; he spoke Japanese; an extremely good self-taught engineer. Everybody liked Barry, and Barry liked everybody. In live interviews he'd say the most outrageous things and get away with it, when anybody else would have given grave offence. I consider myself extremely fortunate to have been a part of this era.'

Murray's passion for motorcycle racing had not been lost on Suzi Perry, the British presenter of motorcycle racing, specifically MotoGP – and later Formula 1 – on various TV channels. When Perry began her journalistic career in print, she needed very little excuse to interview her hero.

'I was writing for a bike magazine,' said Suzi. 'I had my own page which allowed me to go and interview anybody vaguely related to bikes. Murray was obviously going to be one of my subjects. I couldn't wait.

'I arranged to meet him at his home in Hampshire. There's quite a big step up and into the house. I rang the bell, Elizabeth opened the door, looked down at me, shouted for Murray, and then disappeared. I think I was twenty-seven at the time and I was so excited about meeting my hero. I didn't want to trip over my words; I was rehearsing my lines.

'Murray came to the door, looked down on me, and these were his exact words: "What's a girl doing talking about bikes?"

'I was flabbergasted. It took the wind right out of my sails. Thinking as quickly as I could, I said: "Well, if you let me in, I'll show you."

'He let me in. I went into his office – the most beautiful office in the world, I thought, with all its memorabilia and paintings and books. I sat down with him and said: "Let me answer your question." I just talked about my passion for bikes. Within five minutes we were chatting. I spent two hours there and walked out as if I was his best friend. That was the start of a relationship in which I would come to look upon Murray as a grandfather and a very best friend.

'I wrote the article – I never mentioned the awkward start – and talked of his love of bikes and how dedicated he was to bike racing at that time, which was the era of Mick Doohan [five-time 500cc world champion 1994–98]. Very soon after the magazine was published, I received a beautifully written letter. It was the most incredible apology from Murray – which actually might make me cry now when I talk about it. He wrote: "You are so gracious. I really loved the article you wrote, I think you have some big days ahead of you. It was wonderful to meet you."

'Ever since then, I was always in love with Murray. I did so much work with him; I interviewed him a lot during my MotoGP days. I always thought of him as being an extremely good friend; someone I could pick up the phone to, someone I could email. The first few words we'd had together were long forgotten. It was like they'd never happened.'

Perry's initial startling encounter on the Walker doorstep would have been no surprise to Louise Goodman. While working with Murray, ITV's pit lane reporter had to come to terms with an attitude that was born of a different generation and meant no offence.

'Murray would sometimes come out with stuff because he was old school,' said Louise. 'A classic example occurred at the British Grand Prix one year. As happened a lot when it came to his home race, Murray had been the subject of a big spread in one of the national newspapers. In it, he said – and I'm paraphrasing here – "The pit lane is no place for women". I took it in the same way that a teenager today would listen to some of the things I might say and think: Oh, bloody hell, she's a bit old-fashioned! I knew Murray's comment hadn't come from a bad place. But there it was, in black and white: the pit lane is no place for women.

'I said to Murray: "Nice piece in the *Mail on Sunday*" – or whatever paper it was. "Oh, thank you, dear. Thank you," he said. "But this little bit here, Murray, where you say the Formula 1 pit lane isn't a place for women . . ." "Yes, dear. Well, it's not really, is it?" "Murray! *I'm* a woman." "Oh, no! No! I didn't mean *you*, dear! Goodness, no!"

'He would have been absolutely mortified if he actually thought he had done something to offend me. He was simply of a different generation and, obviously, some of those attitudes are looked upon differently by my generation. He probably thought women shouldn't be working full stop! His face when I said "*I'm* a woman" was an absolute picture.'

Suzi Perry would see an expression of a different kind when she set up an intriguing interview at a British round of MotoGP.

'I knew Murray liked coming to the British Grand Prix,' said Suzi. 'I suggested it would be great if he interviewed Valentino [Rossi] and get the two generations talking about racing in their different eras. We did that, and the interview was brilliant; it was magical. Valentino was hanging on every word. He knew exactly who Murray was. He didn't need to be briefed; he was very excited. And, of course, Murray was obsessed with Valentino. So, you had this really intense, respectful and interesting conversation that was wonderful to watch.

'When I left MotoGP at the end of 2009 [due to illness], *Motorcycle*

News did a big front-page spread on me – it must have been a slow news day – and there were interviews and comments inside. Murray had written them a letter, saying why he thought it was bad for the sport that I would no longer be there. It was so kind and caring. He went out of his way to support me.

'When I got a job in Formula 1 [in 2013], he was the first to call, asking if I needed any help. We did some filming with him at one stage. He turned up with a thick book of notes. He would have been ninety, and he had more energy than me by a million miles. The job was to sit and talk about races and what was happening at the time from his point of view. He hadn't broadcast for a long time. But you could see that it ignited his whole being to talk about racing again; to just be there and be a part of it. It seemed as if he really resumed part of his old life during that show.

'At one point he had been asking me about social media. I was trying to explain about Twitter, Instagram and so on. He was fascinated but he obviously didn't really understand it and didn't want to get involved in anything. I suggested I did a tweet about him. We did a recording with him saying: "Four lights, five lights . . . It's go, go, go!" I put that up – and Twitter just melted; went absolutely berserk. "There you are, Murray," I said. "Everybody loves you; they really do." He looked on and shook his head in complete and utter disbelief. And then that smile broke out.'

Murray's passion for motorcycle racing in general, and the Isle of Man TT in particular, would prompt an immediate call to Neil Duncanson when Murray heard about the producer's latest plans.

'We got the contract to produce the TT,' said Duncanson. 'It didn't take long for the call to come through from Murray! His words were: "This is the most wonderful thing!" He was even more excited than we were because he was such a huge bike fan. In a quiet moment, he would confide that he thought bike races were way better than

Formula 1 races, and bike racing in general was far better than Formula 1. For Murray, the TT was the absolute pinnacle.

'Each year when we were on the Isle of Man, he would come and see us. He just loved it. For him, it was like being in a theme park. And everyone wanted a piece of him. Just as we had found in F1, it was like being with Bono – but in this incredible place. He would reminisce a lot and tell these amazing stories. He remembered sitting on his dad's bike outside one of the hotels on the seafront after winning the TT in the thirties.

'One occasion I'll never forget occurred when we did an interview with him at a statue in memory of Steve Hislop [eleven-time winner of the TT, killed in a helicopter crash in 2003]. The memorial overlooks the bay at Douglas. It was a beautiful day – clear sky, blue sea; absolutely wonderful. While we were there, he got quite emotional, became quite teary. When I asked what had triggered this, he said: "Oh, just remembering Mum and Dad. I remember them having a row while driving down there" – and he pointed towards Douglas. He continued: "My dad wanted to move here. And my mother didn't. I remember sitting in the back of the car, driving along the front down there, with them rowing and my mother telling my father: 'It's all very well, you wanting to move here when you're here two weeks and you are a hero winning races. But what are you going to do for the other fifty weeks of the year?' Of course," Murray went on, "there were no aeroplanes in those days, only the Liverpool ferry. My mother won the day and we never moved."

'He was quite wistful for a minute or two. I got the impression that, looking back on it, he wished that maybe they could have moved to the island because, in his head as a kid, he thought every day was like TT Day. He absolutely adored it.'

32

QUIET RETREAT

Murray had been a proud member of the Royal Automobile Club (RAC) and its private club, as had his father before him. Located in London's Pall Mall and known affectionately as 'The Parliament House of Motordom' when opened in 1911, the imposing clubhouse offered Murray an old world charm – starting at the front door with the gentle reminder that gentlemen must wear 'a collared shirt – tucked in'. The grand rooms inside, with their lofty ceilings, mahogany and brass accoutrements, bore names such as St James, Mountbatten and Segrave, indicating historic, imperial and motoring affiliations. A refurbishment programme over the years covered the major rooms, leaving just a smaller one housing a television for the use of members and guests.

'It was difficult to decide just what to do with this room,' said Tom Purves, vice-president of the Royal Automobile Club. 'Murray Walker is a wonderful individual and a real gentleman. Actually, he personifies everything that's good about this club. We decided – if he agreed – to call it the Murray Walker Television Room.'

Murray had no hesitation in agreeing.

'I find it very difficult to find the words to say how humble and how delighted and how proud I am,' he said. 'I'm very conscious of the Segrave Room and how it carries the name of someone significant from motor racing [Sir Henry Segrave held world land speed and water speed records and was the first Briton to win a Grand Prix in

1923]. To somehow be associated with the club in this way, to have my name on this room, with some of my memorabilia and my name on the sill plate as you go in the door, is beyond my wildest hopes and dreams. I'm very, very proud indeed.'

In a small and informal ceremony in July 2019, Murray cut a tape in the room before adjourning for dinner with a group of colleagues and friends including Bernie Ecclestone, Martin Brundle, Jonathan Martin, Derek Warwick, Simon Taylor and Sir Jackie Stewart.

'I was terribly chuffed to be invited,' said Simon Taylor. 'I was asked to introduce the dinner and, after we'd eaten, go round the table and have each of the guests say a few words about Murray. Martin Brundle is the most brilliant speaker: he was charming and delightful, quite humble when he said that anything that he knew as a commentator, he had learned from Murray.

'Derek Warwick said the thing about Murray was that if you were a driver in the paddock, you trusted him. You knew that he was an honest, honourable man, to the extent that, if you told him something was private and off the record, Murray respected that. Derek said there were very few people in the media he could say that about.

'Jonathan Martin told some funny stories about Murray working with James Hunt. When I asked Bernie what he thought, he said: "All of us have been involved in Formula 1 for quite a long time and Murray was a very important part of that. But I don't believe Formula 1 would have been as successful as it is without Murray Walker."

'Once I had been round the table, I handed over to Murray. He rounded off a brilliant evening with the perfectly balanced, sincere and funny speech we had all come to expect over the years.'

'Apart from doing a small piece with him on Sky, that was the last time I saw Murray,' said Brundle. 'They made a really nice job of what had been a pretty dingy room that no one bothered with. It was a fascinating dinner, only about a dozen of us around the table. I sat opposite Murray and Bernie. Murray may have been on a stick but you could see that, while Bernie may have had the mobility, Murray's mind was sharper. He stood up and addressed us all with an impromptu speech of about fifteen minutes. He included everybody around the table, without repetition and in a really entertaining way. Straight off the top of his head – boom! So impressive.'

'It was a lovely occasion,' said Jonathan Martin. 'We stayed in the club that night. The next morning at breakfast, Murray and Elizabeth came and sat with us. I reflect on that now, because it was the last time I would ever see him. And I miss him. Obviously I knew lots of BBC commentators but Murray was the one I used to ring – I wouldn't say regularly, but every two or three months. He remained as sharp as ever. And the thing is, that voice did not change, even in his last years. It was the voice of Murray Walker. Unmistakable.'

Jonathan Legard was one of the last journalists to formally inter-view Murray, in 2019, continuing a relationship that had flourished when Legard had become F1 commentator for BBC Radio 5 Live in 1997 and, twelve years later, when he moved on to BBC Television as lead F1 commentator.

'In 1995,' said Legard, 'I went to the Monaco Grand Prix to inter-view Murray about James Hunt and Nigel Mansell for a series on British champions for BBC 5 Live. I'd never met him before, but he was magnificent in his hospitality and his concern for me. He gave me almost an hour of his time – and time on a Thursday afternoon is really precious because getting around the paddock to see people at Monaco is challenging. He didn't just answer my questions, he wanted to make sure I could find my way around and get to where I needed to be. He was like a concerned uncle.

'He was seventy-one at the time. So, this was when most people are slowing down. His energy wasn't just in the commentary, it was also within him. The thing that struck me as much as the voice, was his eyes: they were alive. There was that sparkle; that sense of fun; and the slightly crooked smile. He was just so alert all the time.

'When I moved into commentary on radio and later television, he was always someone I felt I could talk to. It's not that he gave instructions, nothing like that. It was gentle advice and words of encouragement. He was always so positive, so accessible, so approachable. You felt a positive charge whenever you saw him.

'The last time I met Murray was in August 2019,' Legard continued. 'We wanted to do a piece on Niki Lauda [who had died in May 2019]. I rang and asked if I could come down for a chat and he agreed straight away. We did about forty-five minutes; even aged ninety-five, his conversation could flow. He was so happy to talk.

'When we finished the interview and I was preparing to leave, he and Elizabeth invited me to lunch in the local pub. We talked about a whole host of subjects, their lives together, and so on. Nothing about F1. The time just flew by. Murray was fragile by then. We said goodbye and Elizabeth drove them back. On the journey home, I remember thinking just how lucky I'd been. It had been a magical couple of hours.'

In early 2020, Elizabeth became ill and they moved into a care home.

'In the last few months, I was communicating with Murray; we'd probably swap an email once a month on various topics, and so on,' said Steve Rider. 'Suddenly, in December 2020, the emails started coming back from Elizabeth. "Murray's fine and sends his regards." I began to think that didn't sound good.

'You had to say that it was Anno Domini, time marches on. It was the same with Peter Alliss [who passed away in December 2020]. I always bracketed them together because I had probably spent as much time with Peter as I did with Murray. Peter would always ask after Murray because I think he admired a different style of commentary and the demands of having to call coverage when the camera shot changed about every twelve seconds and the storyline changed about every thirty seconds in F1. Whereas Peter had the luxury of being able to spin yarns over long, lingering shots. They were different kinds of characters, and yet, in many ways, very similar: both were absolutely devoted to their sport and both were the greatest communicators of not just stats, facts and technology, but the very spirit of their sport.'

'The last time Murray and I were together was in March 2020,' said Nick Goozée. 'It was not long before he and Elizabeth moved into the home. I was due to go and see him but lockdown started that week. That was it; I was never able to see him again. But we spoke every week.

'This is just my personal view, but I think he was a little bit sad. In motor sport, unfortunately, when you're finished, you're finished. Of course, people will have memories, but the world moves on very quickly. Because Murray was so embedded in it, there was – and he never actually said as much, but you got the impression – a huge hole in his life because he couldn't be active. He'd had his time and was quietly saddened by the fact that he couldn't be as deeply involved as he always wanted to be.

'That probably explains why, at the end of his life, he wanted to disappear in complete obscurity. He didn't want any form of fuss or ceremony for his funeral; he didn't want anybody to know where he would be buried. He was totally strict about that.'

In marked contrast to the extraordinary frenetic and global life he had lived, Murray Walker died peacefully in rural Hampshire on 13 March 2021, at the age of ninety-seven.

33

ONE LAST SHOUT

Murray Walker's company at the races was like being with your favourite uncle. The paddock seemed to be complete when he appeared, this stocky figure with everlasting enthusiasm and an ever-ready smile. For Murray, no part of F1 was dull, no matter how humdrum it may have appeared to the rest of us.

There was an occasion at one Grand Prix when a team press officer asked for our help. A new sponsor had come on board and wished to make his presence known to the media. He represented a particularly dull product – something to do with a brake pad material that could apparently survive on the surface of the sun, or some such. Our PR colleague accepted he was asking a big favour to have us stop by for coffee during a busy time following free practice. But since our media relations friend was well liked and always helpful, it was readily agreed that working in the F1 paddock was a two-way street. At the appointed hour, the press officer was to be as grateful as his sponsor was impressed by a room full of journalists and broadcasters apparently keen to learn more about the coefficient of friction – whatever that was.

Clearly enthused by the size of his audience, the sponsor seized the moment and launched into a technical discourse that had lost most of us after the first sentence. Twenty minutes or so later we emerged, thankful that at least the coffee and cookies had been palatable.

As we stepped outside and attempted to clear our heads, Murray suddenly piped up: 'Well, incredible! Wasn't that jolly interesting?' And he meant every word, as witnessed by copious notes in his usual neat handwriting. You could only applaud and respect such remarkable diligence and fervour.

Despite his vast experience and global reputation, Murray Walker, as has been noted countless times in the preceding pages, remained self-effacing and relentlessly professional. As a summarizer on F1 for BBC Radio 5 Live in 2007, I was to discover this at first hand when Murray was persuaded to make a brief comeback as a stand-in when our lead commentator, David Croft, was forced to miss the European Grand Prix at the Nürburgring.

There were no airs or graces; no prepared excuses for being rusty or out of touch after six years away from the microphone. Murray arrived early and insisted on being a part of our team at every turn, both business and social. He never came close to playing the 'Well, in my experience' or 'I think we should do it this way' cards you might have expected of somebody with more than five decades of broad-casting experience. If anything, he was mildly apprehensive. But it didn't take long for the adrenalin to kick in. In fact, he couldn't wait to get going at the start of qualifying.

The Open Championship was on at the same time and BBC 5 Live Sport that Saturday afternoon was being presented by John Inverdale from Carnoustie. Inverdale began the handover to the Nürburgring with an effusive welcome for a broadcasting icon who was returning to his radio roots.

Meanwhile the cars were leaving the pits, and I could see the longer this gushing introduction continued, the more agitated Murray was becoming – to the point where he thumped his fist on the table in frustration. When the big moment finally arrived, rather than thank Inverdale for his very kind words and describe how much going back to BBC Radio genuinely meant to him, Murray, at peak revs, launched straight into: '*ROUND TEN OF THE CHAMPIONSHIP! Qualifying HAS BE-GUN!*' And we were off!

It was to be a truly memorable weekend and a privilege to sit alongside the maestro and watch him at work. This was the first radio broadcast he'd done since – well, he couldn't remember, but he reckoned it was in the late 1970s. He immediately adapted to the different discipline, one in which the commentator had to paint the picture for the listener, a role he would relish during a wet race.

Here are a few classic Murray excerpts from that broadcast:

'*And it's not raining – it's DELUGING down. STAIR RODS are falling out of the sky. I'm looking at three cars now – and one of them is a McLaren, and it's off – and it's LEWIS HAMILTON! Lewis Hamilton is off at the same corner as Jenson Button. And they're flying off. There's another one. Straight into the side of Jenson Button's car. And another! ONE! TWO! THREE! FOUR! FIVE cars off at the same corner.*'

Later in the race: '*My goodness! It's exciting now! Lewis is eighth. WELL DONE, LEWIS!*'

And, finally, this one: '*Alonso is practically sawing Massa's Ferrari in half!*'

'I enjoyed it enormously,' said Murray, once the headset had been removed for a final time. 'Not just because it was coming back and doing something I enjoyed doing. But because it was radio, which was where I cut my teeth in 1949 when I started with the British GP. Going back to something that involved you just talking, and not relating to pictures, was wonderful.'

Before the start, our producer, Jason Swales, had cleverly resurrected 'The Chain'. When the familiar beat hit the airwaves, the hairs on the back of many a neck stood up. It was the prelude to hearing an equally evocative voice motor sport fans had taken to their hearts – where it will forever remain.

Incredible, Murray. Just incredible.

34

MEMORIES

Linda Keen (journalist and press officer)

In the early eighties, I was working for *Motoring News* as editor of Sporting Scene, which covered a wide range; my favourite events were hot rods and rallycross.

Lydden Hill was very much the home of British and European rallycross and the race meetings were action-packed. I would go there, reporting and gleaning stories for the weekly paper. The bigger championships were televised by BBC *Grandstand*.

Lydden Hill didn't have any sort of media centre, so I used to climb the rickety stairs to the creaky wooden commentary box situated on the start/finish line. It was always dirty in there but it was a great place to sit and watch the action.

I went up there for one British Rallycross Championship meeting and was surprised to be confronted by Murray, who was already there with all his papers in front of him. Of course, I knew who he was and introduced myself. He welcomed me very warmly and made it clear another pair of eyes would be enormously helpful. He soon found, as a journalist, I had lots of information I could share with him. We developed a delightful relationship, and I thoroughly enjoyed my time 'spotting' for him at Lydden. The relationship continued at Brands Hatch, and during the course of the British Rallycross Grand Prix weekend Murray and I would often go for dinner together along with others.

Murray was always fun to be around, had a lovely sense of humour, was a superb raconteur and told incredible stories. I found his 'Muddly Talker' mistakes hilarious and he could always laugh at himself too. When I left Brands Hatch to pursue a freelance career at the end of 1988, he kindly gave me a letter with a glowing reference, which I still have to this day. Whenever I met him in the years after, he would greet me like an old friend.

Graham Ogden (F1 chef)

In 1996 I was head chef for MSL, the F1 catering company, cooking for half the teams in the paddock, along with various TV crews. As a distraction for my kitchen staff, we ran a fantasy F1 league every Saturday night, betting on the next day's race as a bit of fun. To make it even more random, we decided to use a bingo machine to choose two drivers and two cars each.

By the time we got to the last European race in Portugal, this simple premise had snowballed. We started doing the draw of the bingo balls live over the circuit TV feed. Mechanics eating in their motorhomes cheered and shouted abuse as their entries failed to score. We even had F1 drivers opening envelopes (like the national lottery) to say which machine or set of balls we were using. Because most crew in those days didn't go on the flyaway races, we decided Portugal would be the final episode.

While cooking breakfast (and mulling over what new level of silliness we could add to proceedings) there was a knock on the kitchen door and Murray appeared looking rather disappointed – the porridge had run out. Murray would eat huge amounts of porridge to see him through the day. I often dispatched a Tupperware full of porridge across the paddock to wherever he found himself.

Jumping at the chance, I made him a deal: more porridge in

exchange for ten minutes of commentary that evening? Once I explained the game, he drew out his notebook and started a series of very insightful questions. I provided him with a printout of the fantasy team managers, points, and so on. Then he disappeared, promising to return at five o'clock sharp. Bang on time, this familiar voice boomed out behind me: 'Right then, chef, where do you want me?'

We grabbed a passing cameraman and sat down to the most surreal five minutes of my life. Murray suggested that we shoot it as a pre-recorded round-up of the standings, from which we could then cut to me live, hosting as usual in the kitchen. After I joked my way through a little introduction about giving a 'young broadcaster' his first real break, I handed the microphone over to Murray.

Without any notes, other than the points standings, Murray set off on a hilariously deadpan delivery, calling out previous results team by team (often with very crude pub quiz-style names). Then he improvised quotes from team managers and drivers, never missing a beat. Much of Murray's own language and double entendres was certainly not fit for the BBC, but always within pantomime boundaries of decency!

As he finished and passed the mic back to me, I thanked him for his efforts and suggested we would get back to him about the job! He disappeared off to a sponsor event in Lisbon, wishing me luck for the show.

Half an hour later, three hundred mechanics and crew were tucking into their dinner as the TVs switched over live to the kitchen. The roar that went up when Murray's face appeared on-screen was genuinely startling. Followed by huge roars of laughter and 'Shhh! Shhh!!' as they told each other to shut up and listen. Once finished, a chant of 'More! More! More!' was heard around the paddock – so we played it again, twice more!

I still have a grainy video version on CD. Looking at my face on that old footage, it is clearly hero worship and love that beams out from the screen. I couldn't believe I was sat with him twenty-five years ago, and twenty-five years later I instantly smile when thinking of him. Contrary to popular advice – always meet your heroes.

Holly Samos (BBC pit lane reporter)

Lovely memories from the 2007 European Grand Prix when Murray sat in for 'Crofty' (David Croft). We all stayed together and it was a wonderful opportunity to really get to know him. I particularly recall teaching Murray how to text, as he had never done it before! Then, when driving to the track, he was telling me how he remembered driving over the same hills in his tank. It's a powerful and priceless memory of a really wonderful man.

Chris Witty (journalist and press officer)

My friend (and fellow journalist) Ian Phillips was about to turn forty. My wife, Megan, worked for Thames TV and suggested we create a spoof *This Is Your Life* video using Murray as the Eamonn Andrews/ Michael Aspel MC. I drove down to Murray's house in Hampshire, rang the doorbell and gave him our copy of the famous 'Red Book'. He took it, turned to camera and said: 'Ian Phillips, This is Your Life!'

Doug Nye (journalist)

Murray was commentating on a motorcycle GP, around 1953–54, in which the 125cc and 250cc NSU world champion Werner Haas was riding. Murray told me he suddenly realized he'd just said: 'And here they come, round the final corner of the opening lap – Haas first'!

Or there was the time he stood with Charles March at Goodwood, addressing the members before dinner on the evening before the Festival of Speed began. We had just put up our first big carriage-circle sculpture, a kind of Roman arch with a Ferrari on top. Murray said: 'Oh, I can't end now without making mention of Lord March's magnificent erection ...'

Tim Edwards (Jordan chief mechanic)

We were sponsored by Stoddy's (Paul Stoddart) European Aviation and flew to many races with them. One of the antics on his plane was aisle surfing. Essentially, Stoddy would sit on two plastic safety cards with four victims doing the same behind him and brace himself against seats 1C and 1D. As the plane lifted its front wheel on take-off, Stoddy would release his brace and five people would shoot to the rear of the plane. We'd just won the 1999 French Grand Prix and, on this particular flight, Murray was in behind Stoddy. As they fired down the aisle, he shouted his famous line: 'And it's go, go, go!' He was seventy-five. What a legend!

Mark James (broadcaster)

I was helping to run the radio service at the 1994 British Motor Show at the NEC. We hooked up celebrities visiting the show with local radio stations. Murray was there with BMW and agreed to do some 'down the line' interviews. I looked after him, made sure he was in the right studio at the right time, ensured he had a glass of water etc. His last interview of the day followed much the same pattern as the others. Everyone wanted to know about Senna and the accident at Imola and Murray was serious, rather downbeat. The famous excitable Walker voice was completely absent. He finished the interview and was about to take off his headphones when the presenter asked him if he would do the station a small favour. Murray immediately agreed, asked what he needed to say and, after a short pause, launched into a full-on classic commentary style: 'Hello, this is Murray Walker. Remember to listen and give generously to *Children in Need* on BBC Three Counties Radio' (or whichever station it was). Once he'd finished, there was another short pause before asking, in his 'normal' voice: 'Was that all right?' I think it took the hairs on the back of my neck a good twenty minutes to go back down ...

Scott Brownlee (communications director)

When I was at BMW GB in the first half of the nineties, we took over supplying a car for Murray from the dealer who had gone bust. I made the contact and once a year he'd come in to swap over, have a quick chat. I'd also see him occasionally at BTCC meetings and he'd say hi, but nothing beyond the usual pleasantries. So, I was touched to receive a note from him when he heard I was leaving BMW to join Cosworth. Murray's note was just a few lines, one of which was 'I don't know why you're going there, but all the best'. It seemed a bit odd but rang no alarm bells. Weeks later, after I'd moved the entire family north to Towcester and swapped the BMW M5 for a Mondeo Estate, I started to realize there wasn't really a job at Cosworth. They had no money, refused to say anything in public, and the divisions were at war with each other and owner Vickers. Murray had warned me, but I failed to listen.

Bob McMurray (broadcaster)

In October 2002, we were asked to host a lunch to launch Murray's autobiography in Eden Park, home of rugby in New Zealand. Prior to the lunch we were approached by a chap who owned what he said was Murray's father's first (or very early) bike. We decided to get the bike up to Auckland for this event. The plan was to get Murray to the edge of the stage to answer questions from the floor and for me to carefully, and quietly, wheel the bike on to the stage behind him. All went well, and then we asked him to turn around for the surprise.

I had never known him being stuck for words, but he was completely rendered dumb and totally blindsided, such that he had to sit down as his face turned a very whiter shade of pale. We honestly thought he was having some sort of seizure!

He did recover and became really quite emotional for a while before reverting to full-on Murray again. It was a precious moment, albeit a worrying one – but all ended well.

Michael Wilson (architect and amateur racing driver)

Murray Walker was such an enthusiastic commentator. I was at a Formula 1 garden party and the TV was on in the sitting room. About ten enthusiasts were drinking in the garden during the quieter part of a not-so-exciting race when we suddenly heard Murray's voice on full noise. Beers were spilled as we rushed back to the sitting room in time to hear Murray say: 'This is INCREDIBLE! I don't think I have ever seen this situation before. There is absolutely NOBODY on the track!' Drinking quickly resumed in the garden.

Stuart Dent (journalist)

The first time I spent quality time with Murray was in 1984, when we met at a recording studio in the West End. I was on *Grand Prix International* magazine and he was voicing a radio commercial for our forthcoming British GP issue. It was extraordinary to see him working at first hand. He nailed it with the first take, but wasn't completely happy with it, so recorded it again. Down to a split-second again, and that was it!

We spent a while chewing the cud, then went our separate ways. From then on, I always made a point of saying hello whenever our paths crossed and have always been proud of the fact that, for the next couple of years, each time he called me 'Steve'! Once he was politely corrected, he never got my name wrong again – and it always staggered me that, in spite of some lengthy gaps as time went on, he always remembered me and greeted me with his infectious smile and a firm handshake. What a lovely man he was.

Derek Warwick (F1 driver)

Murray was a very proud member of the BRDC (British Racing Drivers' Club). He didn't take it lightly. He never failed to wear the lapel badge or, when he could, the BRDC cap. When we had evenings with our young drivers, he would be there to talk to them and encourage them. He had such a lovely way of putting it across with such excitement and humour. For those of us who were a bit older, Murray Walker had been an integral part of our racing lives; we'd listened to his voice from when we were enthusiasts, right through to when he was commentating on races we were in. He totally understood the sport and its importance, particularly to his audience. I don't know a single person who had a bad word to say about him.

Frank Dernie (F1 aerodynamicist)

Murray obviously spoke mainly with the drivers. But he would always come to me and ask what changes we may have made to the cars. And to be honest, you couldn't always say because we didn't want the other teams to find out what we were up to. Murray was on top of everything. He kept his notes. He knew what was going on but, in the heat of the moment, he didn't always quite get it right. But that was part of the joy of Murray.

You won't get a bad word from me – or anyone else, I imagine – about Murray. He was just fantastic. Such a gentleman. He didn't come blundering in and get in the way when you were in the middle of some meeting, or whatever. He was able to get all the information he needed without being a pain in the arse. And that's because he had such a depth of understanding of how the whole process worked.

Max Mosley (F1 team owner and FIA president)

There is no question that Murray was responsible for drawing many, many people to the sport because he was such a personality. And, of course, his sayings – Murrayisms – were part of the attraction. As were his mistakes – which were almost as good as the bits he got right! Apart from that, he was just a very, very likeable person.

When we had the very last Grand Prix in South Africa in 1993, people from the then government turned up. As did people from the ANC. And one of the leading ANC lights was its general secretary and I volunteered to take him round, show him everything and introduce him to people. As it turns out, it was Cyril Ramaphosa, who is now the president. When I met him, I said: 'Now, who would you like to meet?' I thought he'd say Ayrton Senna, or someone like that. He said Murray Walker! We went into the press room together and stood in front of Murray's desk, where he was writing. I introduced Ramaphosa to him. Murray seemed as surprised as I was but, of course, he was absolutely charming and Mr Ramaphosa was delighted!

The thing about Murray is that he managed to do all those commentaries, make all those comments and do all those interviews without giving anyone cause for complaint. That's very rare, particularly in this business. What a talent to have.

Sir Jackie Stewart

It was interesting that my father and his father knew each other. My father used to go to the Isle of Man and one of his friends was Murray's father. He talked a lot about that friendship.

Murray did the commentary of me winning the 1969 Italian GP – a close finish that gets played a lot because Murray was really going for it! I did quite a few races with him as a commentator. The very first one, I was told to be in the commentary box at Silverstone at a certain time. I arrived to find Murray sorting out pages and pages of information. When it came time to do the race, he never sat down. I was used to sitting down when doing commentaries with ABC in America. But because Murray was standing up, I felt I had to stand up.

I've got nothing but nice things to remember him by. He was so good to me. He said what he wanted to say to you, even if it was embarrassing – but it was never, ever oily. I don't know anyone who had a bad word to say about him. Such a gentleman.

Paul Stewart (F3 driver and F1 team owner)

When I was racing in Formula 3, it felt like an honour to have Murray commentating on your race. He always had such a kind disposition. We had been running the Stewart Grand Prix team for a couple of years when, in 2000, I was in chemotherapy back in the UK and keeping track of how the team got on in the Monaco Grand Prix. I wasn't feeling 100 per cent. Murray was commentating and he got something wrong. I was immediately thinking: 'Not again! C'mon, Murray. Get it right!' And, literally, within thirty seconds of that, he said: 'Meanwhile, Paul Stewart is not here this weekend, and we want to wish him well for a good and speedy recovery.' I'd barely finished cursing Murray and he came out with this typically kind thought. I was absolutely mortified that I could even think such a thing – particularly of Murray.

Phil Cant (F1 mechanic)

I went to the loo at Suzuka and there was a notebook sitting on the side. It was full of all sorts of stats, facts and anecdotes, so I figured a journalist or commentator had left it. I took it back to our garage [Tyrrell] and told one of the TV guys what I had found. A short time later, Murray came into the garage, so relieved and grateful that he'd been reunited with his notes. He was such a lovely guy. He always asked how the cars were going – and I always told him. I would see him as an enthusiast, not the bloke on the telly. You always knew you could trust him.

Simon Sanderson (advertising manager)

As the advertising manager of *Autosport* magazine, I was responsible for our stand at the 1990 Racing Car Show held at Olympia in London. I wanted to add a bit more to the stand rather than the usual show cars and magazine sales, so I asked the publisher of *Murray Walker's Grand Prix Year* if we could sell his book – but we wanted Murray to come along and sign a few. To my amazement, the queue for Murray's signature went all around the top floor at Olympia.

After a day's hard work of signing and chatting to his fans, I asked Murray if he'd like to come out for dinner, with my wife Fiona. We had a lovely evening chatting about many things not racing-related. Murray was particularly interested to hear stories from Fiona as she was then the buyer of wardrobe and bathroom accessories at Harrods in Knightsbridge. She regaled Murray with a story about one of her customers who bought three thousand wooden coat hangers, then priced at £16.50 each (they were handmade!). He was totally amazed that someone would want that many and spend that much money on them.

Fast forward to the Japanese Grand Prix at Suzuka in 2006. I was walking down the open corridor above the pits and bumped into Murray. 'Hello, Simon, how's Fiona? Is she still selling coat hangers?' I was flabbergasted that he could remember that conversation, and Fiona's name, from sixteen years earlier.

Stuart Codling (publishing manager)

He was such a nice bloke in real life. Being Murray Walker was a job he seemed to revel in. When he came as a guest to the Autosport Show, he'd be escorted round the various stages to 'do his thing' and answer questions. But what he really enjoyed was taking in the sights of the show and talking to all the punters. Sometimes we'd collude so I distracted his 'minders' while he slipped away to have a little wander around.

What really impressed me was his work ethic and his capacity to soak up knowledge from everywhere. There was something unique in the way he imparted it to the audience: he wasn't showing off how much he knew, he was just kind of releasing it into your ears. To my mind, the things that made Murray great – on top of being able to carry the broadcast with hardly any live data coming in – were that he never confused opinion with fact, and he was never afraid to admit when he'd got it wrong. Unheard of these days.

Andy Hallbery (journalist)

In October 1986, just days after my twentieth birthday, I started my dream job on the bottom rung at *Autosport* magazine. That summer I had graduated from the London College of Printing. By 1989 I was attending Formula 1 Grands Prix in my role covering the F1-supporting Opel Lotus Euroseries, and being an extra pair of hands at the track. I was still the shy junior, being shown the ropes by my journalist colleagues. Over lunch, Murray would often sit next to me, chat like he'd known me for years, and ask which youngster had been fastest that day in Opel Lotus. He never took notes, but it was clear he was storing the information for the future, 'just in case'.

Fast forward to February 1992. At the age of twenty-five, I was appointed editor of *Autosport*, at the time the youngest member of the

Autosport team. To say I was a rabbit in headlights at the rapid promotion is an understatement. The day following the announcement in the magazine, a beautifully handwritten letter arrived in the *Autosport* office, personally addressed to me.

I opened it, read it. Then I'll admit I had to make my excuses and go outside to get some fresh air, and wipe away a tear or two. Murray Walker, the guy I'd grown up listening to and learning so much from, had written not only to congratulate me, but to confirm that I now had the best job in the world – with his full support. I may still have been a rabbit in headlights, but those headlights felt a lot further away from that moment on, thanks to Murray's kind words.

Ian Flux (racing driver)

When I was racing in the BTCC (British Touring Car Championship) in 1993, my gran thought I'd really made it when she heard Murray commentating and mention my name!

Sir Lewis Hamilton

No one could come close to Murray's commentary. I just remember hearing this voice when I was growing up, watching all the Grands Prix. He really made the sport exciting. There's been no one like him that I've seen on TV – that even without watching the TV, if you're out of the room and you hear him, you're excited and it makes you want to run back in and see what's happening. He was very much loved around the world, and particularly in the UK. His contribution to the sport was huge. Obviously, me growing up watching him through that early phase of my life, and hearing him, no one can come close to that. Murray Walker was the iconic voice of our sport and a great man. Thank you for all you did. You will never be forgotten.

MURRAYISMS

Either that car is stationary, or it's on the move.

Tambay's hopes, which were previously nil, are now absolutely zero.

I've just stopped my start watch.

That was exactly the same place where Senna overtook Nannini that he didn't overtake Alain Prost.

Martin Schanche's car is absolutely unique, except for the one behind which is identical.

Two laps to go, then the action will begin, unless this is the action, which it is.

The young Ralf Schumacher has been upstaged by the teenager Jenson Button, who is twenty.

It's a sad ending, albeit a happy one here at Montreal for today's Grand Prix.

Prost can see Mansell in his earphones.

The first four cars are both on the same tyres.

Unless I'm very much mistaken – yes, I am very much mistaken.

A mediocre season for Nelson Piquet, as he is now known, and always has been.

There's nothing wrong with the car except it's on fire.

With the race half gone, there is half the race to go.

I imagine the conditions in those cars are totally unimaginable.

The atmosphere is so tense you could cut it with a cricket stump.

And now, the boot is on the other Schumacher.

Do my eyes deceive me, or is Senna's car sounding a bit rough?

Damon Hill is leading. Behind him are the second and third men.

He is shedding buckets of adrenalin in that car.

There is only a second between them. One. That's how long a second is.

There is no doubt in my mind that if the race had been forty-six laps instead of forty-five, it would have been a McLaren first and second. But it didn't, so it wasn't.

He's obviously gone in for a wheel change. I say obviously because I can't see it.

Anything happens in Grand Prix racing and usually does.

Alboreto has dropped back up to fifth place.

Murray: What's that? There's a body on the track.
James Hunt: Um, I think that's a piece of bodywork from someone's car.

★

Murray: There's a fiery glow coming from the back of the Ferrari.
James: No, Murray, that's his rear safety light.

And the first five places are filled by five different cars.

You can't see a digital clock because there isn't one.

And we've had five races so far this year – Brazil, Argentina, Imola, Schumacher and Monaco.

And Damon Hill is coming into the pit lane. Yes, it's Damon Hill coming into the Williams pit and Damon Hill is in the pit—no, it's Michael Schumacher.

As you look at the first four, the significant thing is that Alboreto is fifth.

I can't imagine what kind of problem Senna has. I imagine it must be some sort of grip problem.

And this is the third-placed car about to lap the second-placed car.

One red light, two red lights, three red lights, four red lights, five laps ... and it's go, go, go!

Andrea de Cesaris is the man who has won more Grands Prix than anyone else without actually winning one of them.

And Mansell is slowing down. He is definitely taking it easy. Oh no he isn't – that was a lap record.

And now, excuse me while I interrupt myself.

ACKNOWLEDGEMENTS

I must start by offering sincere thanks to Elizabeth Walker. I can only hope this narrative of Murray's extraordinary and well-loved life invokes warm memories in return for her gracious support for the book.

I owe a debt of gratitude to a great many people. They may have been very willing to recall predominantly, if not exclusively, happy recollections of such a wonderful man but considerable time in their busy lives was given over to sessions on Zoom. In every case, the interview quickly developed into a chatty stroll down Memory Lane – a recommended tonic for anyone in these straitened times, particularly when such a congenial character is the subject of discussion. Nonetheless, I am deeply grateful for such an enthusiastic response to my call for help.

I must, however, single out Martin Brundle and Oliver Owen for their valuable support: Martin for contributing a foreword only he could write with such personal eloquence; and Oliver for continuing a skilful editorial stewardship that began over thirty years ago during our time together on the sports pages of the *Observer*. I must also pay special tribute to Richard Wiseman, whose remarkable ability to seek out archive footage has been incredibly helpful.

Sincere apologies if I've omitted any significant names from such an esteemed list.

James Allen, Jonathan Ashman, Brian Barwick, Matt Bishop, Scott Brownlee, Rupert Bush, Phil Cant, Stuart Codling, Stuart Dent, Frank Dernie, Mike Doodson, Neil Duncanson, Ben Edwards, Tim Edwards, Ian Flux, Louise Goodman, Nick Goozée, Andy Hallbery, Sir Lewis Hamilton, Damon Hill, Mark James, Tony Jardine, Bob Jennings, Linda Keen, Jonathan Legard, John Lemm, Nigel Mansell, Jonathan Martin, Bob McMurray, Roger Moody, Max Mosley, Doug Nye, Graham Ogden, Jonathan Palmer, Andy Parr, Suzi Perry, Steve Rider, Jim Rosenthal, Holly Samos, Simon Sanderson, Sir Jackie Stewart, Paul Stewart, Simon Taylor, Ian Titchmarsh, Derek Warwick, Mark Wilkin, Michael Wilson, Chris Witty.

And last, but not least, I must mention the team at Transworld Publishers for their valued support and professional skill in putting together a wonderful book that was originally hatched by my ever-perceptive literary agent, David Luxton.

Thank you all for helping make this book happen. It has been a joy and a privilege to write.

SOURCES

Books

Autocourse (Hazleton Publishing, Icon Publishing)

Damon Hill, *Watching the Wheels* (Macmillan, 2016)

Steve Rider, *My Chequered Career* (Haynes, 2012)

Murray Walker, *Bedside Wheels* (Collins Willow, 1986)

Murray Walker, *Unless I'm Very Much Mistaken* (Collins Willow, 2002)

Murray Walker Scrapbook (Porter Press International)

Newspapers

Advertiser (Adelaide)

Daily Telegraph

Guardian

Observer

Sunday Times

The Times

Magazines

Autosport

F1 Racing

Motor Sport

Startline

PICTURE ACKNOWLEDGEMENTS

The publisher would like to thank the following for kind permission to reproduce images. While every effort has been made to trace the owners of copyright material reproduced herein, the publishers would like to apologize for any omissions and will be pleased to incorporate missing acknowledgements at the earliest opportunity.

Plate Sections

Page 1: top with special thanks to Keig for the gift; middle © Maurice Hamilton. Page 2: top with thanks to the BBC Archive Photo Library/BBC Sport F1; bottom left © Maurice Hamilton; bottom right Murray reporting © Darren Heath/Getty. Page 3: top left and right both © Maurice Hamilton; middle and bottom © Motorsport Images. Page 4: top © Motorsport Images; middle with Louise Goodman © LAT Images; bottom left with Nigel Mansell © PA Images/Alamy; bottom right image of Murray with Michael Schumacher courtesy of Motorsport Images. Page 5: top © Michael Cooper/Getty Sport; middle courtesy of Jon Nicholson Photography; bottom with thanks to Hoch Zwei/Getty Sport. Page 6: top left © F1 Racing; top right with Bernie Ecclestone © Darren Heath/Getty; bottom left © Motorsport Images; bottom right with Suzi Perry with special thanks to Charlie Day and Suzi Perry. Page 7: top with thanks to Motorsport Images; middle and bottom courtesy of Motorsport and Sutton Images. Page 8: middle © Motorsport Images; bottom courtesy of Maurice Hamilton.

INDEX

ABOUT THE AUTHOR

Maurice Hamilton was a friend and colleague of Murray Walker. He has been a full-time Formula 1 journalist since 1977, and has attended over five hundred Grands Prix as a working journalist. He has also been an award-winning writer for leading British newspapers, including the *Observer*, the *Guardian* and the *Independent*; Grand Prix editor for *Racer* magazine; editor of the *Autocourse* Grand Prix annual; and commentator for BBC Radio 5 Live at Grand Prix events. He is the author of more than thirty books.